Peacekeeping Under Fire

ALSO BY ROBERT A. RUBINSTEIN

Doing Fieldwork: The Correspondence of Robert Redfield and Sol Tax (editor)
The Social Dynamics of Peace and Conflict: Culture in International Security (co-editor)
Peace and War: Cross-Cultural Perspectives (co-editor)
Epistemology and Process: Anthropological Views (co-editor)
Science as Cognitive Process: Toward an Empirical Philosophy of Science (co-author)

Peacekeeping Under Fire

Culture and Intervention

Robert A. Rubinstein

Paradigm Publishers
Boulder • London

Published in the United States by Paradigm Publishers, 3360 Mitchell Lane, Suite E, Boulder, CO 80301 USA.

Paradigm Publishers is the trade name of Birkenkamp & Company, LLC, Dean Birkenkamp, President and Publisher.

Library of Congress Cataloging-in-Publication Data

Rubinstein, Robert A.
 Peacekeeping under fire : culture and intervention / Robert A. Rubinstein.
  p. cm.
 Includes bibliographical references and index.
 ISBN-13: 978-1-59451-547-7 (hardcover : alk. paper)
 1. Peace-building—Cross-cultural studies. 2. Peacekeeping forces. I. Title.
 JZ6374.R83 2008
 341.5'84—dc22

                               2008003525

Printed and bound in the United States of America on acid-free paper that meets the standards of the American National Standard for Permanence of Paper for Printed Library Materials.

Designed and typeset by Beth Wright, Trio Bookworks

12 11 10 09 08   1 2 3 4 5

For
Sandy and Helen

All of the author's royalties from *Peacekeeping Under Fire* are donated to the Ploughshares Fund, Fort Mason, San Francisco, CA 94123, http://www.ploughshares.org.

Contents

Figures and Tables

Figures

Tables

Acronyms

DOMREP	Mission of the Representative of the Secretary-General in the Dominican Republic
DPKO	Department of Peacekeeping Operations, United Nations
IGO	Intergovenmental organization
IPA	International Peace Academy
MINURSO	United Nations Mission for the Referendum in Western Sahara
MSF	Médecins Sans Frontières / Doctors Without Borders
NATO	North Atlantic Treaty Organization
NGO	Nongovernmental organization
OGE	Observer Group Egypt
ONUC	United Nations Operation in the Congo
ONUCA	United Nations Observer Group in Central America
ONUSAL	United Nations Observer Mission in El Salvador
PARC	Program on the Analysis and Resolution of Conflicts, Maxwell School of Syracuse University
PKI	Peacekeeping Institute, United States Army War College
SWAPO	South West African Peoples Organization
UN	United Nations
UNAMIC	United Nations Advance Mission in Cambodia
UNAMIR	United Nations Assistance Mission in Rwanda
UNAVEM	United Nations Angola Verification Mission
UNDOF	United Nations Disengagement Observer Force
UNEF	United Nations Emergency Force
UNFICYP	United Nations Peacekeeping Force in Cyprus
UNGOMAP	United Nations Good Offices Mission in Afghanistan and Pakistan
UNICEF	United Nations Children's Fund
UNIFIL	United Nations Interim Force in Lebanon
UNIIMOG	United Nations Iran-Iraq Military Observer Group
UNIKOM	United Nations Iraq-Kuwait Observation Mission

UNIPOM	United Nations India-Pakistan Observation Mission
UNMIK	United Nations Mission in Kosovo
UNMO	United Nations military observer
UNMOGIP	United Nations Military Observer Group in Pakistan
UNOGIL	United Nations Observations Group in Lebanon
UNOSOM	United Nations Operation in Somalia
UNSF	United Nations Security Force in West New Guinea (West Irian)
UNTAF	United Task Force
UNTAG	United Nations Transition Assistance Group
UNTSO	United Nations Truce Supervision Organization
UNYOM	United Nations Yemen Observation Mission
USAWC	United States Army War College
USIP	United States Institute of Peace
WHO	World Health Organization

Preface

In 1986, I began what I thought would be a more or less traditional anthropological study of peacekeeping. As an anthropologist, I initially saw peacekeeping as an interesting arena for exploring how an international organization creates a common sense of purpose among its participants. It was particularly appealing because peacekeeping is a transnational social institution; it brings together people from the militaries of many countries, international civil servants, staff of a wide variety of nongovernmental organizations, and individuals from many walks of life. Conducting such transnational research would require developing methods for working across those boundaries. I took this as an engaging challenge. As well, studying peacekeeping is an opportunity to study people involved with powerful institutions and to examine the institutions themselves, what Laura Nader memorably described as "studying up." Just as a transnational research endeavor would require methodological innovation, so too would studying up.

During the next two and a half years, I interviewed diplomats and military officers from many countries who had participated in peacekeeping missions around the globe. This was made possible by the International Peace Academy (IPA), a New York City–based nongovernmental organization working to improve peacekeeping, which also allowed me access to their off-the-record meetings. In 1988 and 1989, I participated in the IPA's two-week-long Vienna Seminar, and used that as a place for interviews and for developing contacts within the peacekeeping community.

In 1988, I moved to Egypt with my wife, Sandra Lane, a medical anthropologist then working for the Ford Foundation. This gave me the opportunity to see how the findings from my interviews were realized within a particular peacekeeping mission. In anticipation of our move to Cairo, I asked for permission to study the United Nations Truce Supervision Organization (UNTSO) with a special focus on its Observer Group Egypt (OGE). I eventually was given that permission and was able to do fieldwork with OGE, as well as with other UNTSO observer groups. I conducted that ethnographic research from late 1988 through mid-1992. During this time I refined a model of how members of peacekeeping missions develop a common sense of purpose and a shared identity.

I decided not to publish a full ethnography of OGE when peacekeeping itself appeared to change dramatically, which led me to question the relevance of the work I had done with UNTSO to the evolving institution of peacekeeping. The missions of the 1990s seemed to be radically different from those that had gone on before, and indeed much of the scholarly and policy writings about them asserted that this was the case. These new missions were fraught with problems. Peacekeeping now appeared to be the locus of disaster for the peacekeeping troops themselves and for the peoples they were protecting. Mogadishu. Srebrenica. Rwanda. Each of these places became emblems of the failings of peacekeeping, and these collectively came to represent the sea changes taking place in peacekeeping.

Following each of these missions a flurry of policy studies sought to identify the lessons that could be learned from them. These missions also provoked considerable scholarly analysis, especially in political science and international relations. This work suggested that there were major discontinuities in the circumstances, structures, and operations between peacekeeping missions in the 1990s and those that had been conducted before. Based on these and other analyses, scholars, policymakers, and laypeople began speaking of peacekeeping in the 1990s as so different from traditional peacekeeping—in the ways that it more frequently used force and dealt with intra-state conflicts—that all we had learned from traditional peacekeeping was called into serious question, or said to no longer apply.

As I continued my own peacekeeping research, interviewing people who had served in military or civilian roles in the new missions, I recognized that many of the new challenges and complications had resonances with earlier peacekeeping activities. Indeed, it seemed to me that the range of functions carried out by observer missions and early peacekeeping forces was quite wide and actually involved considerable civilian effort. I began to suspect that traditional peacekeeping could help us understand and improve the new peace operations. Work with colleagues at the United Nations Department of Peacekeeping Operations, the IPA, and the US Army Peacekeeping Institute at the US Army War College convinced me that this was the case.

Despite the now growing recognition of their importance, the cultural aspects of peacekeeping (and of postconflict stability operations) have received relatively little attention in the literatures that examine peacekeeping, although there are signs that this is changing. While there are a few very useful studies in this area, they primarily focus on one aspect of the many ways in which culture affects peacekeeping. For instance, they look at how peacekeepers' lack of cultural understanding of the societies to which they are sent leads them to make mistakes, or they examine how organizational cultural differences complicate cooperation among military and civilian elements of a mission. In contrast, yet building upon these kinds of studies, in this book I explore why a broad understanding of the role of culture is critical to preparing for and conducting effective peacekeeping operations.

My approach is to show how cultural processes at each level of analysis are essentially linked to those at the adjacent levels. To adequately engage the cultural side of peacekeeping requires developing a model of peacekeeping that provides a conceptual scaffold through which this linkage can be understood and then used for improving peacekeeping. The reason this scaffolding is important is that the microlevel and macrolevels at which peacekeeping is experienced affect each other quite profoundly. Being alert to the mutually affecting aspects of these interactions is critical to improving the planning and execution of peacekeeping missions.

This book is neither a traditional ethnography nor a work of applied social science that describes how to do peace operations better. I have published both of these kinds of scholarly works in academic journal articles, and I have spoken about them at numerous trainings, in-service events, and scholarly meetings. What I offered in those venues was grounded in my broader understanding of how culture affects peace operations. Also, this book is not intended as a guide to specific policies or as a compilation of up-to-date case studies of the most recent missions. Rather, my aim is to present an anthropology of intervention by giving a framework for understanding culture in peacekeeping and to illustrate the value of taking a broad view of culture that embraces all levels at which it affects peacekeeping.

Acknowledgments

My late friend and collaborator, Mary LeCron Foster, first suggested to me that peacekeeping would be an interesting and important subject of anthropological research. She introduced me to the International Peace Academy, where my research began. We both believed that symbolism plays an important and substantive role in international security. Her influence is reflected throughout this book.

Sol Tax encouraged my work on this project. Before he died in 1995, Sol was a pioneer of transnational anthropology, single-handedly building in the 1950s and 1960s the international anthropology community, focused around the journal *Current Anthropology* and connected to the Wenner-Gren Foundation for Anthropological Research and to the International Union of Anthropological and Ethnological Sciences. He was deeply concerned that anthropological voices be heard in public policy, and committed to the basic interconnectedness of people and to the need for effective international organizations and global governance. During the decade and a half that we worked together, Sol was a constant interlocutor in my efforts to understand peacekeeping.

My debts to my wife and daughter, Sandra D. Lane and Helen Lane Rubinstein, are too great to leave to the end of these acknowledgments, the space authors traditionally reserve for thanking their families. In addition to the care and nurturing and enthusiasm that Sandy brings to everything she does, she is also an anthropologist. So, she is my most important professional colleague and collaborator. Quite literally, for reasons described in chapter 4, without her my ethnographic research with the United Nations Truce Supervision Organization (UNTSO) and its Observer Group Egypt (OGE) would have been much different, if I had been able to conduct it at all. She has also listened to, read, and critiqued the materials presented here. As a result, many of the ideas and perspectives offered in this book were developed jointly with Sandy. But I have made many of these work in ways with which she might disagree, so she is not jointly responsible for any places in which I might have erred.

In ways of which she cannot yet be aware, our daughter, Helen, also gave new depth to my understanding of peacekeeping and to the communal and cultural aspects of that enterprise. A few months after I began working with UNTSO, Sandy and I conceived a child. That pregnancy was noted by my "informants" at OGE. Sandy was well advanced in her pregnancy when we left Egypt for our annual leave toward the end of my first year of fieldwork at OGE. During our time back in the United States, that child died from a listeriosis infection. We returned to OGE childless; all our informants at OGE consoled and supported us. When Sandy became pregnant again, many of our OGE informants emerged as caring friends. Helen's birth deepened those bonds and brought us into many OGE activities in which we had not previously been included. This expanded my perspective on, and deepened my understanding of, OGE.

I began this project at a time when it was not yet fashionable in anthropology to study multinational institutions, to study among the military, or to address too directly the macrolevel questions of international relations or security policies. I am especially grateful for the early financial support from the Ploughshares Fund in San Francisco. This grant funding supported my initial work, thus opening for me the possibilities of studying peacekeeping. To express my deep gratitude, I have arranged for all royalties from this book to be paid to the Ploughshares Fund. Support from Ploughshares was instrumental in my gaining additional support for my research from the Wenner-Gren Foundation for Anthropological Research in New York. Later a grant from the United States Institute of Peace (USIP) allowed me to convert my fieldnotes to a computer database, broaden my work by looking at other peacekeeping missions, and interview NGO staff who had participated in those missions. I am thankful for this additional support. Under the USIP grant, Kristi Simkins, Linda Heilmann Curran, and Christos Kyrou helped turn my fieldnotes into computer databases and code them for analysis, and Michael Nobleza gave bibliographic assistance.

I began this project while I was associated with the Department of Anthropology at Northwestern University. This gave me access to an excellent library and an institutional review board, which helped me get this work started. I am grateful to the department and to my colleagues there for that support. At Northwestern, I benefited especially from conversations with Timothy McKewon, Mary Anna Thornton, Jeffrey Ward, and Oswald Werner.

From 1989 to 1994 I was an associate research medical anthropologist with the Francis I. Proctor Foundation for Research in Ophthalmology at the University of California at San Francisco. I had already begun my peacekeeping research when I joined the Proctor Foundation, and did so with the understanding that I would be continuing that work. Although they did not always understand how a researcher could work on both the prevention of infectious eye disease and international security, my Proctor Foundation colleagues and our Egyptian collaborators always respected the constraints that my peace-keeping work placed on my ophthalmologic work. I am especially grateful to Chandler Dawson, then Proctor Foundation director, for making this dual focus possible.

This work began through the good offices of the International Peace Academy (IPA). I was extremely fortunate that the late General Indar Jit Rhikye and Thomas Weiss, then president and vice president of the IPA, responded favorably to the suggestion that anthropological analysis could add an important dimension to our understanding of peacekeeping. I thank them for allowing me to work through the IPA meetings and for twice inviting me to the IPA's Vienna Seminar. It was at the 1988 Vienna Seminar that I was able to speak with General Martin Vadset, then UNTSO chief of staff, about my desire to do ethnographic research with UNTSO. I appreciate greatly his openness to this request and his subsequent support for it. It was also at the 1988 Vienna Seminar that I met Pasi Patakallio, currently Finnish ambassador to Canada. Since that time, I have had a few opportunities to speak and visit with Pasi and found at each opportunity his reactions to be insightful, informative, and helpful.

At Observer Group Egypt, I am especially indebted to Lieutenant Colonel Alen D. Clarke, then OGE chief of staff, and to Lieutenant Commander James Robinson, then senior liaison officer, United Nations Liaison Office, in Cairo, and to their wives, Susan Clarke and Fran Robinson, for helping us enter the OGE community and for the kindnesses and friendship they extended to Sandy, to Helen, and to me. My thanks also to Father Constantine-Paul Michael Belisarius, hieromonk of the Melkite Greek-Catholic Patriarchate of Antioch and All the East of Alexandria and Jerusalem, for many conversations about my project at OGE and for sharing his observations of the life of the observer group, which he recorded in his capacity as informal chaplain there.

Midway through my fieldwork with UNTSO, Sir Brian Urquhart, then recently retired from his post as undersecretary-general of the United Nations, came to Cairo for a Ford Foundation–sponsored meeting. I am very grateful to him for having made time in his schedule to meet with me. We spent an afternoon together in Cairo discussing my project, and I gained considerable insight from him. After our meeting in Cairo, Sir Brian arranged for me to have access to other missions. Our most recent meeting was on another afternoon, this time in Syracuse, New York, during his visit to us in connection with the Ralph Bunche centenary. At that time we had a chance to speak about the project as it was taking its present shape, and I once again benefited greatly from that conversation.

Much of the analysis in this book derives from anthropological lessons I first learned from H. Stephen Straight and Charles D. Laughlin Jr. I am especially grateful to Steve for introducing me to the analysis of language and for leading me through the literature on the neurological basis for language. Charlie introduced me to symbolism and ritual studies, and nurtured my commitment to the development of multilevel analyses and to connecting anthropology with adjacent disciplines. I thank him for those lessons and for years of collaboration though his informally constituted biogenetic structuralism research group.

When I began this project, only one other anthropologist, Marianne Heiberg, was studying peacekeeping. Happily, this situation has changed. Now there is a small and constantly expanding group of anthropologists who are engaged in this work. Among these, I have benefited especially from conversations and the exchange of manuscripts with Tanjia Hohje Chopra, Carolyn Nordstrom, Anna Simons, and Donna Winslow. More recently, I have gained from conversations with Kevin Avruch, Keith Brown, and Matthew Gutmann and Catherine Lutz. Also, I have benefited from correspondence and exchange of papers with Eyal Ben-Ari, David Last, David R. Segal, Boas Shamir, and Liora Sion.

I was prompted to think of my work as reaching beyond the anthropological community by a request in the mid-1990s from Jarat Chopra, of Brown University's Watson Institute, and Colonel James McCallum, then professor at the United States Army Peacekeeping Institute, to write a chapter on culture and peacekeeping for a manual they were preparing in order to assist special representatives of the secretary-general in their organization and management of peacekeeping operations. I am deeply grateful to them for opening the path that led to my rethinking of the relationship between "traditional" and contemporary peace operations, and for many ensuing years of friendship and collaboration. In the years following their invitation I have had opportunities to visit and work with colleagues at the US Army Peacekeeping Institute and with colleagues at the United States Army Center for Strategic Leadership. My thanks to Colonel Joseph Cerami, Colonel Mark Walsh, and Colonel George Oliver, then director of the institute, for their reactions and conversations about the materials in this book.

My thanks also go to Joelle Tanguy, US executive director of Médecins Sans Frontières (MSF) from 1994 to 2001, for many conversations about MSF and humanitarian action in general. Those conversations helped greatly as I developed the views expressed in this book. I have been encouraged from the start of this project also by Christopher Coleman, first while he was at the IPA and subsequently during his tenure at the United Nations Department of Peacekeeping Operations (DPKO). I am grateful also to Anja Kaspersen, then of the Best Practices Unit of the DPKO and now at the Norwegian Ministry of Foreign Affairs, for her interest in and suggestions for this project.

Since 1994, I have been on the faculty of the Maxwell School of Citizenship and Public Affairs of Syracuse University, where I am a member of the Department of Anthropology and where, until 2005, I directed the Program on the Analysis and Resolution of Conflicts (PARC). I am indebted to a number of colleagues for discussions of the material I treat in this book. In anthropology, I thank John Burdick, Christopher DeCorse, Michael Freedman, William F. Kelleher Jr., and Deborah Pellow. My thanks also go to my colleagues at PARC, who have discussed this material with me and helped me to develop my thinking about peacekeeping. I am grateful in particular to James P. Bennett, Jerry Evensky, Louis Kriesberg, Elizabeth Mignacca, John Murray, J. David Richardson, and Susan Senecah for encouraging me in this work.

I conducted much archival and documentary research and many interviews for this project in New York City, at the United Nations, and in visits to UN permanent missions, UN specialized agencies, and nongovernmental organizations. I am fortunate that Syracuse University has a facility in New York, the Lubin House, where I was able to arrange meetings and stay while conducting this work. For the many ways they facilitate my research, I am grateful to the staff of the Lubin House, especially, Patricia Dombrowski, Lynn Clarke, Svetlana Sagrin, Oscar Mendez, and Raymond Sanchez.

I have presented aspects of this work to my students at Syracuse University and in seminars elsewhere, including at Yale University, Brown University, Colgate University, the University of British Columbia, Sabanci University, and Gent University. I am grateful for all of the comments and suggestions I received from colleagues in those settings, especially from Rik Pinxten and Linda-Anne Rebhun. I have had valuable discussions about the issues treated in this book with George Farag, Kerry B. Fosher, Cornelius (Neil) Funk-Unrau, C. Esra Cuhadar Gürkaynak, Fethi Keles, Svetlana Peshkova, Béatrice Poligny, and Brian Selmeski.

A number of colleagues read all or parts of the manuscript. Thanks to Michael Bhatia, Clementine Fujimura, Diana M. Keller, and Elizabeth Mignacca for their comments on the early chapters of the manuscript. I thank Michael Apter and Martin Hébert for their comments on chapter 6. For comments on the entire manuscript I am indebted to Deborah Goodwin, Matthew Gutmann, Tanja Hohe Chopra, David Last, Catherine Lutz, James McCallum, and James (Tim) M. Wallace. I am grateful to each of them for their very careful reading of and many suggestions for improving the entire manuscript.

Finally, my thanks to Dean Birkenkamp at Paradigm Publishers. Dean encouraged me to write this book and has watched over its development from the start. This is the third book I have been fortunate to work on with Dean's support, and, as before, I have benefited greatly from his suggestions and insight.

1

Introduction

While I was growing up in suburban Long Island in the late 1950s and early 1960s, the most common evidence of the United Nations was the orange, milk-carton-sized donation boxes that school children carried with them as they went door-to-door on their Halloween rounds. With those boxes, my class-mates and I collected spare change to help other children around the world. The first school day following Halloween, we would bring the boxes, heavy with pennies, nickels, dimes, and the occasional quarter, to school so that they could be sent to UNICEF in New York City.

As with most things at school, there was a lesson attached. For these orange collection boxes, the lesson was about the good that the United Nations was doing throughout the world—how it was fighting disease and poverty, help-ing to ensure that the world became a better place for everyone, and working to prevent war. We learned that UNICEF was just one way that the United Nations was carrying out its vision and mission to free the world from the scourge of war and to ensure that people everywhere lived better lives.

The UNICEF box was more than just a vehicle for collecting spare change. It was a symbol that represented UNICEF, and UNICEF, in turn, stood for the entire United Nations.[1] Like any symbol, the meaning of the little orange box came from its being embedded in a larger way of thinking. This larger system of meanings entailed seeing the United Nations as an institution of hope and cooperation and as a force for the development of a new and better world.

The lessons we were taught about the founding of the United Nations emphasized how, following the Second World War, the world was able to look beyond political differences and band together to create an institution whose vision of a world free from war and pestilence could be made a reality through cooperation and the setting aside of narrow national self-interests. The cre-ation of the United Nations, the lesson continued, represented the emergence of an institutional embodiment of a moral force for the development of a bet-ter world—a world in which business-as-usual could be set aside for the com-mon good. These meanings were crystallized and condensed into the little

1

cardboard boxes, carried about by school children as they pursued their quest for Halloween treats.

To be sure, the United Nations did not emerge simply from the selfless impulses of good people. Its design and development involved great diplomatic jockeying and many trade-offs among the interests of the great powers.[2] But this politics-as-usual aspect of the organization's founding receded into the background. Much of the diplomatic work upon which the United Nations rested took place in private, so it was outside of public view, and once the Charter was ready for signing, it slipped discretely from the general public's awareness to be replaced fully by an optimistic narrative of possibilities for a new and better world.[3]

The fruits of UNICEF's work were not the only evidence that the promises of this narrative were being made a reality. Real accomplishments could be seen in the work of the World Health Organization (WHO), a United Nations specialized agency, which led the campaigns to eradicate smallpox and malaria. The massive smallpox vaccination campaign and the antimalaria efforts coordinated the work of scientists and health care workers around the world. In the ten years between 1967 and 1977, WHO efforts led to the elimination of smallpox, a disease that had regularly devastated human populations for millennia.[4]

In its efforts to preserve or restore peace to areas of conflict around the globe, the United Nations developed the mechanism of peacekeeping. In the next chapter, I give a brief history of the development of peacekeeping. Here it is enough to say that beginning in 1948 the United Nations has deployed peacekeeping missions to areas of conflict. These missions sent unarmed or lightly armed military observers and troops, along with their civilian support staff, to conflict areas to observe that cease-fire agreements were kept, and, in conjunction with that task, sometimes to administer civilian populations in those areas.

By the late 1980s peacekeeping's currency could not have had higher value. In 1988, United Nations Peacekeeping was collectively awarded the Nobel Peace Prize. In awarding the prize, the Nobel Committee cited the work peacekeeping accomplished in diffusing and mediating difficult situations. In presenting the prize, Egil Aarvik, chairman of the Nobel Committee, offered a portrait of an instrument of international action that depended upon moral force for its effect. He said although it mixed military observers with military forces that, "the description 'Forces' is in itself inadequate since it conjures up the idea of a military operation in the traditional sense, while the reality is in many ways the diametric opposite."[5] Peacekeeping had emerged as an important element for realizing the promise of the United Nations.

The UNICEF box is largely gone from my experience, and from that of many others.[6] In a decade of Halloweens lived in Chicago, and two decades in suburban neighborhoods in New York and Ohio, I cannot recall a single Halloween when even one trick-or-treating youngster held out a UNICEF box and asked for a donation. The little orange UNICEF box is no longer the most familiar representation of the United Nations.

Now, United Nations Peacekeeping is arguably the most common and salient symbol of the United Nations, and "many perceive the role of the United Nations as all but synonymous with peacekeeping activities."[7] The symbolic artifacts of peacekeeping—images of blue berets, white vehicles with large black UN letters painted on them, and, of course, the United Nations flag—appear frequently on television, in magazines, and in newspapers. These pictures and reports most often come from places torn by conflicts or disasters.

The disappearing UNICEF box has been accompanied by a shift, in the United States at least, in the way many people think about the United Nations in general. The earlier view of the United Nations as a moral, normative force for change in the world now seems mainly trumped by a view that sees the United Nations as an inefficient, ineffective, corrupt, and bureaucratically moribund institution. Almost no aspect of the United Nations system is exempted from this criticism, be it the Secretariat, the specialized agencies, or peacekeeping operations.

During the 2000 US presidential campaign, for example, then candidate George W. Bush advanced his bid for the presidency by strongly attacking American participation in the United Nations, and especially in arguing that peacekeeping (and the nation-building that it often entails) is an enterprise in which the United States ought not be involved.[8] Throughout the 1980s and 1990s, the US Congress has also made unsympathetic decisions regarding the United Nations, and the United States has withheld payments to the organization. Peacekeeping often bears the brunt of these attacks.

Of course, negative views of the United Nations were not new. Anthropologists observe that all societies contain within them considerable variations, and their cultures embrace alternative ways of valuing actions and institutions. The alternative that holds the greatest sway, and thus characterizes the normative nature of the society's culture, largely emerges from the confluence of historical, political, economic, and other factors. Although cultures can be relatively stable, they also undergo significant shifts over time. How these shifts are triggered is a matter of considerable research showing that there are many ways to bring them about.[9] So, even while the view of the United Nations as a force for moral good was the normative narrative within the United States, from the very beginning there was also opposition and derision of the organization.[10]

The shift in the perception of the promise of the United Nations built up over many years, but it accelerated with the end of the Cold War and in its aftermath. During this period the negative images and critical voices gained real traction, seemingly tipping the balance in their favor and against the United Nations. In fact, the negative shift in the normative perception of the United Nations came at a relatively well-bounded moment in the 1990s.

The early 1990s are critical to understanding the change that took place in perceptions of the United Nations. Although there are many pathways to this shift, two divergent events captured the attention of the international community during this period. The first was the keen anticipation with which the international community greeted the end of the Cold War, and the active role for peacekeeping that was envisioned as a result. The second is the United Nations engagement in Somalia in the 1990s, an experience that played a particularly pivotal role in the perceptual transformation.[11]

As it became clear that the Cold War would soon be over, there was a tremendous burst of optimism for what the United Nations might accomplish now that it was to be freed from the shackles of the Soviet-American standoff. Even astute and long-term observers of the international system expressed a kind of euphoria of anticipation as they contemplated how, with the Cold War over, the international community would be able to act through the United Nations in ways that it could not before.[12] This assessment was widely shared throughout the United Nations and its specialized agencies. Then Secretary-General Boutros Boutros-Ghali submitted a report, *An Agenda for Peace*, to the Security Council at the end of January 1992; in it he set out a broad activist vision for the prevention, cessation, and amelioration of conflicts, through an elaboration of the instrument of peacekeeping. His vision would expand the scope and kind of operational tasks peacekeeping would perform.[13] It was in this optimistic context that the United Nations engagement in Somalia took place.

The United Nations in Somalia in the 1990s

In the late 1980s, as the Cold War was winding down, Somalia, a country in the Horn of Africa of considerable geostrategic importance due to its location at the entrance to the Red Sea, was experiencing both famine and political turmoil. Somalia had been run by an authoritarian, centrally controlled government under the leadership of Siad Barre. The Siad Barre government had held political power in Somalia since 1969, mainly by keeping clan rivalries under control, first with support from the Soviet Union (until 1977) and later with support from the United States.

As the end of the Cold War approached, client states of both the Soviet Union and the United States (and the West more generally) received less support. As a result of their dwindling resources these governments lost the power to keep local political rivalries in check. Local political factions—often ethnic, religious, or clan based—pushed hard against the central governments.

In Somalia, the central government's control began to splinter in 1988, as clans in the north rebelled against the Siad Barre government, resentful of their long exclusion from sharing power and benefits within the country. A widespread and heart-rending humanitarian crisis ensued during which hundreds of thousands of Somalis starved to death, and living conditions deteriorated horribly. The international community responded to this crisis when nongovernmental organizations and United Nations specialized agencies rushed to Somalia to provide aid and assistance.

But the situation worsened. Government services functioned with increasing difficulty and eventually not at all. The government could not provide for the day-to-day security of its citizens (law enforcement and judicial sectors collapsed) or for their basic needs (food and health care became increasingly scarce). In the context of a deteriorating political and security environment, the efforts of humanitarian workers were often thwarted by violence and theft, or they were blocked by one of the clan-based political factions competing for power within the country. The situation continued to deteriorate for humanitarian efforts, for humanitarian workers, and for the Somalis themselves.

In January 1991, the Siad Barre government fell, and Somalia became a "failed state," a term in vogue at that time for describing nations where public authority was no longer effective in providing for the security and welfare of the country's citizens, and where competing factions were often involved in violent power struggles.[14]

Following the Somali government's collapse, the political and security situation continued to decline, making the delivery of humanitarian aid even more difficult. By the end of 1991, humanitarian organizations found themselves unable to operate effectively, and nearly all shut down their operations.[15] The Security Council, which had been monitoring the situation in Somalia, authorized a United Nations peacekeeping mission in Somalia. United Nations missions were in Somalia for the next three years, from April 1992 through March 1995.[16]

Initially, the Security Council authorized a mission to facilitate humanitarian deliveries within the capital, Mogadishu. This mission, the United Nations Operation in Somalia (UNOSOM I) later was expanded to include the entire country. UNOSOM I began its work with a small contingent of fifty military observers. As with earlier peacekeeping missions, UNOSOM I was under the operational command of the United Nations. Conditions in the country continued to deteriorate, and violence continued to interfere with humanitarian efforts. The Security Council twice increased the strength of UNOSOM. But by the end of 1992, it was clear that this approach to providing support for humanitarian efforts was not working.

In response, the Security Council turned to another mechanism. It authorized the United States to lead a multilateral task force to use "all necessary means" to create a secure environment that would allow humanitarian aid to be delivered. This force, the United Task Force (UNTAF), under US command, overlapped with UNOSOM I, still under UN command. When UNTAF established the necessary level of security it would hand off responsibilities to a new UN commanded mission, UNOSOM II.[17]

This handoff took place over a period of two months between March and May 1993. At that time operational control was returned to the United Nations. UNOSOM II included US military personnel, whereas UNOSOM I had not. Many considered the handoff to be an example of bad planning and execution. A separate US commanded force remained in Somalia to support the UN mission, creating some role confusion.

Many analysts view the UN engagement in Somalia as a failure.[18] During the three years very little seemed to go right. Early successes in getting competing warlords to cooperate in a scheme for effectively distributing aid and reestablishing governance slipped into chaos. Bureaucratic politics, personality differences, and careerism at all levels led to a shifting cast of leaders, which complicated rather than alleviated the problems in the country. Relations between UN personnel and the local populations waxed and waned, between the welcoming reception of the missions as life-saving to resentment and hostility on the part of the local population, and between impartiality and partisanship on the part of UN personnel. Humanitarian aid did not get to where it was needed most. National contingents, although technically under UN command, took direction from their national capitals, sometimes resulting in their not participating in actions where they were needed.[19]

In the face of these difficulties, 1993 turned out to be a fateful year for international intervention in general, and for United Nations peacekeeping in particular. The year began amid growing tensions between the United Nations and local warlords, especially Mohammed Farah Aideed and his clan. Despite these rising tensions, few were prepared for what happened, or for the aftershocks that those events would produce.

Canada has been a staunch supporter of United Nations peacekeeping since its beginning. During my early research on peacekeeping in the late 1980s and early 1990s, it was common for Canadian officers and troops to narrate their participation in peacekeeping with a special sense of pride. In part, this sentiment related to a sense of contribution to the work of maintaining peace and security, but it was also in no small measure associated with a bit of nationalistic pride in the major role that their former Prime Minister Lester Pearson played in creating peacekeeping. But the mission in Somalia did not go smoothly for Canadian forces. On 16 March 1993, a sixteen-year-old Somali, Shidane Arone, was tortured and beaten to death by Canadian peacekeepers.[20] Horrible though this episode was, there were indications that it was only one of several ongoing problems. An allegation was made that Canadian troops carried out execution-style murders of Somali intruders, often young men seeking to pilfer supplies from the Canadian camp. These events plunged Canada into a period of intense self-examination. Some analysts concluded that the inhumane treatment of the Somalis resulted from an underlying racism.[21] The Canadian forces undertook an investigation of these events and, following a period of political contention, on 20 March 1995 the government established the independent Commission of Inquiry into the Deployment of Canadian Forces to Somalia. The work of the commission was ended before the commissioners could complete their mandate. Yet they produced a report that included some 160 recommendations.[22] The report also led to much public discussion and several books.[23]

This inauspicious start to the year was hardly preparation for how disastrously it would close. Throughout 1993, tensions continued to rise as the missions in Somalia intervened more aggressively in the local politics of the country. Some saw this growing assertiveness as necessary to try to ensure that humanitarian aid reached its intended targets. But others viewed some of this heightened action as attempts to set an example by bringing Aideed's faction to heel. In early October 1993, for example, US forces attempted to snatch Aideed's senior aides from a meeting they were known to be planning in downtown Mogadishu.

It is not my purpose to recount here in detail the events of that failed mission or to analyze fully how it came about.[24] I want only to note that the mission went badly wrong. The mission culminated in a fifteen-hour-long battle during which many peacekeepers were killed, and the pilot of one of the American Black Hawk helicopters, Michael Durant, was held captive. The most shocking turn of the day for those in the West came in the form of reports and videos of jubilant Somalis dragging American corpses through the streets. These images were perhaps especially shocking for those in the West, because they could not understand how the Somalis could act so violently against people who were "only trying to help them."

As had the murder and abuse of Somalis at the hands of Canadian peacekeepers, the battle in Mogadishu provoked widespread reaction. The initial response of both the American and United Nations communities was to appeal for resolve and steadfastness in pursuing the noble goals of the intervention. Then US Secretary of State Warren Christopher was quoted as saying, "In the face of these kinds of attacks, it's time for Americans to be very steady in our response and not talk about getting out."[25] But the actions of the United States and others did not measure up to such appeals for steadfastness. Instead, in the United States, the Clinton administration reevaluated its position vis-à-vis peace operations and developed a restrained policy, reluctant to deploy US troops in interventions. Naturally this had consequences for how the international community in general approached peacekeeping. This general reluctance to intervene or to fully commit to interventions, for fear of casualties and the political consequences that would follow, was called the "Somalia Syndrome." This syndrome, then, became an explanatory shorthand for the failure of the international community to act in the face of subsequent crises, such as that in Rwanda.

The Somalia experience was something of a watershed for United Nations peacekeeping. As UN peacekeepers had come under fire in the streets and alleys of Mogadishu, so too United Nations peacekeeping, lauded with the Nobel Prize just five years before, came under fire as an instrument of international action. United Nations peacekeeping had gone badly wrong not only by failing in its attempt to make suffering people safer but at times even by exacerbating their plight. The question was, how did this happen?

Lessons Learned and the Rethinking of Peacekeeping

A satisfying explanation of how culture affects peacekeeping requires both an underlying understanding of culture and an overarching account of the fundamental aspects of peacekeeping in general. What is called for, then, is the integration of a general analysis of peace operations that contextualizes culture-specific problematic events in an understanding of the broader cultural context of how and why peacekeeping works, when it does. I undertake this task in this book.

In response to events in Somalia, as well as those in the former Yugoslavia and Rwanda, those who saw an expanded role for peacekeeping in the end of the Cold War needed to take stock. This was done in a context where domestic political expediency in the United States and elsewhere made for greater caution about participation in peacekeeping, if not outright rejection of such involvement. There were at least two paths that this stock-taking could follow. The first was a reassessment of the wisdom of assigning to the instrument of peacekeeping the set of expanded roles envisioned for it in *An Agenda for Peace*. That path would entail going back to basics and figuring out what made peacekeeping successful—when it was successful—and how to build on those findings. The second path was to consider the failures of Somalia, and later in the former Yugoslavia and elsewhere, as a problem for which technical solutions could be worked out. That is, the alternative to a thorough reassessment was to tinker around the edges of the instrument. This alternative focused, for instance, on the need for more robust mandates, better financing, and quicker deployment.

In what I think was an unfortunate turn in peacekeeping studies, for reasons described in this book, it was largely by traveling this second path that analysts sought to make sense of what had happened. This did not serve well the clear need for developing missions to deal effectively with new circumstances. My view is that developing missions with an understanding of the power of the symbolic and cultural aspects of peacekeeping could help make those missions effective, in ways that technical fixes could not. However, such lessons-learned studies examined a wide set of factors that affected peacekeeping—the use of force, new geopolitical relationships, challenges of adequately financing peacekeeping, the complex nature of missions undertaken in the post–Cold War period. While some analysts saw one or another set of these factors as making the crucial difference, nearly all agreed that peacekeeping had entered a new phase.

John Mackinlay and Jarat Chopra introduced the term "second generation peacekeeping" to indicate that peacekeeping was being asked to take on a new range of operational functions and to set this new kind of peacekeeping apart from the way it had been done before 1990.[26] The idea of second generation peacekeeping captured something in the imagination of the international community. The term became widely used by those interested in the future of peacekeeping. Describing the new missions as second generation peacekeeping implied that the missions of the 1990s related in some important though unspecified ways to earlier peacekeeping. However, the narrative of great differences between traditional peacekeeping and the complex missions of the 1990s and later soon moved the community away from speaking about generations of peacekeeping. In place of that concept, terms were used that explicitly or implicitly embraced the idea that post-1990 peacekeeping was a new phenomenon, often invoking two main sets of considerations.

The first theme in the narrative was that the conditions facing new missions are radically different from those in which faced pre-1990 peacekeeping. Traditionally missions were fielded in situations of inter-state conflicts; most post-1990 missions dealt with internal conflicts or collapsed states. The second theme in the narrative was that the new missions were multifunctional in ways that first generation peacekeeping was not. Taken together, these considerations meant that post-1990 peacekeeping required different operational capacities than had first traditional peacekeeping, and that much of what was learned in traditional peacekeeping no longer applied. Thus, multifunctional peacekeeping was different in that it required, for example, more robust rules of engagement (that is, instructions that allowed peacekeepers to use more force and to use it more freely), larger military forces, and tighter coordination between the military and humanitarian organizations, whether specialized UN agencies or nongovernmental organizations.

As a result of following this second path, many fine studies have been written about the technical aspects of peacekeeping. Since the mid-1990s, scholars, militaries, and agencies have published thousands of such studies. These studies focus on such features of peacekeeping as the use of force in peace operations,[27] financing peace operations,[28] the challenges of providing for law and order in mission areas,[29] challenges to and methods for military-humanitarian coordination,[30] and the role of information campaigns in peace operations.[31]

A smaller, but still substantial, literature treats issues that are slightly removed from the policy and technical analyses of peacekeeping and thus moves toward consideration of its foundational aspects. This literature treats topics such as how the organization of the United Nations affects peacekeeping,[32] the nature of neutrality and impartial action in peacekeeping,[33] the role of conflict resolution within peacekeeping missions,[34] and the broader questions of when and how the international community ought to intervene to protect people when sovereignty is an issue.[35]

There are relatively few studies that follow the path of going back to basics and self-consciously examining the fundamental underpinnings of peacekeeping. If that path were pursued, it would inevitably lead to considering, at least in part, the cultural context of peacekeeping. During its first forty years of operation, peacekeeping developed deep organizational cultural roots that propelled its practice. These practices, in turn, communicated to populations where missions were deployed and to the national and international constituencies from which peacekeeping drew its support.

Although peacekeeping has been a presence on the stage of world affairs since 1948, until the mid-1980s the literature about peacekeeping contained no significant treatments of its cultural aspects. Possibly this was because most of those concerned with peacekeeping prior to that time were political scientists, sociologists, military professionals, or international civil servants. Whatever the reason, the earliest sustained work treating peacekeeping as a cultural phenomenon was Marianne Heiberg's empirical studies of the Norwegian contingent of the United Nations Interim Force in Lebanon (UNIFIL), and my own theoretical and programmatic treatments of peacekeeping from an anthropological perspective, as well as my subsequent empirical study of the United Nations Truce Supervision Organization (UNTSO).[36]

Since 1993 there has been a growing interest in culture and its relation to peacekeeping and an increasing number of anthropologists have come to the field. Missions in Kosovo and East Timor, the United Nations's first attempts during the 1990s at extensive state-building, were troubled by a lack of understanding of local structures and of the cultural contextualization of those structures. This led to important work urging that international interventions, especially those that involve state-building, respectfully engage local culture.[37] This interest grew exponentially after the events of September 11, 2001, and the subsequent invasions of Afghanistan and Iraq, because in these cases the initial expeditionary activity was followed by "nation building" that is also thought of as a "peace operation." The difficulties that are still being experienced in Afghanistan and Iraq are partly attributed to a lack of cultural knowledge. This has, in turn, created a frenzy of activity aimed at defining just what kind of cultural understanding a military engaged in peacekeeping—and more problematically engaged in counterinsurgency or occupation—might develop that could make a difference in their activities in these places.[38]

As in the past, when anthropologists turned their attention to development or other applied projects that have gone awry, they invoke culture to show why the projects did not turn out as expected.[39] Thus, anthropological analyses of peacekeeping either tend to show how inattention to culture caused the problem or are used to give a metacultural analysis critiquing the enterprise of peacekeeping as a whole. For example, anthropological work helps us to understand what went wrong in Somalia. Donna Winslow provides an anthropological account of how a failure to understand the organizational cultures of the Canadian Airborne contributed to its failings in Somalia, and Tamara Duffey describes a number of cultural mistakes made by the peacekeepers during their efforts in Somalia.[40] Based on his brief encounter with the United Nations mission in Cambodia, Amitav Ghosh wrote off the entire enterprise of United Nations Peacekeeping as a neo-imperialist canard.[41] Sociologist David Segal applied a cultural analysis to the Multinational Force and Observers in Sinai.[42]

For the most part, however, these studies have been conducted in a somewhat ad hoc manner in that they are offered in reaction to specific circumstances but lack an overall framework for understanding peacekeeping in general. Thus, as useful as these kinds of cultural analyses are, they run the unfortunate risk of reinforcing, for nonanthropologist audiences, the notion that culture is a stable and homogeneous "thing," the shortcomings of that view I address in chapter 3. As I write, there is a frenzy of activity that reflects just such a static notion of culture, and is aimed at figuring out how to include "culture" in the training of troops who will be deployed to peacekeeping and stabilization operations.

While it is too early to know what the doctrinal outcome of these efforts and expenditures of resources will be, early indications suggest the results will engage fairly superficial forms of cultural understanding at the level of common travelers advice. Travelers advice provides a list of "facts" about the other group's ways of dealing with the world and a basic list of things a person engaging members of the other group should or should not do. It focuses on things like how to count in the other group's language, how to recognize divisions among members of that group that are salient to them (but might not seem so to an outside observer), and, classically, advice about what gestures to make and postures to avoid: never show the sole of your foot, don't eat with your left hand, and so forth. These are stereotyped instructions that focus on the surface elements of culture, most often on those surface aspects that are different or exotic from the perspective of the person giving the instruction. The "Iraq Culture Smart Card" (produced by the United States Marine Corps) and the advice to Japanese soldiers deploying to Iraq (given by the Ministry of Defense) that they grow mustaches so that they will fit in better with Iraqis are instances of such engagement.[43] They continue to take culture—both the local culture and the culture of peacekeeping—as a stable homogeneous thing and as organized in the form of rules for action and interpretation. Even if the increasing interest in cultural aspects of peacekeeping leads analysts to use more sophisticated theories of culture—which see it as, for example, partial, political, emergent, and contested—the ad hoc nature of this engagement will remain problematic.

A Multilevel Approach to Peacekeeping

In placing peacekeeping in the context of a broad understanding of culture, I use three interrelated theoretical commitments. The first is that understanding the cultured nature of peacekeeping requires a multilevel approach. This follows the theoretical idea that to adequately account for any human activity, analyses must extend to levels of organization above and below the activity of interest.[44] Thus, in order to understand how peacekeeping works it is necessary not only to give an account of the particular activities of a peacekeeping group but also to show how those activities and the symbolic system within which they take place affect individuals and at the same time affect meaning and actions at higher levels of social organization.

The second theoretical commitment is that the accounts offered at each of the levels of organization must link essentially. Analyses at one level must at a minimum be consistent with those at adjacent levels and, if possible, support and enhance those analyses. I call this *theoretical scaffolding*. But, this multilevel approach is not just theoretically important. It also has important practical implications for the training for and organization of peacekeeping missions, where this approach is necessary for coordinating activities at the strategic, operational, and tactical levels. I refer to this as the need to construct a *strategic scaffold*. I show that when peacekeeping runs into trouble, it does so partly because the scaffolds of understanding and action have been destabilized.[45]

The third theoretical commitment this book accepts is that cultural systems are dynamic. They change through the practice and experiences of those who enact them. Because cultures always incorporate competing, sometimes antagonistic, frames of reference, a cultural analysis must provide flexible tools for understanding. Otherwise, cultural descriptions are taken to be stable and static, resulting in a false sense of knowledge of the system, and what I previously called the fallacy of detachable cultural descriptions.[46]

In addition to these three theoretical commitments, the analysis in this book proceeds from the perspective that nonmaterial and moral factors play important roles in matters of international security. I have developed this view in detail elsewhere in analyzing various episodes in US security policy.[47] The argument in this approach is that nonmaterial considerations play important and fundamental roles in shaping world events. While acknowledging that the traditional foci of security analyses such as economics, power, logistics, and legal contexts all contribute importantly to international affairs, it is also evident that symbolic and moral considerations have real force in human activities. Symbolic and moral considerations are less easily studied, quantified, and presented in neat policy papers than are the other factors usually considered by analysts. As a result, discussions of the symbolic and moral dimensions of international security form a small minority in the analytic literature, and such factors are often swept aside as insubstantial, as icing on the cake, rather than treated as contributing to events in critically important ways. While acknowledging the importance of material matters, the analysis of peacekeeping presented in this book shows the critical importance of moral and symbolic elements to peacekeeping.

This book is not intended to serve as an up-to-the-moment guide to contemporary peace operations. Nor is it a survey of the scholarly or policy literatures on peacekeeping, although I draw on both of these literatures. And, most certainly, it is not intended as a prescription for fixing peacekeeping *tomorrow*, although I do think that the material in this book will help those seriously thinking about the reframing and restructuring of peacekeeping efforts. Much of the material in this book deals with military aspects of peacekeeping. This may seem odd, since much of peacekeeping is carried out by civilian actors. Indeed, that this has always been the case is one of the arguments of this book. Yet, it is the military aspects of the enterprise that have shaped the symbolic contexts in which peacekeeping takes place, and for that reason foregrounding the military aspects of this work helps to sort out the complex processes involved in peace operations.[48]

My aim is to set out a dynamic, multilevel, cohesive approach to under-standing the ways in which peacekeeping is a cultured human activity. In doing so, I hope to show that the reason peacekeeping is under fire—both in the actual sense of peacekeepers being shot at and in the metaphorical sense of peacekeeping being under political fire—results from failures to act from such an understanding.

To accomplish this I move freely among a number of levels of analysis and sources of information. These include theoretical analyses, reports of ethno-graphic data that I have gathered through fieldwork and ethnographic inter-views, historical and documentary sources, and news reports and analyses. In the next chapter, I describe the origins and development of peacekeeping with a special focus on the symbolic nature of the institution. I pay special attention to the development of peacekeeping before the mid-1990s. I do this in order to highlight that these missions created processes and structures that critically affect missions today. The range of functions of observer missions and early forces discussed in chapter 2 was quite wide and predated the "second genera-tion" and "multidimensional missions" of the 1990s and beyond. In chapter 3, I discuss culture theory as it applies to peacekeeping and describe a variety of theoretical perspectives that help illuminate the dynamics of peacekeeping. In particular, I highlight the critical importance of political symbolism and ritual for peacekeeping. I argue that these cultural phenomena create a sym-bolic inversion, connected essentially to the symbolism of the United Nations, from which peacekeeping derives legitimacy.[49] In order to illustrate how the materials in chapters 2 and 3 merge, I describe some of my fieldwork with UNTSO. This involves considering the methodological challenges of that work (chapter 4) and a description of how everyday practice at UNTSO forms a web of symbolic meanings.

Following this, in chapter 5 I turn to showing how peacekeeping groups and forces adopt and reinterpret military symbolism and ritual so as to facilitate cooperation and coordination. This involves the construction of the shared identity of peacekeeper, which then shapes and channels the ways that mission members perceive, think about, and feel about their work. This is a complex set of social and cultural activities that affects the local group level. In addi-tion, the activities also affect individual motivation and perceptions of a mis-sion and of peacekeeping in general at levels above the local group. Chapter 6 extends the analysis to the level below the group and focuses on how the individual is affected by, and effects, peacekeeping. This chapter focuses on the importance of individual motivation in peacekeeping and on how appropriate motivational frames interact with other aspects of culture and experience in peacekeeping.

The material I develop in earlier chapters shows the importance of cultural understanding for cooperative action. Thus, in chapter 7, I consider how organizational cultures enhance or impede peacekeeping. Chapter 8 discusses how the lack of a broad cultural understanding of peacekeeping has resulted in calamities, for peacekeeping as an instrument of international action, for the troops and civilians who have served in missions, and for the populations that the missions were meant to serve. I consider atrocities like the Canadian troops' torture and murder of a young Somali, recent revelations of sexual exploitation, and the purposeful and inadvertent destabilization of local communities in which peacekeeping operations have been deployed. I show how such actions destabilize the symbolic inversions upon which peacekeeping depends for its legitimacy. I conclude in chapter 9 by discussing what my analysis suggests about the future of peacekeeping and how it might move from being under fire to reclaiming a position as an important and respected instrument for supporting international peace and security.

2

A Brief and Selective History
of Peacekeeping

United Nations peacekeeping emerged in the wake of the Second World War and in the midst of the solidification of the Cold War. Never envisioned in the United Nations Charter, peacekeeping was forged in the crucible of practical diplomacy. In 1948, a small number of unarmed military observers were sent to Palestine to monitor the truce that had been called for by the Security Council.[1] These observers were sent in a hurry and with no firm plans for how they would operate. The task of organizing these observers, determining their functioning, and supervising their activities fell to Ralph Bunche in his capacities first as the assistant to the UN Mediator in Palestine, Count Folke Bernadotte, and later as UN Acting Mediator in Palestine. In establishing the practice of using military officers from countries that could be viewed as honest brokers in a conflict area, Bunche set up the foundations of peacekeeping. It was Bunche's insights that led to the use of officers from many countries, who would be viewed as impartial observers of actions on the ground.[2] For his work in Palestine, which included the nascent instrument of peacekeeping, Bunche received the 1950 Nobel Peace Prize.[3]

It is from this humble beginning that United Nations peacekeeping evolved. In this chapter I give a brief and selective history of peacekeeping. Several more extensive and systematic treatments are available, and a full discussion of the intricacies of peacekeeping's development is outside the purpose of this book.[4] Rather, my aim in this chapter is to describe just enough about peacekeeping so that there will be a general context for my later discussion of some of its social and cultural characteristics.

The military observers deployed in Palestine in 1948 formed the basis for the United Nations Truce Supervision Organization (UNTSO). When it was authorized in June 1948, UNTSO became the first United Nations peacekeeping operation. UNTSO, in its turn, set the basic pattern for the development of peacekeeping over the next four decades. During that time, the popular perception of peacekeeping missions was that they used international military forces to observe that cease-fire agreements were honored, to supervise the withdrawal of troops, and sometimes to promote conciliation and confidence building between beleaguered parties. In 1984, General Indar Jit Rikhye, then the president of the International Peace Academy—a nongovernmental organization dedicated to the promotion of peacekeeping and the training of diplomats, military officers, and others—wrote that peacekeeping involved "the prevention, containment, moderation and termination of hostilities between or within states through the medium of third-party intervention organized and directed internationally, using multinational military, police, and civilian personal to restore and maintain peace."[5]

When Rikhye was writing, there was no generally accepted definition of peacekeeping. (Indeed, even today there is no single definition that is agreed to by all.) The definition he offered is noteworthy because he was writing from the vantage of someone who had participated in several peacekeeping missions, had served as the military advisor to the secretary-general, and was directing the only organization then dedicated to advancing the conceptual and practical aspects of peacekeeping. Since it will later emerge as a point much cited in discussions of how missions established in 1992 and afterward differ from those established between 1948 and 1991, note that Rikhye's definition explicitly includes civilian personnel. This is contrary to the widely held view that early operations were purely military and that later operations were complicated by the inclusion of civilians.

Two general types of peacekeeping missions were developed: observer missions and peacekeeping forces. Both of these grew from the patterns that were established early in the UN experience with the peaceful settlement of conflicts. Observer missions deploy unarmed military officers to verify that the terms of a truce agreement are maintained. Observers do this by patrolling designated areas, inspecting troop and weapons concentrations, and providing independent verification of reported breeches of such agreements. Peacekeeping forces began as lightly armed military units that administered an area, usually a buffer zone between belligerents, and provided the separation of forces, security for civilians, and the calm necessary for the pursuit of negotiated settlements.

Between 1948 and 1992, the United Nations established twenty-three peacekeeping missions. In addition to a number of missions related to the Israel-Arab conflict, UN peacekeeping missions also took place in Kashmir, Cyprus, the Congo, Yemen, Afghanistan, Pakistan, and in Central America, among other places, as shown in table 2.1.[6]

These missions usually monitored or brokered cease-fire or other agreements, supported governmental transitions, and generally provided a measure of stability in conflict areas. Some were brief, like the mission in Yemen (July 1962–September 1963), or the mission in Namibia (April 1989–March 1990). Others have been ongoing for many years. UNTSO and UNMOGIP (United

Table 2.1: United Nations Peacekeeping Missions, 1948–1992

Dates	Mission Acronym	Mission	Region
June 1948–	UNTSO	United Nations Truce Supervision Organization	Middle East
Jan 1949–	UNMOGIP	United Nations Military Observer Group in India and Pakistan	Asia
Nov 1956–June 1964	UNEF I	United Nations Emergency Force	Middle East
June 1958–Dec 1958	UNOGIL	United Nations Observation Group in Lebanon	Middle East
July 1960–June 1964	ONUC	United Nations Operation in the Congo	Africa
Oct 1962–April 1963	UNSF	United Nations Security Force in West New Guinea (West Irian)	Asia-Pacific
July 1963–Sept 1964	UNYOM	United Nations Yemen Observation Mission	Middle East
March 1964–	UNFICYP	United Nations Peacekeeping Force in Cyprus	Europe
May 1965–Oct 1966	DOMREP	Mission of the Representative of the Secretary-General in the Dominican Republic	Americas
May 1965–Oct 1966	UNIPOM	United Nations India-Pakistan Observation Mission	Asia
Oct 1973–July 1979	UNEF II	Second United Nations Emergency Force	Middle East
June 1974–	UNDOF	United Nations Disengagement Observer Force	Middle East
March 1978–	UNIFIL	United Nations Interim Force in Lebanon	Middle East
May 1988–March 1990	UNGOMAP	United Nations Good Offices Mission in Afghanistan and Pakistan	Asia
Aug 1988–Feb 1991	UNIIMOG	United Nations Iran-Iraq Military Observer Group	Middle East
Jan 1989–May 1991	UNAVEM I	United Nations Angola Verification Mission I	Africa
April 1989–March 1990	UNTAG	United Nations Transition Assistance Group	Africa
Nov 1989–Jan 1992	ONUCA	United Nations Observer Group in Central America	Americas
April 1991–Oct 2003	UNIKOM	United Nations Iraq-Kuwait Observation Mission	Middle East
May 1991–Feb 1995	UNAVEM II	United Nations Angola Verification Mission II	Africa
July 1991–April 1995	ONUSAL	United Nations Observer Mission in El Salvador	Americas
April 1991–	MINURSO	United Nations Mission for the Referendum in Western Sahara	Africa
Oct 1991–March 1992	UNAMIC	United Nations Advance Mission in Cambodia	Asia

United Nations Department of Peacekeeping Operations, http://www.un.org/Depts/dpko/dpko/.

Nations Military Observer Group in India and Pakistan), the observer mission in Kashmir, begun in 1948 and 1949 respectively, are still on the ground, as is the mission in Cyprus, which began in 1964.[7]

Peacekeeping's Early and Changing Fortunes

As it developed as an instrument of international action, peacekeeping went through periods characterized by almost opposite evaluations of its utility. Bunche's success in bringing the parties of the Palestine conflict to a settlement depended in part on the deployment of military observers. His being awarded the Nobel Peace Prize was an indirect acknowledgment of the high value that such operations could offer. Yet between 1948 and 1991, peacekeeping was sometimes derided as hopelessly ineffective, a waste of resources and efforts, and a potential threat to the capacity of nations to exercise their own sovereignty. Peacekeeping came in for particular criticism in the wake of its 1960 mission in the Congo, which failed to successfully midwife the Congo's independence, and in the failure of the mission in the Sinai to prevent the 1967 Arab-Israeli War.

The Congo, 1960

In 1960, the Security Council established the United Nations Operation in the Congo (ONUC). The original mandate for the operation was to facilitate the withdrawal of Belgian forces from the newly independent country and to help the Congolese government establish law and order. At the same time, the Security Council stated explicitly that ONUC would have no role in the internal affairs of the newly independent country.[8] Events unfolded quickly. Soon the internal situation in the country deteriorated, ONUC became embroiled in the conflict, and its mandate was strengthened to allow it to play a more active role in establishing a peaceful and secure environment.[9] ONUC began as a mission legitimated by Chapter 6 of the United Nations Charter, which calls for the pacific settlement of disputes, but transformed into a mission where force was applied. Thus, the mission in the Congo was authorized to support intervention in an active conflict, as allowed in Chapter 7 of the Charter.

The mission in the Congo was the first UN peacekeeping mission authorized to use force in order to help a "collapsed state" regain order. I note this because in discussions of missions established from 1992 onward, it is often asserted that the authorization to use force marks those missions off from earlier ones. I do not want to dwell on this issue here, since I will return to it later, but note that the use of force within peacekeeping missions has been evolving throughout peacekeeping's history, much like the institution itself.[10]

The Congo achieved independence in a complex political setting.[11] The Belgian colonizing powers left only reluctantly in June 1960. The Congo was a source of considerable economic wealth. As they left, many Belgian interests were in the hands of local proxies. As well, the United States and the Soviet Union coveted the resources of the Congo, and both sought to control them. This American-Soviet contest was overlain on local political factions, which carried it out both as surrogates for the superpowers and in their own self-interests. As independence approached, a series of political struggles and compromises led to political rivals Patrice Lumumba and Joseph Kasavubu gaining the posts of prime minister and president, respectively. Lumumba, a charismatic and popular figure, had been in the forefront of the Congo independence movement. He was widely viewed in the West as pro-Soviet, though some dispute this and portray him as a dedicated, but inexperienced and politically naïve, nationalist.[12]

The situation was unstable and became increasingly chaotic and violent when, only a month after independence, the mineral-rich province of Katanga seceded, with the complicity of the Belgian mining cartel that had interests in the area. On 9 September 1960, President Kasavubu dismissed Lumumba, who reacted in kind, but without the constitutional authority to do so, by dismissing Kasavubu. On 14 September, Joseph Mobutu, Lumumba's chief of staff, seized control of the government, further complicating the situation.

Increasingly worried about Lumumba's safety, the UNOC sought to protect him by placing a large number of troops around his house. The way to characterize that action is still a matter of contention. Depending upon the perspective taken, either the UNOC offered Lumumba protection or he was held there under house arrest to better control his movements. In any event, one evening Lumumba left his UNOC-protected house. Soon he was captured by the military controlled by Mobutu, and over the next days he was brutalized and murdered.[13]

Following Lumumba's capture and assassination while ostensibly being protected by UNOC troops, criticisms of the mission became intense.[14] Especially important for the fortunes of peacekeeping was the stinging criticism of the United Nations and of Secretary-General Dag Hammarskjöld by the Soviet Union—in concert with many African and nonaligned nations—as the situation deteriorated and the United Nations' role became increasingly messy. These critics accused the organization and the secretary-general of serving as agents of the United States, playing a part in the superpower realpolitik of the day, and thus acting outside of the moral order the United Nations was intended to establish. The firestorm of protests and accusations about the Congo mission greatly affected peacekeeping.[15]

The United Nations in Sinai

Only four years earlier, under Hammarskjöld's leadership, the United Nations had demonstrated its capacity to act against the interests of the big powers when it deployed the United Nations Emergency Force (UNEF).[16] But this victory against realpolitik was to prove temporary. In 1956, Britain and France joined with Israel in attacking Egypt after Egyptian President Gamal Abdel Nasser nationalized the Suez Canal. Each of the attacking countries had substantial interests in having free access to the canal, particularly Britain. The United Nations intervened to end the fighting, and in doing so worked against the interests of two permanent members of the Security Council. It did this by establishing UNEF as a key element in ending the fighting among the parties. Because Britain and France were involved in the fighting, UNEF was authorized by the General Assembly, rather than through the Security Council where both hold the veto. For the next decade UNEF was a model peacekeeping operation, maintaining peace and order in a buffer zone in the Sinai and Gaza Strip between Israel and Egypt.

Only a few years after the Congo crisis and its diminishing of the United Nation's political and symbolic capital, UNEF shifted from being a model mission to being highly problematic.[17] In 1967, President Nasser demanded the withdrawal of UNEF from Gaza and from the Sinai, where critical UNEF troops were stationed at Sharm el-Sheikh, on the tip of the Sinai peninsula. Access to the Gulf of Aqaba could be controlled from Sharm el-Sheikh. This was especially important to Israel because its port city of Eilat depends upon access to the gulf.

United Nations Secretary-General U Thant sought to persuade Nasser to allow UNEF to remain, since the replacement of UNEF troops by Egyptian troops at Sharm el-Sheikh would be viewed by Israel as a casus belli.[18] U Thant stalled for time, sending urgent cables and representatives to Cairo to try to dissuade Nasser from this path.[19] Nasser remained steadfast in his course of action.

UNEF's forces were arrayed on Egyptian territory, Israel having refused to have troops stationed on its territory. U Thant decided that, because the basis of the deployment included Egypt's consent to UNEF troops on its sovereign territory, the proper course of action was to withdraw UNEF.[20] He complied with Nasser's request and recalled the force. UNEF troops left Sharm el-Sheikh on 22 May 1967 and it was then immediately reoccupied by Egyptian forces. Nasser imposed a naval blockade that would prohibit Israeli ships from the Gulf of Aqaba. This took place a day before U Thant's planned arrival at Cairo on 23 May 1967, thus foreclosing his diplomatic efforts.[21] Events developed so quickly that, rather than completing the orderly withdrawal they had planned,

UNEF troops were caught in the hostilities that followed Nasser's actions—finding themselves amid Israeli air bombardment of Egyptian targets, and Egyptian, Palestinian, and Israeli troop engagement.[22]

The ensuing war led to the Israeli occupation of much Arab land, including the West Bank and Gaza, the Golan Heights and the Sinai. Many argued that UNEF's withdrawal was a key factor leading to the June 1967 Arab-Israeli War. The action was widely cited as evidence of the failure of the United Nations' peacekeeping.[23]

Critics of the decision to withdraw UNEF argued that doing so was a major political miscalculation, one that resulted from a lack of appreciation for the rules of political rhetoric in the Arab world. This line of criticism suggests that much in Nasser's public pronouncement was intended for a domestic audience, which would expect and appropriately discount the hyperbole and overstatement. In any event, the collapse of the United Nations Emergency Force in the Sinai brought renewed and deep pessimism about the potential for peacekeeping, as a tool of collective action, to maintain peace and international security. Indeed, some saw this episode as signaling a "requiem for United Nations Peacekeeping."[24]

Peacekeeping Continues

Despite these two difficult episodes, the Security Council continued to use peacekeeping as an instrument for addressing threats to international peace and security. During the two dozen years following the UNEF debacle, UN peacekeeping missions were deployed in multiple areas of the Middle East, Asia, and Central America. It was these, along with earlier UN missions, that were collectively awarded the 1988 Nobel Peace Prize.

Close analysis of the development of individual missions shows that a considerable amount of improvisation and ad hoc development was involved in each mission. In 1990, having recently retired from his long-time post as under secretary-general for special political affairs where he was the primary person overseeing United Nations peacekeeping, Brian Urquhart wrote, "Care should be taken in attempting to generalize and improve upon what has been part of the recipe for success [of United Nations peacekeeping], namely improvisation."[25]

Nonetheless, certain regularities developed in UN practice that imparted common attributes to all of the missions. By the mid-1980s, a kind of informal peacekeeping doctrine was in the air that would soon be set down by scholars and practitioners as the elements of effective peacekeeping. Claims that peacekeeping after the Cold War is distinct from the peacekeeping that took place prior to 1992 are based in part on identifying how newer missions do not conform to this doctrine. For that reason, it is worth a brief review of the principles underlying peacekeeping from 1948 to 1991.

Early Peacekeeping Principles

By the mid-1980s, a small but significant literature about peacekeeping had developed. Three genres contributed to this literature. First, a number of books and articles distilled lessons from past experience. These focused on the nitty-gritty aspects of peacekeeping and offered advice and procedures for carrying out technically effective missions.[26] Second, nearly from the beginning, participants in peacekeeping operations published memoirs about their own experiences. This memoir literature offered summary advice about what makes for effective peacekeeping, and sometimes these also sought to account for the author's retrospectively controversial decisions and actions.[27] And third, a number of studies examining a variety of peacekeeping missions drew general principles and lessons about peacekeeping and discussed the political and economic constraints under which United Nations peacekeeping operated.[28] In this literature, and in the hallway conversations of diplomats and military personnel, a kind of received view of peacekeeping developed. This received view consisted of a set of nine understandings and principles about what made for good peacekeeping practice.[29]

"Ripeness" for Resolution. Generally, when a threat to international peace and security was noted by the UN Secretariat or by the Security Council, the organization's main reaction was for the Security Council to pass a resolution calling for the immediate end of fighting and for a cease-fire. Security Council resolutions enter into force as an element of international law. They are sometimes followed, and often not. By the mid-1980s, it was commonly recognized that parties responded to Council actions mainly when their situation had reached a point where they realized that it would be more harmful for them to continue fighting than it would be for them to agree to a cease-fire. When this occurs in a conflict, the state of affairs is generally referred to as being "ripe for resolution." Ripeness is a necessary but not sufficient condition for a conflict to move from hostilities to negotiated settlement.[30]

As I described earlier, during the fighting between Israel and Egypt in the 1967 war, Israel captured the Sinai peninsula and as a result controlled the east bank of the Suez Canal. The occupation of the Sinai, and especially the loss of sovereignty, was keenly felt by the Egyptians. Their desire to reassert control over these areas and to reestablish a sense of national efficacy was one of the reasons why on 6 October 1973, Egypt attacked the Israeli positions at the Suez Canal.[31]

Having caught the Israelis by surprise, Egyptian troops crossed the Suez Canal, overran the Israel positions on the east bank, and pushed a small distance into Sinai. Egyptian military success was a genuine source for the renewal of national pride in Egypt. The Egyptian strategy called for its troops to cross and hold the canal, but for them not to advance beyond a perimeter where they could be protected by Egyptian air power. This strategy was successfully put into action. Soon, however, overeager commanders on the ground advanced their troops beyond that perimeter. With that turn of events, the Israeli army was able to counterattack. Israeli forces retook their positions on the Sinai side and then crossed the canal. This allowed Israeli forces to surround the Egyptian Third Army and advance toward Cairo, the Egyptian capital. Early calls for cease-fire went unheeded. It was not until both sides faced situations in which further fighting would bring unwanted consequences that they agreed to a cease-fire and the United Nations mediated negotiations. In this case, Israel did not wish to occupy Cairo, since doing so was bound to create impossible challenges, and the Egyptians did not want their Third Army to perish. Only when the situation was thus ripe for resolution did the parties turn to the United Nations.[32]

Similarly, the UN initiatives in other conflicts took hold only when parties to the conflict arrived at a hurtful stalemate—when neither side can win outright and the costs of remaining at war are too harmful for each side to bear.

Reputation Considerations. Reaching the point of mutually hurtful stalemate, the parties to the conflict confront an immediate difficulty. Having publicly fully committed themselves to victory in the conflict—sometimes using florid rhetorical demonizing of the enemy, and perhaps with overoptimistic assessments of how the fighting was going—the parties could not very well sue for a cease-fire without harming their reputations with their own people and with the international community. Grasping that continued fighting would not be to their advantage, the parties find themselves caught in a dilemma: either continue fighting and suffer unacceptable losses while saving face or stop fighting and lose credibility. Neither option is palatable.

The received view was that United Nations peacekeeping provided a very practical, diplomatic way out of this dilemma. By acceding to the demands for a cessation of hostilities made by the Security Council, parties to a conflict could reframe their decision to stop fighting as a response to the concerns of the international community, and as the act of a responsible member of that community. The introduction of a peacekeeping mission further allowed them to maintain that they were protecting their people, without having to recant any of their earlier demonizing of the other party to the conflict.

Attaining a situation in which parties to a conflict are willing to accept that continued fighting is not in their self-interests and to see that the least damaging way out of the fighting would be to reframe their decision in terms of international concerns, provides necessary but not sufficient conditions for missions to be successfully employed. The prevailing wisdom was that an additional six considerations needed also to be met.

Security Council Support. Any United Nations peacekeeping operation needs to be appropriately authorized by the world body. Of the twenty-three missions authorized by the United Nations between 1948 and 1991, nearly all were authorized by the Security Council. Thus, support within the Security Council was seen as essential to designing and fielding a successful peacekeeping mission.

While it was not absolutely true that missions needed to have Security Council endorsement, it became a practical reality. Indeed, the expected failure to achieve Council support for the envisioned peacekeeping mission between Israel and Egypt when they negotiated their peace demonstrated that going outside of the Council was not an easy or common response to an impasse in the council. In Article IV of the "Treaty of Peace between the Arab Republic of Egypt and the State of Israel," signed 26 March 1979, the parties agreed to request that the United Nations deploy a peacekeeping mission in the Sinai in order to support the treaty. These forces were to operate check points within and between buffer zones, periodically verify the implementation of the treaty, provide on-the-spot inspections at the request of either party, and ensure freedom of navigation through the Strait of Tiran.[33] Significantly, in light of the 1967 experience with UNEF, both parties agreed that UN personnel would be removed only with the consent of the Security Council, and with all five permanent members voting in the affirmative.[34]

It soon became apparent that the Arab states disapproved of the treaty and that the Soviet Union would block the United Nations from implementing it. The suggestion to use UNTSO to fulfill the peace observation functions specified in the treaty was rejected.[35] Ultimately the Security Council was unable to provide the specified force and observers. As a result, Egypt, Israel, and the United States formed the Multinational Force and Observers as an independent peacekeeping mission. It is still functioning today.[36]

Consent of the Parties. Peacekeeping missions put military and civilian personnel on the ground in tense and dangerous situations. The ability of peacekeepers to carry out the tasks assigned to them requires more than the legitimacy bestowed on their actions by Security Council resolutions. Indeed, that the parties to the conflict must give their consent to the mission was seen as an essential element for UN peacekeeping.

Earlier I noted that much about peacekeeping developed in an ad hoc manner and through trial and error. This is true for the understanding of consent, which over time came to be seen as having at least four required levels of consent: for the mission, for the mandate, for the force commander, and for troops to be deployed. Each of the four levels of consent presents practical political challenges.

At the broadest level, at least one party to a conflict had to consent to the deployment of the United Nations peacekeeping mission in its sovereign territory. While the consent of all parties to the deployment of the mission was considered ideal, missions could go forward with forces placed only in the territory of one of the parties. As was the case for UNEF, having the force deployed on one party's territory meant that the revocation of that consent could lead to the effective end of the mission. The UNEF experience suggested that in the absence of the agreement by all parties, care must be taken, as it was in the Egypt-Israel treaty, that the parties agree to specific criteria for how the mission might be ended.

Determining the mandate of a mission requires a more specific level of consent by the parties than does their simple agreement that a peacekeeping mission be authorized. What the mission will be authorized to do—maintain a buffer zone, observe and report that a cease-fire is being honored, aid in elections, maintain an area in which a civilian population continues to reside, for example—affects greatly the nature of the deployment that will follow. Whether the mission will be a small observer group, a larger multinational force, or a ubiquitous presence derives from the mission's mandate. The size and responsibilities of the deployment are set out in the mandate. According to the view current by the mid-1980s, parties needed also to give their consent to the mission's mandate.

The mandate gives strategic guidance to the leadership of a mission. That guidance is translated into tactical instructions under the direction of the mission leadership. Those tactical instructions are made operational by the peacekeepers on the ground, whether they are staffing an observation post or administering a particular sector of the mission area. The military components of a peacekeeping mission are drawn from a number of countries. This introduces two further levels at which the parties' consent that the received view deemed necessary.

The military component of a UN peacekeeping mission is under the direction of a force commander who is appointed by the secretary-general with the concurrence of the Security Council. The choice of the force commander is complicated by political considerations. No force commander would be appointed should he or she be objected to by one of the parties. Likewise, the troops that will deploy as part of the mission come from a variety of countries. The process of raising the troops for a mission involves considerable behind-the-scenes negotiation, sometimes hard and creative negotiation by members of the Secretariat. Typically, there is an effort to get as broad a mix of national troop contributors as possible, since this adds to the legitimacy of the mission:[37] "The more flags you have on the table . . . the more the legitimacy."[38] A practical corollary of this was that superpowers did not contribute troops, and, often, troop contributors did not have a colonial past.

Countries that contribute large contingents may set conditions on their participation, including that the force commander be one of their nationals. Whether these conditions are agreed to is a matter of negotiation and calculation by the Secretariat. But beyond this internal negotiation the parties to the conflict must agree to the origins of the troops deployed. There are many reasons that parties to a conflict might reject the inclusion of particular troops in the mission. The potential contributor might be seen by the parties as having their own interests in the conflict and thus being intrinsically incapable of being a fair broker.[39] Also, historic antagonisms—such as those deriving from shared colonial histories—might lead one of the parties to reject offered troops. Thus, parties' consent to the force commander and to the troops was also considered essential for a mission to go forward successfully.

A Clear Mandate and Its Careful Specification. By the mid-1980s, one of the most common assertions about UN peacekeeping missions was that they could not succeed if the Security Council did not give a clear mandate setting out what the mission was to accomplish and providing sufficient resources for achieving those ends. Thus, in shaping the mandate, the Security Council considered whether or not member states would be willing to provide the necessary financial support for the responsibilities outlined in the envisioned mandate. The mandate sets out what the mission will do in general terms, and usually the force commander and a technical team specifies how the mandate will be translated into actions on the ground. This is done in negotiation with the parties.

In my early interviews with military officers who had been involved in various peacekeeping operations, I heard frequently how frustrated they had been by mandates that had been purposefully kept ambiguous so that diplomatic objectives could be reached. They reported that this made their job of translating the mandate into rules and procedures more difficult. They would underscore the point that however clear or unclear the mandate, it had to be implemented. And they stated that in the process of agreeing to implementation plans, carelessness or inexperience could introduce additional difficulties to the mission. To make this point, they related stories about how using maps with too broad a scale or drawing demarcation lines using blunt pencils caused later confusion on the ground. And they told about how parties to the conflict had restricted movement within the mission area because initial negotiations failed to specify adequately who could go where, or even who could legally drive a vehicle in the country.

In short, by the mid-1980s the received view held that for peacekeeping to succeed, mandates ought to be as clear and unambiguous as possible and translated carefully into operational instructions that met the needs of the mission.

Multinational Troops. Article 26 of the United Nations Charter established the Military Staff Committee, consisting of representatives from the permanent member countries of the Security Council, which was to be "responsible under the Security Council for the strategic direction of any armed forces placed at the disposal of the Security Council." Article 45 envisioned that "members shall hold immediately available national air-force contingents for combined international enforcement action." So according to its Charter, the United Nations was to have at its disposal troops from member countries to be used for maintaining international peace and security, and to be deployed and directed by the Security Council. The Military Staff Committee meets every two weeks, but as a consequence of the Cold War, and the resulting inability of the permanent members of the Security Council to reach agreement, the Military Staff Committee has never had any significant operational responsibilities. Likewise, the standing availability of national troops for United Nations use has also never been realized. Most observers agree that it is unlikely that the Military Staff Committee will ever assume a meaningful operational role or that significant standing military resources will be put at the organization's disposal.[40]

In light of this circumstance, whenever the Security Council authorizes a new peacekeeping mission, the members of the Secretariat have to negotiate with individual states about whether they will contribute troops to the mission. Of course, there is first a need to be sure that troops from potential contributing countries are acceptable to the parties. Beyond this there is the difficulty of finding countries that are willing to contribute troops. And not just any troops will do. Those assembling the mission must ensure that they can raise a sufficient number of troops, and that those troops will have the skills needed for the purposes of the mission.

Authorizing a mission, defining its mandate, and securing troops is actually not a linear process. As a crisis builds toward intervention, all of these issues are subjects of informal discussions at the United Nations. From these discussions, it is often possible to gauge the number and kinds of troops that will be available for the mission, and possibly what skills they will bring. This influences the way the Council defines the mission and its mandate, which introduces many of the ambiguities and troop shortfalls decried by peacekeepers and commentators.

Those interested in peacekeeping recognized that the multinational character of United Nations peacekeeping was an essential element of its potential success. This tenet made it worth grappling with the practical and political difficulties encountered in raising the required troops.

Rapid Mission Deployment. In conflict settings, things develop quickly. As a result, a situation that may provide an opening for intervention today may rapidly dissolve as the facts on the ground change. By the mid-1980s, it was recognized that the period between a Security Council mandate and troop deployment was extremely volatile and critical to the success of a mission. Thus, rapid deployment of the peacekeeping mission became an element in the received view of what makes for successful peacekeeping. Unfortunately, throughout the period from 1948 to 1991, such rapid deployment was more of an ideal than a reality. Often, a few advance troops would start the mission while troop contribution negotiations were finalized.

Non-Use of Force. Between 1948 and 1991, the view developed that peace-keepers should not and do not use force as part of their mission. In their first missions, peacekeepers were deployed with no weapons or with only sidearms for self-defense. Later missions, like the 1960s Congo intervention, used more significant weapons.

Just what role, if any, the use of force actually had in peacekeeping was more complex. As I suggest in chapter 3, the idea that peacekeepers did not use force—indeed, that they were unarmed—is a powerful component in the system of symbolism from which peacekeeping gains its legitimacy. The symbolism of the unarmed peacekeeper is a powerful and compelling image. It became incorporated into the general perception of peacekeeping in part because occasional news stories described how an unarmed peacekeeper had carried out a particularly heroic act, placing himself or herself in grave danger in order to enforce a mission's mandate. For instance, "the story is told of the Israeli tank in the vanguard of the 1982 invasion that was to drive out the Pal-estinians that halted in front of a French UNIFIL officer standing alone and very isolated in the middle of the road. He informed the tank commander that he had no right to pass."[41]

Yet the situation on the ground was always more complex. The kind of arms present in each mission varied considerably. Conversations about the use of force spanned discussions that focused on exactly how the meaning of self-defense should be construed. Is it self-defense only when a peacekeeper was in danger of personal harm, or is it also when the physical assets of the mission are at risk, or when civilians in mission-controlled areas are threatened? Although it is not ordinarily acknowledged, these kinds of discussions began prior to 1991, yet they became more public in the context of post-1992 missions. This is just one example of how missions post-1992 share more with pre-1991 missions than is ordinarily acknowledged. The complexity of discussions concerning the proper role of force in peacekeeping missions is certainly one such area of resonance.

Impartial Nature of United Nations Missions. Perhaps the sine qua non of the received view of peacekeeping was that it was impartial. The idea that the United Nations would deploy troops who would carry out their mission in an impartial manner—stating accurately what they observed and reporting this evenhandedly to the world community—was a keystone of peacekeeping since its earliest missions in the Middle East. It is often supposed that for missions prior to 1991, impartiality was a clear-cut thing to achieve. In fact, impartiality turns out to be a less straightforward concept than it appears at first blush.[42]

All peacekeepers arrive in the mission area with ideas about the conflict. Even in observer missions, these conceptions are sometimes challenged by what the peacekeeper finds on the ground. Sometimes they are reinforced. In every mission, peacekeepers have built up social relationships with people in the mission area, and these affect how they feel about and understand the conflict.

In UNIFIL, for instance, battalions from different nations administered discrete areas in southern Lebanon. All relied on their relationship with the local population to maintain order and to carry out their mission. As Marianne Heiberg put it, "Stated in a nutshell: a relationship to local civilians built on communication and confidence is a necessary factor for success; a relationship characterized by mounting hostility, suspicion and lack of communication is a sufficient cause for failure."[43] Yet national contingents built those relationships differently, and each acted differently in its engagement with the local population. Since the local population in southern Lebanon included parties to the conflict, the development of empathy with the population meant that observations were affected by bonds of friendship. Indeed, some observers asserted that "with some of the U.N. contingents, there was silent cooperation with the P.L.O. They were ready to close their eyes to P.L.O. infiltration."[44]

Military observers I interviewed at UNTSO stressed how their role was an impartial one. But the majority of those interviewed indicated that their views had shifted because of their experiences with UNTSO. Many said they had developed sympathies for one or the other parties that differed from the attitudes with which they had arrived, while others said their original views had been reinforced. Most of the military observers did not acknowledge that this had an effect on how they evaluated and reported the things they saw. But some did, and one stated plainly, "I don't think I could deal with them in a fair and impartial manner at this point."[45]

As was the case for the non-use of force principle, the experience of peacekeeping missions concerning impartiality differed from the ideal. This too was already a topic of discussion in relation to pre-1991 missions. And again, it resonates with the post-1992 conversations about United Nations impartiality, even as the pace of post-1992 deployments brought an increased tempo and scope to the conversations.

Taken together, the nine elements of the received view of pre-1992 peace-keeping create an ideal for the institution from which actual missions may depart. Anthropologically this is not surprising. In nearly all societies, ideals of behavior are associated with the society's institutions. Yet anthropological fieldwork shows that people depart from those ideals. A classic example is postmarital residence. In many societies, people describe how newly married couples move to the home of one of the couple's parents. If they move to the groom's home, this is patrilocal postmarital residence rule. However, upon investigation the researcher will invariably find that some proportion of newlyweds do not follow that rule. Nevertheless, the ideal is robust, and members of the society continue to describe themselves as having patrilocal postmarital residence patterns for a long time. Change in this self-description takes place only after massive and prolonged departure from the ideal has occurred.[46] For this reason, the way peacekeeping was actually conducted could differ from how it was thought about institutionally.

Normative Tensions regarding Traditional Peacekeeping

Even while the principles of the received view of peacekeeping were setting out the normative ideals to which the institution ought to conform, there were dissonant voices in the discussion. This too is not surprising from an anthropological perspective. Anthropologists have long observed that within any society there are always points of tension between opposing normative views. For instance, Mary Catherine Bateson shows that in the mid-1970s in Iran there were two competing normative idealizations of the "good man." One characterized him as a pragmatic entrepreneur, the other as a person of faith and principle. One was dominant within the society, the other a minority view. This is an example of intracultural variation recognized as present in all societies.[47]

Similarly, a tension existed between those who saw peacekeeping that conformed to the ideals of the received view as a strong instrument for maintaining international peace and security and others whose perspective was based on two negative observations: (1) that peacekeeping did little, if anything, to move belligerent parties toward resolution of their conflicts and (2) that the superpower competition between the Soviet Union and the United States meant that meaningful United Nations intervention could not take place because on serious issues Soviet and American interests would clash, and agreement would be impossible. In the former view, some peacekeeping operations appeared to freeze the status quo and provide no incentive for belligerents to negotiate in good faith or to move toward normal relations. Prime examples subject to this criticism were the two original observer missions, UNTSO in the Middle East and UNMOGIP in Kashmir, each of which had been in continuous operation by the 1980s for more than a quarter century without significantly altering the conflict. Another example, the UNFICYP in Cyprus, had been established in 1964 in reaction to communal violence between Greek and Turkish Cypriots had done little to alter that situation. In 1974, in response to internal developments in Cyprus, the Turkish government launched a large military intervention. So not only had no progress been made in managing the intercommunal conflict during the first decade of UNFICYP's presence, the situation had worsened. Through the 1980s, and despite continued efforts to use the good offices of the secretary-general to address the conflict, little progress was made toward resolving the Cyprus situation. To some commentators, the presence of UNFICYP is a screen that has allowed the parties the luxury of not engaging one another in meaningful dialog. UNFICYP remains in place at this writing.[48]

The second criticism rested on the fundamental structure of the international system and the potential problems that resulted from the basic structure of the Security Council. The five permanent members of the Security Council hold the power to veto resolutions. For peacekeeping, this means that any contemplated mission that is sufficiently out of touch with the interests of one of the permanent members faces a veto. As a result, action might not be taken, or, if it is, the scope of the mission might be more restricted than desirable. For example, this difficulty was realized when the British and French exercised the veto against the formation of UNEF in response to the Suez crisis, causing UNEF to be authorized by the General Assembly.[49]

For most of the first five decades of the United Nations' existence, the competition between the Soviet Union and the United States pervaded all aspects of its work. For the Security Council this made cooperation difficult in major projects. Only limited kinds of peacekeeping operations could be authorized. The Cold War competition poisoned chances for meaningful cooperation on conflicts that were viewed by the powers as close to the core to their interests. In this event only relatively limited operations would win approval in the Security Council. Those that were complex and involved in the East-West competition would fail. The mission in the Congo, for instance, faced significant problems shortly after being authorized by the Council. As the situation changed on the ground, the Soviet Union found ONUC's actions objectionable. This led to a political context in which authorizations for necessary action were impossible to obtain, causing much trouble for the ONUC mission and making it even more difficult.[50]

Despite the tension in these discussions, by the middle of the 1980s peacekeeping was widely viewed as a useful instrument of international action that provided new hope for the pacific settlement of conflicts. Peacekeeping had achieved significant successes in spite of the difficult constraints under which it had developed.

A Glimpse Ahead

The awarding of the Nobel Prize to United Nations peacekeeping came at about the same time as the dissolution of the Soviet Union. The enthusiasm for peacekeeping merged with a rush of optimism about the possibility that the United Nations would play the positive role in world affairs that its founders had envisioned. In place of the paralysis resulting from the political maneuverings of the United States and the Soviet Union, there was much anticipation that the following years would be an era of cooperation and that the United Nations would finally fulfill its potential for constructing a new and better world for all.

This optimism was extremely widespread, and even seasoned observers of the United Nations joined in it.[51] As head of the institution, it falls to the secretary-general to shape the vision of the organization and to provide the leadership that will move it toward achieving that vision. Secretary-General Boutros Boutros-Ghali seized on the confluence of confidence in peacekeeping and the possibility of post–Cold War action. In his June 1992 report to the Security Council, *An Agenda for Peace*, Boutros-Ghali set out a sweeping vision of United Nations action to ensure international peace and security.[52] And he identified the more active role for the United Nations with the expansion of its peace operations.

The functions of peace operations envisioned in the agenda suggested action at all points of the natural history of a conflict. Thus, the report described United Nations leadership in preventive diplomacy, peacemaking, peacekeeping, and postconflict peacebuilding. Although these are defined as discrete activities, the report notes that they are "integrally related."[53] To some extent, all of these functions could be identified in earlier peacekeeping missions, although, as my presentation of the received view of peacekeeping suggests, they were not part of their core activity. Peacekeeping, as the monitoring of agreements to end hostilities, is the raison d'être of United Nations actions and the core function of many of the early missions, such as UNTSO, UNMOGIP, and UNFICYP. The other functions are seen, for example, in the Congo mission, ONUC, which involved peacemaking; in the United Nations Transition Assistance Group (UNTAG) in Namibia, which was a form of preventive diplomacy; and in UN actions in Lebanon (UNIFIL), which exhibited postconflict peacebuilding.[54] The critical point is that while these activities were all present in traditional peacekeeping missions, only rarely were the noncore activities a preoccupation of missions in the field.

Because each of these functions had been part of earlier missions, and because *An Agenda for Peace* was written during the early and very hopeful stages of the United Nations engagement in Somalia, the report was relatively warmly received. As its vision was implemented, the activities were grafted onto peacekeeping and the related functions were added to the responsibilities of the small staff within the Secretariat charged with managing peacekeeping. A record of failed interventions in failed states soon developed.

In this chapter I have sketched briefly the history of United Nations peace-keeping from 1948 to 1991 and foreshadowed events that followed. This period has been called by many names—traditional peacekeeping, first generation peacekeeping, and peace observation—to list just three. There are many technical reasons to favor each name and the characterization of peacekeeping that it connotes. My purpose has not been to enter into that debate. Rather, I have described the principles of what I call the "received view" of peacekeeping as it existed in the literature and among military and diplomatic practitioners during this period. Despite considerable collective agreement about these principles at the time, particular missions departed from the ideal and there was a contrary conversation taking place.

My sketch of the history of peacekeeping and of the principles that operated during the pre-1992 period has two purposes. First, in this book I am suggesting that there is more of a connection between these early missions and later missions than is commonly supposed and that this link is culturally important. Moreover, although it is commonly presumed that the kinds of missions deployed prior to 1991 are no longer put into the field, this is not actually the case. This is part of the reason for the continued relevance of the early missions. Second, this historical and analytic sketch describes missions about which earlier discussions were restricted to "policy relevant" topics, such as the operational basics of peace operations, as reflected in discussions of best practices, or on economic, political, or organizational issues.[55] The result was that the cultural factors affecting those missions were inadequately examined. Yet those cultural factors are perhaps now even more important. It is by going back to those missions, which are not so obscured by today's realpolitik, that the cultural context of peacekeeping can be clarified. In the next chapter, I present a conceptual framework for understanding the roles of culture in peacekeeping.

3

Culture and Peacekeeping
A Conceptual Framework

In 1957, following the truce that ended the Suez War, the United Nations Emergency Force (UNEF) was deployed to monitor the separation of Egyptian and Israeli troops in Gaza and the Sinai. On the first evening of their deployment in Gaza, UNEF troops sprayed a minaret with machine gun fire from which a muezzin was calling Muslims to prayer. The UNEF soldiers, not understanding Arabic or Islam, had mistaken the call to pray as a call for civil disorder.[1]

On New Year's Eve day in 1992, a recently deployed detachment from Operation Restore Hope arrived in Wanwaylen, Somalia, to secure a Red Cross food warehouse that was being looted.[2] Initially, the force dispersed a large crowd around the warehouse with only minor injuries to the troops and the Somalis. After gaining control of the warehouse, the detachment faced a large, apparently unorganized crowd. Some people in the crowd explained that, rather than distributing the food fairly, the Somali Red Cross official in charge of distributing the supplies in the warehouse had been giving food to his own people and selling what remained. The crowd increased in size as it was joined by curious onlookers, but it showed no sign of belligerence. Soon, however, the officer in charge realized that his detachment was too small to hold off the crowd should it recommence its efforts to get the food.

The major decided that the way to disperse the crowd—the first obviously hungry people he had seen since his recent arrival in Somalia—was to distribute the food in an orderly and even-handed manner. The officer acted without knowing the local tribal patterns of competition and reciprocity that shape the distribution and sharing of resources in the area, and also without understanding the local uses and meanings people there attached to relief aid during the crisis. As a result, the well-intentioned food distribution provoked rather than calmed the crowd, which became increasingly agitated and violent. Ultimately, with the aid of reinforcements, the unit withdrew from Wanwaylen, having stacked the remaining food supplies outside of the warehouse, where it was freely plundered by the now much larger, somewhat violent, and uncontrolled crowd.

Peacekeeping and Local Culture

In the Gaza and Wanwaylen incidents, peacekeepers' efforts were frustrated because they did not understand the local cultures and thus could not interpret correctly or respond properly to the actions of the people they were sent to assist. These are examples of one way in which culture is important to peacekeeping. Without knowing local cultural patterns of behavior and interpretation, peacekeepers too easily react in inappropriate ways, even when they mean well. These examples from Gaza and Wanwaylen are but two of literally thousands of examples of intercultural misunderstandings that lead to conflict between peacekeepers and local populations.[3]

In Gaza and Wanwaylen, the cultural mistakes involved groups of peacekeepers acting corporately. Even more common is for civilian and military members of peacekeeping missions to engage local populations alone or in pairs. Whether they are patrolling, maintaining an observation post, working a checkpoint, attempting to resolve peacefully a minor local dispute, interviewing victims of gender violence, or seeking to engage local institutions, individual peacekeepers make myriad decisions each day. Those decisions depend upon their interpreting correctly what they see and the interactions in which they are engaged. As I discuss below and in later chapters, those interpretations frame the actions they take. In turn, the effects of those actions are immediate, and they can have a larger, strategic importance that affects the entire course of the mission for good or ill.

Colonel (Retired) Mark Walsh, the zone director of Southern Somalia during UNOSOM (United Nations Operation in Somalia), says he knew nothing of the local culture when he arrived in Somalia. Needing to get to his post, he managed to get a ride in the back of a pickup truck with a small group of Somali men. He later learned that he was well regarded by local elders because his behavior and actions during that ride had conveyed an appropriate sense of respect. Their initial evaluation of him was transmitted from person to person, building for him a positive reputation that facilitated his work for the rest of his stay. When he relates this story, Walsh stresses that this happy outcome could easily have come to grief if he had acted in ways that offended his hosts. He says, because he acted in ignorance of Somali culture, that could just as easily have been the case. For example, he gave no thought to the gender of those in the pickup truck. It was happenstance that the truck he approached had no women or girls in it. But since he was simply looking for transportation, had the available truck had women in it, then his actions might, inexplicably to him, have had a different result. Similarly, if the ages of the occupants of the truck had happened to be different, his actions might have been seen as inappropriate and offensive.[4]

Although it did not take place within the context of a United Nations operation, the importance of individual action in such operations came into stark relief during the second US-led invasion of Iraq. When forces entered Baghdad in April 2003, they arranged for the "spontaneous" pulling down of a massive statue of Saddam Hussein. During the process, Corporal Edward Chin covered the face of the statue with an American flag. With this simple act, the image of the coalition troops as liberators of Iraq instantly transformed to an image of them as a triumphal invading army. Although the American flag was quickly replaced with an Iraqi flag, the consequences of this act were swift and long lasting from the strategic perspective. Despite the military's stage-management of the event, some crowd members understood the triumphal meaning of the flag draping, responding not with the desired grateful cries of support but with "shouts of 'Yankee murderers.'"[5]

The first level at which culture is important to peacekeeping, then, is the interface between the mission and the local culture. This happens through both the corporate actions of the mission and in individual encounters of peacekeepers with people they are deployed to help. At this level as well are questions of how the mission engages local culture when developing programs that, for instance, promote the rule of law, manage conflict, or attempt to establish mechanisms of local governance. What happens at this interface can either facilitate or compromise the mission's effectiveness, since it influences the ways in which the peacekeeping mission is perceived and received by the local population.[6]

Organizational Culture and Interoperability

A second level at which culture affects peacekeeping is in the interaction among and between the many individuals and organizations that make up a peacekeeping mission. Even the earliest, "simplest" missions brought together troops from countries with diverse cultural backgrounds and from militaries with different traditions, ways of approaching their professions, and understandings of what they are supposed to do in the field. Thus, from the start peacekeeping missions brought these diverse military elements into interaction with civilians working in the mission area, including, for example, people working as international civilian employees of a mission (both locally recruited individuals and expatriates), employees of United Nations specialized agencies, diplomats, and civilian nongovernmental organizations (NGOs).

Interactions among these diverse constituencies can be difficult. Attempts at cooperation can break down because people bring to their work different organizationally derived ways of thinking about their mission and of doing their work. Sometimes these differences are troubling but relatively innocuous. During my fieldwork with UNTSO, I was often told about—and I observed—problems of coordination between the civilian side of the mission and the military side, including problems created by different bureaucratic structures and approaches. Also, organizational cultural issues sometimes made it appear that diplomatic and UNTSO personnel were working at cross-purposes.

These kinds of difficulties did not lessen in the subsequent "more complex" missions of the 1990s. In Somalia, for example, attempts at coordination between the military elements of the mission and the humanitarian organizations frequently foundered on issues of specific organizational cultural differences. As I explore more fully in chapter 7, those I interviewed described how different organizational cultural meanings attached to the word *security* led to misunderstandings and conflicts between these groups. They told me that as the situation around the Somalia intervention deteriorated into further disorder, the military redoubled its efforts to coordinate its actions with those of the humanitarian agencies. They had formal coordinating meetings that covered many topics, one being the need for improved and increased security. All at the meetings acknowledged the desirability of better security. But for reasons originating from their different organizational cultures, some humanitarian organizations and the militaries acted in diametrically different ways to implement security increases.

For those humanitarian agencies that understood security as deriving from the placing of their operations in the midst of local populations, with the resulting removal of boundaries between aid workers and the people they serve, increasing security meant moving their operations more deeply into the community and increasing the close daily contact between themselves and the local population. In contrast, military units understood security to derive from control and separation. Thus, they further separated themselves from the local population, strengthened their buildings and post perimeters, and controlled entry into their compound more tightly. It is not hard to imagine the frustration that resulted from these differences as one group in the mission undertook security measures that they felt reasonable and appropriate for securing their own safety but that their partners saw as irrational, as placing themselves at risk, or even compromising the mission as a whole.[7]

Problems of coordination recur in all peacekeeping missions. Sometimes they rise to the highest level of concern. General William L. Nash recounted that as the administrator in Mitrovica, Kosovo, the biggest problems he faced were in coordinating the military and civilian components of the international community, not those between the mission elements and local Serbs and Albanians.[8] Likewise, in his memoir of his time as the force commander of the United Nations Assistance Mission in Rwanda (UNAMIR), General Roméo

Dallaire recounts numerous ways in which the interaction between the military and civilian, especially political, components of UNAMIR conflicted because of organizational cultural differences. These differences were not only frustrating but of deadly consequence, arguably leading to the failure of the mission.[9]

There is now a general acknowledgment that problems in coordination between various elements of a mission can be a major obstacle to the effectiveness of that mission. A significant literature specifically examines the differences in work style and structure between military and NGOs. Some of it explicitly acknowledges that these difficulties derive from differences in organizational culture.[10] Culture is important to peacekeeping at the lower levels of organization where individuals and corporate elements of the mission interact with local populations. At the same time, culture is important at the higher levels of the interaction among organizations that play a role in the mission.

Culture in the Broader Understanding of Peacekeeping

It takes little reflection to conclude—if it is not immediately intuitively obvious—that culture is an important factor in the interactions between local peoples and the individuals and groups belonging to a peacekeeping mission. And there are few, if any, who would object to the observation that organizational cultural differences can create opportunities or obstacles for a mission. It is less obvious that culture matters at higher levels of organization as well. Yet, what happens on the microlevels not only affects but is affected by the macrolevel cultural considerations in peacekeeping. There are two important areas in which macrolevel cultural processes affect peacekeeping. The first is at the strategic level of a mission, and the second is at the level of the broad international perception of peacekeeping and the legitimacy given it.

In assessing experiences in missions in the Balkans, Somalia, and East Timor, at least, the importance of cultural understanding at the strategic levels of mission operations and for individuals and groups emerged in the late 1990s as a general area in which culture was important to peacekeeping.[11] For example, some peacekeeping missions have had at their strategic core the idea of reconstituting a functioning central government in an area that has been experiencing violence and conflict. Strategically, the international community has tasked peacekeeping operations with facilitating this process by their carrying out a variety of different kinds of activities. These include demobilizing and disarming combatants, reconstituting law enforcement and judicial systems, developing health and education systems, and promoting economic development. All of these activities are part of a larger strategic vision that supports self-determination by creating the conditions under which free and fair elections can be held in order to create a legitimate indigenous government. The missions in Namibia, Cambodia, and East Timor are examples of this strategic vision.[12] The intervention in East Timor represents the first time that the United Nations had full authority over a sovereign country and made the first steps toward implementing this Western-style (and nonindigenous) vision.[13] The development of this strategic vision has been traced to the privileging of a commitment to a particular form of governance—liberal market democracy—that can be out of synch with the symbolic goals of the United Nations.[14]

Namibia. During World War I, South Africa occupied the German colony of South West Africa.[15] Following the war, the League of Nations extended to South Africa a Class C Mandate, giving it the right to administer South West Africa as an integral part of its own territory but not to formally incorporate it into South Africa. This arrangement continued through the Second World War, following which the United Nations sought to extend its authority over the area. South Africa rejected this assertion, eventually applied apartheid to the territory, and moved to annex it. These moves were resisted by the international community and by Namibians themselves. A number of independence groups formed, but by the mid-1960s the South West African Peoples Organization (SWAPO) emerged as the leading political opponent of South Africa and coordinated military action against South Africa. The General Assembly recognized SWAPO as the legitimate representative of the Namibian people in 1975.

Although Security Council Resolution 435, setting out a plan for Namibian independence, was passed in 1978, it was not implemented for more than a decade. During that time, a protracted, violent liberation struggle continued. SWAPO was supported by the Soviet Union, making for the possible extension of Soviet influence in the region, a situation unacceptable to the United States and other Western states. Thus, the delay in implementing the program for Namibian independence resulted from the issue being refracted through the lens of the Cold War competition between the East and West. It was not until the late 1980s that each side recognized that the fighting had reached a stalemate. This created the conditions that allowed the United Nations to act as a vehicle for mediating the conflict and gave all parties a way to save face.[16]

Security Council Resolution 435 provided the essential outlines for the achievement of an independent Namibia, although it was updated in early 1989. The resulting peacekeeping mission, the United Nations Transition Assistance Group (UNTAG), was deployed from 1 April 1989 until March 1990. Although brief, UNTAG involved a wide variety of military and civilian personnel, including "4,493 [military troops of] all ranks, 1,500 civilian police and just under 2,000 international and local staff; the mission was strengthened by some 1,000 additional international personnel who came specifically for the elections."[17] The tasks assigned to the mission were also varied, including: monitoring the disengagement of South African troops, demobilizing SWAPO fighters, providing oversight monitoring of the South West Africa Police by a civilian police contingent, restructuring the legal system to eliminate discriminatory laws, providing amnesty where appropriate and the release of prisoners and detainees, supervising the return of exiled Namibians who wished to repatriate, and overseeing voter registration of the population. All of these activities combined to form UNTAG's core function, which was to create the conditions necessary for free and fair elections. Thus, the strategic goal of the mission was to achieve elections recognized by the international community that would result in the creation of a legitimate Namibian government. Those elections were held on 11 November 1989. Ninety-seven percent of the registered voters elected a Constituent Assembly, which then drafted a constitution adopted on 9 February 1990.[18] The achievement of "free and fair elections" marked the successful end of UNTAG's mission.

Approaching Culture in Peacekeeping

The cultural aspects of peacekeeping are but one important factor in what makes missions more or less successful. Also important are considerations of logistics, information gathering, economics, politics, and international support, for instance. Several of these other factors are more tangible and apparently more manageable than is culture. Indeed, organizations and individuals and the international community have collectively developed systems for analyzing and managing these elements of peacekeeping missions. In contrast, culture in peacekeeping is most frequently treated in a retrospective manner, called upon to explain why a particular mission or aspect of a mission went wrong. There are some extremely useful examples of cultural analyses undertaken from this perspective.[19] A smaller group of studies looks at how culture works to maintain peacekeeping as a social institution, and thus to keep peacekeeping missions working smoothly, but nearly all of these treat the importance of culture at a single level of analysis.[20]

Analyses of how culture contributes to the failure of some missions or facilitates the functioning of others are valuable in their own right. Yet, to really understand how culture affects peacekeeping it is important to locate these studies within a broader a framework for understanding how the cultural dynamics at each level affect and are affected by what goes on at other levels. This requires understanding peacekeeping itself as a cultural phenomenon; this recognition is the background against which the more local and specific aspects of culture play out. As we saw in chapter 2, peacekeeping emerged as an instrument of international diplomacy through a series of improvisations as a way of seizing opportunities for promoting international peace and security. At some point, perhaps very quickly, peacekeeping transitioned from an act of convenience to a recognizable pattern of social action, which condensed into a relatively stable pattern of behaviors and was eventually formalized. Thus, peacekeeping became not just a mode of international operation but a social institution. Institutions are more than just relatively stable, more or less formalized patterns of behavior.[21] Over time, people invest in institutions in a variety of ways (for example, their sense of identity or common purpose, or material resources), and institutions thus become symbolically meaningful. This means that in thinking about peacekeeping, culture is not a peripheral subject; it should be a core policy consideration. Below I show that the the symbolic meanings invested in peacekeeping depend upon a radical restructuring of political perceptions so that the politically unthinkable is rendered possible and acceptable. But before doing this, a brief discussion of how I understand culture in this context is a necessary background.

Culture and International Affairs

During the Second World War, and for a brief period after it, culture was an important category of analysis in international affairs. Anthropologists and others focused their attention on developing profiles of political culture. The unit of analysis was often quite large, most frequently the political culture of an entire country. In attempting to assist in the war effort, anthropologists applied the theoretical understandings of culture that they had developed earlier in the century. Heavily influenced by the gestalt psychology that was revolutionary in the early 1900s, many of these theories treated culture as a unified whole that formed stable patterns of behavior, belief, and practice. Accounts of particular cultures were developed from personal interaction with communities through ethnographic fieldwork. The length of fieldwork varied greatly among researchers, and the methods employed by fieldworkers were quite disparate, yet it was first-hand accounts of society and culture that marked anthropology in the interwar years.

During the Second World War, it was often impossible to do the fieldwork that would ordinarily inform cultural descriptions. Anthropologists turned to compiling cultural descriptions from a variety of secondary and documentary sources, developing a form of work referred to as studying culture at a distance. Using these sources and techniques, anthropologists described the broad outlines of cultures. Perhaps the most famous examples of this kind of work are Ruth Benedict's pre–World War II book *Patterns of Culture* and her 1946 study of Japanese culture and society, *The Chrysanthemum and the Sword*, and Margaret Mead's national character study of the United States, *And Keep Your Powder Dry*.[22]

Although this reified view of culture was predominant during the war years, even then some anthropologists were beginning to critique it as an inadequate way of understanding cultural practices. These researchers began to see culture less as the stable precipitate characteristic of societies and more as a set of processes. They observed that culture was neither stable nor homogeneously shared by all members of a society and therefore could not be studied solely at a distance. Indeed, conceptions of culture that emphasized intracultural variation expanded forcefully in the 1950s and 1960s.

After World War II, anthropological understandings of culture changed quite rapidly (and indeed, they continue to develop). In general, anthropologists moved away from conceptualizing culture as homogeneous, static patterns of behavior into which a person is socialized and that determine behavior, and toward a view of culture as a dynamic, processual, meaning-based activity that *orients* and *constrains*, rather than determines, behavior and thus allows for considerable intracultural variation. These anthropological discussions of culture moved forward rather quickly amid rich debates within the discipline. Outside observers who saw the contentiousness and detailed criticisms involved in these debates sometimes interpreted them to mean that anthropologists had concluded that culture was not a useful conceptual tool. They mistook the intellectual trees for the forest, which was in fact growing quite healthily.[23]

Within political science and other fields dealing with international policy analyses, there have long been those who argue that culture matters. In early forms, their work too emphasized the stable, homogeneous, and determinative conception of culture, although especially since the 1990s the number of more dynamic and interpretive analyses of specific aspects of international relations expanded greatly. But those who hold the latter view remain the minority and are largely marginalized within their fields. Even now it is still common for discussions of culture to reach back to the early twentieth century for conceptions of it. In almost cliché fashion, these discussions often return to the work of two distinguished anthropologists, Alfred Kroeber and Clyde Kluckhohn, who in the 1950s sought to catalog the definitions of culture used in the field. They reported over 150 definitions, subdivided by their primary emphases.[24] Commentators assert that the culture concept is so diversely defined or compellingly contested that there is no common understanding about the nature and importance of culture. For instance, one contemporary writer, citing Kroeber and Kluckhohn, stated: "The social science literature provides no uniform guidance in conceptualizing culture; on the contrary, what is notable is the diversity of definitions." But then he goes on to assert that "at the core of most definitions, however, is the notion of culture as a set of customs, mores, beliefs and values," emphasizing the "things" of culture.[25] Thus, the first reason that maturing anthropological concepts of culture moved slowly into adjacent fields was that those disciplines mistakenly saw the technical debates being conducted by anthropologists as demonstrating that no useful consensus existed regarding the nature of culture.

A second reason that maturing anthropological concepts of culture moved only slowly into adjacent fields was that, because of their own methodological and epistemological commitments, those in the receiving fields were more comfortable with treating culture as a concrete thing that could be parsed and measured. Thus, as the Second World War ended it was the conception of culture as a homogenous, stable "thing" that was fostered into international relations and political science and policy analyses because it was most congenial to the quantitative and positivist models being developed at the time.

A third reason for the slow movement of dynamic understandings of culture into international relations analyses was that the rapid emergence of the Cold War, which quickly distorted the treatment of culture by refracting it through the lens of East-West competition. The progress being made in anthropology toward understanding cultural processes was both inconsistent with dominant paradigms of analysis and seen as focusing at too fine a level of analysis to usefully inform the realpolitik of the epic Cold War struggle, which focused on large configurations and political groupings.[26]

There was (and to some extent still is) a kind of cultural lag in the way the concept of culture spread through the academic disciplines and into policy analyses. The notion of a cultural lag identifies a situation in interconnected areas of a society where social institutions and understandings in one part of a society change more rapidly than they do in the other.[27] In regard to the understanding of culture, a kind of double cultural lag exists. First, there was a lag in the diffusion of processual and interpretive models of culture from anthropology to other social science disciplines. Second, there was a lag in the diffusion of these revised conceptions of culture from those disciplines into policy analyses.

Most often left behind in this process were anthropological discussions that emphasized the point that patterns of culture are the temporary crystallizations of the organization and interpretation of social life in a group, stable only insofar as social processes did not lead to changes in values and goals leading to the reinterpretation of their experience. The "Iraq Culture Smart Card," mentioned in chapter 1, is emblematic of some of the ways older conceptions of culture have been embraced and reified.

Culture: Meaning and Practice

Human beings everywhere face challenges in their natural and social environments. Like other organisms, we encounter our world and either change that world or change ourselves in response to it. In some cases, the very existence of life depends on successfully meeting these challenges. Under other circumstances, life goes on regardless of how the challenges are met. Some ways of meeting these challenges are experienced as better than others and are seen as leading to a better life than would the possible alternatives. These challenges are rooted in environments that are so complex that it is impossible for human beings to apprehend the totality of information continuously presented to them. Trying to take in all in the information we encounter simultaneously would overwhelm our processing capacities because the amount of information available to a person at any time is so great. In the face of such complex environments, people need some kind of heuristic to help them sort out what matters from what does not matter from among all of the input they receive at any moment. Culture is that heuristic.

All organisms are in continuous interaction with their environment, having to accommodate or adapt to it repeatedly from one moment to the next throughout their entire lives. Humerto Maturana and Francisco Varela describe this as "structural coupling" between an organism and its environment, by which they mean that "there is a history of recurrent interactions leading to the structural congruence between two (or more) systems."[28] Thus, an organism acts repeatedly on its environment, and in turn is acted upon and changed by that environment. People, like other organisms, are in continual interaction with their environments, changing and being changed by them.

Human beings are essentially social animals. Being neither particularly swift nor especially brawny, and bearing young that require an extended period of care before they are sufficiently mature to fend for themselves, people need to work together in groups to ensure their survival. Living in social groups is thus an essential aspect of the human experience. This necessary interdependence creates social environments people live within and with which they interact. Although these social environments do not exist independently of human interaction, their influence can be as far-reaching as that of the physical environment. People are in continuous interaction with their social environments. The structural congruencies created between people and their social environments result not just from the isolated actions of individuals but from the mutual actions of many people. Each group member is affected by and affects their own immediate social environment, and their social environment is affected by and affects other members of their group.[29]

Some aspects of new environments we encounter are the same or similar to ones we have encountered before. Recognizing these similarities increases the efficiency of the interaction and can lead to more successful outcomes. Culture as heuristic is what leads people to define some phenomena as being in the same class of things, events, or experiences as other phenomena they have previously encountered. Sorting experience into sets is what allows people to translate challenging situations into defined problems. Once a challenge is defined as a problem, it can be approached using the solutions defined as appropriate to that particular class of problems.[30]

Conceptualizing the world as containing classes of common elements is a source of the predictability of thought and action that binds people together in successful social groupings. Neurological anthropologists, such as Charles Laughlin and Eugene d'Aquili, suggest that part of this predictability results from the nonrandom patterning of the human brain, especially in newborns. Their work shows that people are born with some initial models of the world that are encoded in neurological anatomical networks they call "neurognosis."[31] These models structure our experience of the world, but are open to modification as the result of that experience. Self-evidently, people have different life experiences from others in their group. What they perceive and how they act are to some extent idiosyncratic. So the coherence of the initial neurological models that structure the encounter between people and the world is elaborated, changed, and channeled, yet the models continue to provide broad parameters within which the human mind works. As well, the basic processes and structures available to all humans constrain the underlying processes that shape and reshape the models.

Human beings are symbolizing animals who derive, construct, and impose meaning.[32] Part of our humanity is that we communicate through and understand our experience in the context of symbolic materials. One need look no further for evidence of this than the centrality of language—perhaps the sine qua non of symbol systems—to human social life. Yet despite the central importance of language, we communicate about and experience our worlds through a myriad of nonlinguistic symbols as well.

It is through the use of symbols that societies structure the ways their members think about the world and how they act upon it.[33] That is, symbols encode both systems of thought and prescriptions for action. Symbols are particularly useful for supporting groups because they have properties that organize diversity into common orientation. Most contemporary accounts of symbolism describe symbols as consisting of a meaning relation in which there is an arbitrary link between the symbol and what it symbolizes. This basic characteristic means that a symbol can be linked simultaneously to many meanings. *Multivocality* is thus an inherent aspect of symbols, giving them a rich capacity for communicating meaning. Symbolic communication involves more than just the broadcasting of a symbol and its meanings. It also involves the active reception and decoding of the symbol. A person engaging the symbol may emphasize one (or a subset) of its meanings and ignore others. As a result, symbols have an essential *ambiguity* built into them. Finally, since so much meaning is packed into a symbol we can say that, like a cooking sauce reduced to enhance its flavor, symbols *condense* and intensify meaning.

People learn the symbols and their various meanings through participation in the daily life of their social group. Symbols encode how the group conceptually organizes the world, and shape what counts as real and what is seen as important. For instance, anthropologists report that human beings are capable of apprehending their worlds while in various states of consciousness. Some societies give ontological status to things encountered and to experiences a person has while in a particular state of consciousness, such as experiences in dreams. Other societies might see those same things and experiences as fanciful and unimportant. Laughlin and his colleagues describe some of this variation and relate it to brain functioning.[34]

Symbols can also convey guidelines for action, valorizing particular ways of behaving and interacting with the world and with other people. They provide a convenient way for holding out certain forms of action as appropriate and effective, or as good or bad. The symbolic condensations of examples for behaving in ways that are highly valued by a group abound in religious systems. Catholic saints, the Buddha, and the Prophet Muhammad are examples of how the actions of a person become valorized, held up as laudatory behavioral norms and mapped into symbols that can then be used to shape group members' preferences and perceptions. This kind of symbolic communication about proper actions and behavior also works in nonsacred contexts. In the United States, behavioral lessons about honesty and integrity are conveyed when, for instance, George Washington is invoked, as a symbol, in discussions of political behavior.[35]

Since some ways of acting toward the world and toward other people are held out as exemplars of the right way to conduct one's life, the structure of how people experience their emotional life is also symbolically communicated. What experiences are sources for joy or despair, for admiration or disapproval, respect or offense, are all things we learn through participating in a world structured through a system of symbolic meanings.

Roy d'Andrade summed up this view when he described culture "as consisting of learned systems of meaning, communicated by means of natural language and other symbols-systems, having representational, directive, and affective functions, and capable of creating cultural entities and a particular sense of reality. Through these systems of meaning groups of people adapt to their environment and structure interpersonal activities."[36]

It is particularly important that symbols do not occur in isolation; rather, they gain their force because they are part of a symbolic system that shapes and is shaped by people's experiences. The fact that culture derives from a complex system of meaning relationships, which can simultaneously embrace characterizations of the world that are not totally aligned with each other, accounts for culture's dynamism and for its relative stability. Each node of the cultural meaning system contributes to maintaining the system as a whole and propels the social and cultural reproduction of the status quo. At the same time, local changes in a node in the system can have ramifications for change elsewhere in the system, and thus for introducing social and cultural change.

The dispositional, rather than determinative, nature of culture is the result of this tension between the press to preserve meaning and its alteration through experience. The result is that the cultural meaning system is an open one that supports the generation of new, appropriate responses to novel situations. That is, the range of possible action and its interpretation is the result of ongoing interactive processes among individuals, communities, and their environments. It is from these repetitive, mutually affecting interactions that cultural practices, durable dispositions, and expected behaviors, emerge, crystallize temporarily, and then change over time.[37]

Seeing culture as a generative system for supporting adaptive behavior is what sets contemporary anthropological approaches to culture apart from those that treat it as a set of stable artifacts. Some symbols emerge as more central than others in establishing parameters within which group activity takes place. Social theorists have variously identified those symbols that are most influential for a group using a variety of terms, including *root metaphors, dominant symbols,* and *key symbols.*[38]

Later, I explore how these deep cultural meanings get expressed in everyday interaction in peacekeeping operations. Here, I want to note only that the central symbols combine to form cultural models that organize how people apprehend language, symbols, rituals, and behavior, and to point out that these cultural models lead to the durable structures often referred to as "cultural styles," which motivate collective action.

Symbolic Inversion and the Power of Peacekeeping

In all societies, people have ideas about the best ways to engage their world and to interact with others. These ideas are shaped by the cultural meaning systems in which they participate, and which they learn growing up or as adults. Those cultural systems are encoded in symbols, and it is through symbolic action that groups of people can be moved to think and act in particular ways. There are many different ways that symbolic action is manifest. It is not my purpose here to explicate the variety of ways that symbols are used to shape social action. Rather, I build my analyses of peacekeeping on earlier work in this area.[39] I find three aspects of symbolism to be particularly useful for understanding peacekeeping. The first is the idea of *conceptual metaphor*, which indicates the process of understanding one area of experience in terms of another area of experience. That is, the characteristics of a source domain are mapped onto the target domain, which is then understood in terms derived from our engagement with the source domain. This allows people to make associations and connections across areas of their experience.[40] (For example, my explanation of "condensation," which employed terms usually used to describe cooking sauces, is a conceptual metaphor.) The power of conceptual metaphor will play an important role later in my discussion, especially in chapters 8 and 9.

The second aspect of symbol use that is particularly helpful in understanding the workings of culture in peacekeeping is the use of symbolism within the context of the *ritual regulation of experience*. Human rituals (religious and secular) can have demonstrable and predictable physiological effects on those who participate in them. These effects tune the autonomic systems of participants to facilitate their adopting of common cognitive, emotional, and action orientations toward the world.[41] In chapter 5, I explore ritual in peacekeeping.

The third approach to symbolism that is essential for understanding how culture affects peacekeeping is *symbolic inversion*. It is axiomatic that culture operates outside of our consciousness. A common conceptual metaphor says that "culture is like water to a fish." So culture is "essential yet not often noticed until the fish is taken out of the water. Culture gives context and continuity to our movements and, like water, buoyancy to our world."[42] Ordinarily, symbolic processes work without our being aware of them. Ritual activity is one way that symbolism gets people into common cognitive, emotional, and action states—by heightening their experience of the symbols. Whether in the context of ritual activity or not, one of the strongest forms of symbolic action is the process of symbolic inversion.

A symbolic inversion is "any act of expressive behavior which inverts, contradicts, abrogates or in some fashion presents an alternative to commonly held cultural codes, values, and norms."[43] Such acts create conditions in which thoughts, actions, and emotions that would ordinarily be considered outside the bounds of what is proper are permitted, even highly valued. Anthropologists have described symbolic inversions in all kinds of societies, all around the globe. Sometimes the conditions created by the inversion are brief and fleeting, as when it is part of a performer's routine in a comedy act. At other times, the inversion creates powerful and longer-lasting effects, as when they are part of religious ceremonies during which they support a feeling of connection and oneness with others. Also, inversions can be found in secular role reversals. When I was an adolescent, one of the symbolic inversions most familiar to my peers and me was the Sadie Hawkins dance, which reversed ordinary gender roles so girls asked boys to dance. Cultural inversions can last even longer and have varying degrees of effect on the individuals who experience them. The behavioral reversals involved in a variety of carnivals—like Mardi Gras—and in some rites of passage last for extended periods. Peacekeeping involves and extended symbolic inversion.[44]

In their 1968 book *The United Nations: Sacred Drama*, Conor Cruise O'Brien and Feliks Topolski offered a complex analysis of the symbolic and ritual basis of the United Nations' standing as an actor in world affairs.[45] Like all symbolic and ritual activity, those involving the United Nations contain complexities and contradictions. Ultimately these complexities combine in essential ways to create the institution's symbolic power and legitimacy. In addition to international laws and treaties that give formal legitimacy to the organization, the substantive legitimacy of United Nations actions rests in major part on the organization's symbolizing a world order not dominated by national self-interests. All of the symbols used in relation to the United Nations reinforce this message and hold out the possibility of a world institution that can be held to different standards—moral, ethical, and practical—than are other multilateral endeavors. NATO, in contrast to the United Nations, for example, gained its legitimacy because it is an institution that explicitly pursues national self-interests through cooperative action.

The root metaphor that structures the United Nations as an institution places it in the service of a pacific world order that empowers the weak, feeds the hungry, conquers disease, and settles conflicts peacefully. The legitimacy of the United Nations rests in part on its encoding a symbolic inversion: it creates a sociopolitical space in which actions that would be unacceptable or foolish for an ordinary state are considered normal and desired.

As peacekeeping developed, under the sway of this root metaphor, traditional military activities were used to support this image of *the world transformed*, thus enacting a symbolic inversion. Table 3.1 displays the symbolic inversions that form the basis for the legitimacy, standing, and authority of peacekeeping missions.[46] In peacekeeping, traditional military ritual and symbolism was appropriated and given new meaning. Through this and the highly ritualized and symbolic actions of the Security Council, peacekeeping contributed to the elaboration of an image of an international community acting in a neutral, consensual manner to sustain a stable world. The use of the military without weapons (a symbolic inversion) in the service of peace is a core image carried forward from the root metaphor of a pacific world order.

Table 3.1: Cultural Inversions in Peacekeeping

Traditional Military: Business as Usual	Peacekeeping: A World Transformed
No foreign troops on sovereign soil	Other countries' troops on sovereign soil
Separate from potential adversaries	Work with potential adversaries
Retain national command of troops	Command officer from other country
Stealth and surprise	Transparency of action
No contact with civilians	Intense interaction with civilians, cooperate with civilian organizations
Use of war-fighting skills	Use of negotiation and persuasion
Victory through force	Conflict management or resolution through pacific means
Strictly observe prerogatives of rank	Officers may perform duties ordinarily done by lower ranks

Adapted from Rubinstein 2005, 537.

At the macrolevel, ritual activity is essential to the establishment of missions. The Security Council creates missions through conventionalized actions. These actions include various forms of consultation and debate among members and the conduct of formal sessions of the Council. Language plays an important role. The language used in resolutions to authorize or reauthorize operations conforms to a ritualized style.

The extensions of this basic inversion can be seen in the on-the-ground practices that characterize peacekeeping. I present this as a model of meaning, not as a description of every empirical peacekeeping circumstance. In a sense, these oppositions represent the orienting dispositions that create the frame of reference within which peacekeeping was conceived by the international community, as well as the frame of reference within which it was interpreted by local actors, even when they are mythic in the standard sense.[47]

These cultural inversions create a space for alternative political representations to develop. In the following chapters, I present descriptions of how these inversions work to support peacekeeping operations by allowing for the construction of community, the alignment of individual motivation, and the organization of collective efforts. What emerges from these analyses is a picture of how the systems of meaning and action work together to reinforce one another across levels of organization. This shows the importance of *theoretical scaffolding* for understanding peacekeeping and *strategic scaffolding* for ensuring the effectiveness of peacekeeping missions. Scaffolding is a structure that links one level of organization to others above and below it. Theoretical scaffolding does this by articulating conceptual frameworks that tie the various levels together, and strategic scaffolding ties the levels together through plans for actions; the actions of individual peacekeepers are linked to the larger symbolic meaning at the group, mission, and national levels.

Taking a Broad View of Culture and Peacekeeping

Because it is a human social activity, and thus communicates meaning, peace-keeping is inevitably affected by cultural considerations. Indeed, culture affects what happens in peacekeeping in a myriad of ways and at all levels of its action. This is as true of the events of particular missions as it is of how the institution of peacekeeping is organized and operated.

For instance, culture conditions interactions with local populations, influencing whether or not the intentions of peacekeepers are effectively communicated to local people. Problems for the mission can develop when the peacekeepers' actions are understood differently than what was meant. This was in part the case when the mission in Somalia was seen by locals as an effort to Christianize their country. Also, the actions of locals need to be understood correctly by peacekeepers if they are to render effective aid. If local actions are not correctly understood by peacekeepers, their response to those actions can undercut the strategic aims of the mission. Firing at the muezzin in Gaza and dealing with the crowd at the depot in Wanwaylen are examples at this level.

As I will discuss in chapter 7, culture also affects how well internal elements of a peacekeeping mission are able to work together, and how well they are able to cooperate with international agencies and nongovernmental organizations that are also working in the area. Successful interoperability within a mission, and between the mission and its partners, is embedded in the need to share understandings about what is to be done, how it should be undertaken, and how each potential action should be valued. While it is not necessary that these understandings be totally shared, there must be a minimal overlap among them to coherently organize their diversity.[48]

Since peacekeeping is an instrument of international action, it is conditioned by cultural considerations at the broadest levels. When, how, why, and by whom missions are authorized and deployed are all affected by the way the symbol of United Nations peacekeeping is understood. As I will discuss in chapter 8, much of the symbolic capital, and the legitimacy that peacekeeping carries, depends upon cultural considerations.

I emphasize once again that the analysis I present in this book is not meant to deny the importance of noncultural factors to peacekeeping. Rather, I offer a corrective to two difficulties in the current peacekeeping literature. The first is that too many analyses of peacekeeping proceed as though culture does not matter at all.[49] The second is that when culture has been considered, it has generally been used to account for locally observed difficulties. The resulting relatively small body of literature, while very useful, has the unintended effect of presenting culture as limited in scope and influence, useful for understanding exotic situations. This book shows that it is important to place the understanding of culture and peacekeeping in a broader framework. Certainly we must do this if we are not to repeat the mistake of trying to understand the whole by looking only at its parts, as poetically exemplified by Saxe's blind men's investigation of the elephant.[50]

At the time I began my research, there were few anthropologists conducting fieldwork on peacekeeping. This was partly because anthropology was focused on meaning and culture, which were then not considered important for peacekeeping. It was also because anthropological methods are different from those ordinarily used for economic, policy, sociological, and political science research, which dominates international security analyses. Doing anthropological research on peacekeeping posed special challenges. In the next chapter, I describe the methodological challenges I met when beginning my ethnographic study of the United Nations Truce Supervision Organization and in my ethnographic interviews of peacekeepers, diplomats, international civil servants, and staff of nongovernmental organizations.

4

"Turn Left at the Mosque"
Anthropological Fieldwork and Peacekeeping

I began my research by interviewing diplomats and military officers experienced in planning and carrying out peacekeeping missions. By late 1987, I was convinced that to really understand the social dynamics of peacekeeping I ought to do ethnographic fieldwork in a particular mission. Ethnographic research involves more than just asking questions or completing survey instruments. It involves observation, participation, systematic in-depth interviewing, and casual interaction, giving richer insight into the lives of those studied. I was most interested in studying the United Nations Truce Supervision Organization (UNTSO) for two sets of reasons. The first related to how I thought I could best gain a better understanding of peacekeeping.

As a site for better understanding peacekeeping, UNTSO was particularly attractive first because, as the oldest peacekeeping mission, it set the basic pattern of United Nations operations. Second, UNTSO had observer groups in a Lebanon, Syria, Israel, and Egypt, so I would be able to see how peacekeeping functioned in different settings. Third, I had learned in my earlier interviews that UNTSO often served as a kind of socializing experience for many military observers who had their first peacekeeping exposure there and subsequently served in other missions. Fourth, UNTSO had become the focal point of United Nations peacekeeping activities. In this capacity it was a reservoir from which officers with experience and expertise in peacekeeping could be drawn for planning and staffing new operations. For instance, during my early fieldwork, it was the UNTSO staff who undertook the technical missions for the peacekeeping operations in Iraq/Iran and Namibia. Finally, UNTSO was frequently the source of the troops initially deployed to new mission areas while other logistical arrangements were being finalized and put in place. Thus UNTSO presented a unique opportunity to get inside United Nations peacekeeping on the ground.

The second set of reasons was related to the development of anthropology as a discipline. Studying UNTSO was attractive anthropologically because it allowed me to engage my long-standing interest in making anthropology relevant to policy in my own society and my interest in anthropological methods.

Like many others, I was deeply concerned that anthropological knowledge was not being used in a meaningful way by policymakers. Many public policies seemed to be articulated in ways that made their lack of success likely, or worse, ensured that they would have an effect opposite of that intended. I was especially concerned about the lack of anthropological perspectives in US national security policy.

In the early 1980s, the risk of nuclear conflict was very real and seemed to be growing, driven in part by security policies that made little if any anthropological sense.[1] To address these lacunae in policy analysis and discourse, as part of the 11th World Congress of Anthropological and Ethnological Science, Mary Foster and I convened four days of coordinated symposia at which we asked our colleagues to address issues of peace and war and public policy.[2]

Many of the papers presented in those symposia studied these issues from the perspectives of those who might be described as ordinary people or those affected by the actions of elites within their societies. This penchant for studying people who were not among the elite or powerful sectors of a society was consistent with anthropology's long experience of working with disenfranchised communities.[3] Yet, as Laura Nader pointed out in 1969, this tradition had the effect of keeping anthropology focused on topics that contributed little to the understanding of contemporary problems and prevented it from contributing to discussions of those problems. As well, the perception of anthropology as irrelevant to the solution of contemporary problems was leading to a kind of lethargy within the field itself. To address this, Nader suggested that to develop more adequate understandings anthropologists had scientific and social responsibilities to study up as well as down: "We are not dealing with an either/or proposition; we need simply to realize when it is useful or crucial in terms of the problem to extend the domain of study up, down or sideways."[4]

No groups are more "up" than diplomats, international civil servants, and militaries with responsibility for maintaining international peace and security.[5] All belong to the upper strata of their own communities, and the organizations they participate in are institutions of power. Peacekeeping missions are an example of their exercise of the prerogatives and power inscribed on those institutions and on the social relations they entail. It would be perfectly respectable anthropologically to approach the study of peacekeeping by focusing on how the people in a particular mission area are affected by and interact with the mission. But that would do little to illuminate the persistent patterns of thought and action among those who deploy and are deployed in peacekeeping operations. Focusing on the people and organizations that participate in UNTSO would allow me to explore those patterns and, when called for, to expand to adjacent levels of analysis. Studying up, in this sense, appealed to me because it provided a way for me to enact my commitment to giving multilevel explanations of social phenomena.[6]

A further anthropological consideration was that the military plays a large role in peacekeeping. Yet the anthropological literature on military organizations was relatively sparse. With few exceptions, after World War II and especially after the Vietnam War, American anthropology had eschewed the study of militaries and other elements of the defense and intelligence communities. There were many good reasons for this. For example, in the 1960s anthropologists participated in counterinsurgency work in Southeast Asia, harming the people with whom they worked and harming the discipline itself.[7] Development of weapons of mass destruction, of more effective ways to deploy them, and the many ways in which militarism distorts societies are all contrary to anthropological commitments to advance the welfare of people, especially those with whom we work. Therefore, the anthropological community saw working with the military as unethical, and the few anthropologists who did study the military reported that they felt like pariahs in the discipline. Some anthropologists had conducted research on military life and on the nature of war, especially "primitive war," and others critiqued the effects of militarization on our own society and on the societies of people whom anthropologists traditionally studied.[8] For the most part, however, anthropology viewed the military as morally contaminated, and even those anthropologists interested in studying military phenomena were fearful that they would be ostracized if they conducted that research. Those who persisted in studying military phenomena kept a low profile within the discipline. As a result, anthropologists spoke about "The Military" in ways that would be unacceptable if they were speaking about other peoples. That "The Military" was (and still is) often discussed as a homogenous and simplistic caricature went mostly unchallenged within the discipline. I found this deeply troubling, especially when troops were involved in nonstereotypic activities like peacekeeping. I wanted to find out how to reconcile these contrasting images.

Finally, anthropology has a long history of studying non-Western peoples. Early in its history this meant studying relatively well-bounded groups of people in faraway places. Then, anthropological expeditions often included arduous travel just to arrive at the field site. It didn't take very long for anthropologists to realize that the people they were studying were often not as isolated as they had supposed. By the 1930s, anthropologists were responding to the reality of regional interaction by adjusting their models and methods.[9] By the 1970s, they faced diminishing opportunities to do research abroad, and there were fewer university positions available for continuing that work. So anthropologists increasingly turned their attention to aspects of their own societies, and we again found that our methods and models needed to change.

Methods of problem-based ethnographic research began to compete with the traditional holistic ethnographies of earlier eras. Similarly, toward the end of the twentieth century anthropologists acknowledged that they needed to develop models and methods to deal with new classes of social phenomena: transnational connections and multilateral institutions.[10] Incorporating both of these classes, anthropological study of UNTSO was interesting because it required working with people from multiple communities with cross-cutting ties who, although interconnected, acted in widely dispersed sites.

Data about the phenomena anthropologists study are contingent on the circumstances under which they are collected, and the resulting perspective affects our understanding and interpretation of those data. My understanding of the role culture plays in peacekeeping is thus affected by the circumstances of my fieldwork. (In fact, because I entered the study of peacekeeping by working with the military, some of my account may overly emphasize its role in peacekeeping operations.) Research on a multisited, multicultural, transnational, elite institution entails challenges no matter what disciplinary or methodological approach is taken. For an anthropologist seeking to make an ethnographic study of the institution and its people, those challenges are multiplied. This chapter describes some of those challenges and relates how I engaged them. In particular I discuss the first nine months of my fieldwork and focus on issues of access and entry to the field, restrictions on my freedom of action, and problems of role legitimization as these affect building and maintaining rapport. After completing my UNTSO fieldwork in 1992, my research activities broadened again, and I collected data from peacekeeping missions in Somalia, the former Yugoslavia, East Timor, South Sudan, Ethiopia, and other areas. I conclude this chapter by describing briefly that new phase of my work.

Challenges of Ethnographic Fieldwork

Anthropological research shares many of its methodological concerns with other social sciences. Anthropologists are concerned about the reliability of our data and whether they are valid, and we devise ways to ensure that the information we gather is collected systematically. For a variety of theoretical and historical reasons, the core method of anthropological research is the ethnographic study. All other data collection techniques anthropologists use compliment that basic approach. Ethnography is what produces the "thick description," "fine-grained account," or "culturally nuanced view" of a particular group, which is what distinguishes anthropology from other social science disciplines.

The ethnographer's main tool is participant observation. Participant observation may start out with an anthropologist just spending time with the people he or she is studying, but it soon evolves into a more planned and systematic observation that may involve participation in the daily life of the group. This requires relatively long-term engagement with the group and the ethnographer's personal involvement. Here, anthropology departs from other social sciences, which do not require such engagement, using instead techniques that call for more well-bounded briefer research encounters. No matter where it is done, anthropological fieldwork presents a number of challenges that must be overcome for it to be successfully carried out. Among these are legal, social, practical, and ethical considerations that must be met.

Special permissions are needed in order to do research in many places. In Egypt, for instance, where I have done sociomedical research, multiple bureaucratic hurdles must be cleared. Often permission takes a long time to be granted (or is not given at all). For some researchers, this process takes so long that they are actually unable to do their proposed study because they no longer have the time or access to financial support necessary for the work.[11] Of course, this is not a problem unique to research in Egypt. In Belize, where I researched education and language acquisition in the mid-1970s, I was required to get research permissions from the Ministry of Education, the district officer (governor), and the schools I wanted to work in before I could do that research. Such legal considerations are not unique to non-Western societies. Indeed, similar constraints affect researchers doing ethnography in the United States, where research is constrained by an elaborate legal apparatus.[12]

The legitimacy conferred by legal permissions may be a necessary condition for anthropological research, but it is not sufficient. Ethnography involves a sustained and integrated presence among the people studied, so it also requires the legitimacy conferred by social relationships. Those relationships affect whether or not it is possible to gain access to a research site, and they make possible the continuation of the research once the researcher is allowed in. This distinction between formal and substantive legitimacy will be important in my discussions in later chapters. Here, it is sufficient to note that for ethnographic fieldwork to be successful, the researcher must be brought into social roles that allow for the gathering of appropriate information and that this requires the active participation of the people with whom the ethnographer works.[13]

No ethnographer can stay in the field long if practical arrangements cannot be made for the basic necessities of living. Food and shelter, at least, must be available to the ethnographer. When ethnographic research meant bringing along one's provisions and pitching a tent in some proximity to the people being studied, these concerns were somewhat minimized, but of course this brought other logistical problems.[14] Especially as anthropologists work in places where such self-sufficiency is not possible, such practical consider-ations are critical. Promising research sites have been abandoned because the practical constraints of doing research there were too great. For instance, Sol Tax's classic research in Guatemala was shaped by practical considerations; he decided to leave a potentially ethnographically rich location because finding food and lodging there was difficult and his presence would have placed an undo burden on the community.[15]

In addition to legal, social, and practical considerations, ethnographers always confront ethical issues. The presence of the ethnographer might put the people among whom he or she works in harm's way. For instance, Tax determined that the harm done by the stress his presence put on the available food supply would outweigh the benefits of the knowledge gained through his stay. Other ethnographers have worked in war zones and had to balance the potential harm caused by their presence and reports against the benefits of the knowledge gained.[16] Research might only be possible if the ethnographer accepted financial support or worked under the auspices of an organization that he finds morally unacceptable. In all anthropological research, ethical questions arise that an ethnographer must confront.

Fieldwork with the United Nations Truce Supervision Organization

My fieldwork with UNTSO shared the general challenges of ethnographic research. The details of many of these challenges are different when one stud-ies up and when research is done in the context of the international security community. In particular, researchers in this area face special issues of access and entry to the field, restrictions on their freedom of action in the research setting, problems of role legitimization, and challenges in building and main-taining rapport.[17] These problems are compounded in studying peacekeeping because there is a considerable amount of turnover in personnel.[18] Because these challenges are most evident in the early period of my fieldwork, I focus mainly on the nine months or so of my work with UNTSO's Observer Group Egypt (OGE). During this time I encountered a series of challenges that had to be overcome in order to gain increasingly broad research access.

Several instances seem to mark points where particular challenges were met. The successful negotiation of each of these broadened the access I was permitted. Although I describe these events as isolated episodes, they were actually part of a continuing iterative process of daily negotiation, much of which defined and legitimated my role as a researcher and member of the community.

Observer Group Egypt

I described the origins of and differences between United Nations observer missions and peacekeeping forces in chapter 2. I add here further details about UNTSO and OGE to provide additional context for my discussion of the challenges of ethnographic fieldwork with this group.

Most UN peacekeeping operations are authorized for discrete periods of time and then periodically reauthorized as needed. When UNTSO was established, it was mandated to monitor compliance with cease-fire agreements and to remain at this task until peace was achieved.[19] UNTSO's activities normally spread over five countries, and sometimes extend beyond these as well. Set up in June 1948, UNTSO's responsibilities and day-to-day tasks have varied considerably over the sixty years of its existence as it has adjusted its operation to the changing environment in the Middle East. In general, however, UNTSO's tasks have involved the use of unarmed military observers from a number of countries to patrol, inspect, verify, and report conditions in areas where truce agreements or treaties have been reached.

At the time of my research, the United Nations military observers (UNMOs) serving with UNTSO were mainly officers with the rank of major and lieutenant colonel. The normal tour of duty with UNTSO is one year, during which a UNMO would ordinarily spend six months in Israel and six months in an Arab country. UNMOs came from seventeen countries and served in five countries in the Middle East (Lebanon, Syria, Jordan, Egypt, and Israel) and in Afghanistan and Pakistan. UNMOs are drawn from all service branches—army, navy, air force, and marine. Thus, a posting to UNTSO is an opportunity for joint and combined service with officers from other countries and services.

Observer Group Egypt was headquartered in Cairo, together with the United Nations Liaison Office in Cairo, and maintained observation posts throughout the Sinai peninsula. There was an average of fifty-four UNMOs serving with OGE. The Soviet, American, and French contingents at OGE each consisted of fifteen UNMOs. The remaining nine came from fourteen other countries. In addition to the military observers who served with OGE, there were several United Nations field service officers, who were civilians serving in support capacities. And OGE had relations with a variety of other organizations.

For at least some portion of their service with OGE, each UNMO participated in the main operational task of the observation group: maintaining a presence in the area by staffing the six observations posts in the Sinai and carrying out routine patrols of the area. The management of time at the observer group revolved around these tasks. Each of the observation posts was occupied by a team of two UNMOs, of different nationalities, for a week at a time.

A few other UNMOs were posted to the Cairo headquarters in staff positions that occupied them with the tasks of running the organization. These officers worked at the OGE headquarters, which was located in an old home in a Cairo neighborhood near the international airport. The building was routinely referred to as "the villa."

Research Access and Entry

It is something of an anthropological truism that how one enters the field has important effects on the entire course of research. Often the manner in which initial contacts are made and auspices under which the researcher acts determine the roles a fieldworker is eventually placed in by the people with whom he or she works. Anthropological literature is full of descriptions of how a fieldworker's introduction to his or her research site affected the future course of their work. The people with whom a researcher works must understand in their own terms who the researcher is and what he or she is doing. So the way a researcher enters the field provides information that is used to place the researcher into an appropriate set of culturally constituted roles.[20]

This observation applies to all forms of social research that involve face-to-face interaction, but it is perhaps particularly salient for researchers who study up. When studying people in professional communities and institutions of power, researchers face special constraints that result from higher degrees of gate-keeping in such settings. For instance, because in the study of peacekeeping the researcher seeks to enter a professional community with a strictly defined and restricted set of roles, there are very few roles the researcher can achieve. Moreover, once having achieved these roles the anthropological researcher is likely to find that the activities of an incumbent in them are restricted in ways that may be inconsistent with traditional anthropological participant observation.

As often happens in anthropological research, my research access resulted from the confluence of a number of practical considerations. In the summer of 1987, I participated in the International Peace Academy's Vienna Seminar, a two-week-long training program for diplomats and military officers. In addition to the daily readings, discussions, and lectures—including guest speakers from the United Nations Secretariat, national militaries, nongovernmental organizations, and from people who had served or were currently serving in UN missions—the seminar was structured around a simulation exercise. The Simulex, as the exercise was called, placed participants in roles that allowed them to experience every aspect of the development of a mission, from the initial crisis to the political negotiations in the Security Council and the definition of the mandate to the logistics and establishment of a mission. I had originally been invited to the seminar as an observer, but at the last moment one of the regular participants dropped out and I was asked to assume his role because the Simulex required a minimum number of actors in order to work effectively.

I returned to the Vienna Seminar the following summer to serve as a co-facilitator of the Simulex. The general who was then UNTSO chief of staff spoke at the 1988 seminar. I was able to explain my interest in studying UNTSO and to sketch for him the work I had done to that point. I explained why I thought an ethnographic study of the mission would substantially enhance an understanding of peacekeeping. And, since I would soon be moving to Cairo, I expressed a special interest in studying OGE.[21] He seemed a bit bemused that an anthropologist should be taking on such a project but nonetheless expressed his willingness to help in any reasonable way. My research could not have proceeded without this modest support, or the support of some other members of the United Nations Secretariat.

During the next three months, the chief of staff and I had a cursory correspondence, and I formally asked for permission to conduct research at OGE. Early one morning a few months after I had moved to Cairo, I received a telephone call from him. He told me that after a visit of some duration he was about to leave Cairo. He added that he had discussed my request with the chief of OGE. Although the UNTSO chief of staff regretted that he could not see me himself, he instructed me to arrange to see the chief of OGE.

This proved to be difficult because the chief's schedule was quite full, and it took a long time to get to speak with him on the telephone. Eventually persistence was rewarded. After three weeks, our phone tag ended, and we spoke briefly about my research. The chief invited me to visit him at the villa so we could review the mission and talk more about my research plans. The villa was located in Heliopolis on the northeast side of the city, and I would be driving from downtown Cairo, so I asked for directions. My notes from that call are striking because of the instructions: "take the airport road; after you go under the overpass with the Misr Insurance sign, turn left at the mosque; you'll see us on the right side, midway down the street." Not wanting to miss our meeting, the day beforehand I drove to Heliopolis to scout out the location. It was on that drive that I realized, this being Cairo, the instruction to turn left at the mosque was not the most precise possible.[22]

Diplomats and military officers are used to scholars, reporters, and others bothering them with questions. Therefore, there is a role into which an anthropologist seeking to do research among them can be assimilated. Unfortunately, at least from the anthropologist's perspective, most of the researchers they have had contact with have worked in traditions that involve brief contacts between the researcher and the officers. Some of these researchers come from the staffs of politicians and are viewed with suspicion because they have produced politically motivated reports that are unremittingly critical of the military and, in the view of some, paint unfair portraits of the military. Because the US government had often taken hostile positions toward the United Nations and peacekeeping, my interest in UNTSO was viewed with particular suspicion. It was against such a backdrop that I approached OGE.

My reception at OGE was cordial but reserved. I checked in with the duty officer and was told to wait in the bar, where the chief would meet me when he was available. He arrived shortly, and we went through security to his second-floor office. He spoke to me about the operation and responsibilities of the observer group. This included examining the large map of the mission area and what seemed to be a rather standard briefing. I explained my research interests and asked permission to conduct research among the observers and to spend a portion of my research in participant observation by accompanying UNMOs on trips to the observation posts and on patrols.

The chief listened without comment to my description of my interests until I mentioned that I wanted to conduct participant observation. At this point, he said that he thought it would be important, if I were to pursue this approach, to spend some time at observation posts in the desert, and he then gave an unappealing description of the rigors of observation post life, including saying that live munitions were still found in the Sinai dessert, even close to the observation posts. It seemed to me at the time that this was intended to discourage my interest. My response that the opportunity to spend as much time as possible with UNMOs at observation posts and on patrol in the Sinai was what I most sought surprised and intrigued him. We parted with his promise to explore whether this would be possible.

In this meeting, I passed one set of gate-keeping controls by demonstrating my earnest interest and sympathetic outlook. But I had stepped outside of the role of a researcher who would pay a brief visit and then move on. This created a new problem in understanding me for my potential hosts. UNTSO in general, and OGE in particular, operated under a considerable amount of international attention. Their activities are restricted by international agreements, national security concerns of its host countries, and the vagaries of diplomatic relations that affect its status. The prospect of having a researcher hanging around for a relatively long time must have been unsettling. So I was encouraged when, several weeks after our initial meeting, I was asked to return to the villa for further discussions with the chief of OGE.

That meeting took place on a Friday morning and was exceedingly brief. The chief informed me that he had consulted with the chief of staff of UNTSO and that I was welcome to conduct my research on an informal basis. I would be welcome to visit the observation posts on my own, if UNMOs invited me to do so. They regretted that because of diplomatic restrictions on its activities, and for security reasons, I could not travel in UN vehicles with UNMOs to the observation posts or on patrol, although eventually this restriction was relaxed.

The chief then called in his senior liaison officer, who he introduced to me as someone particularly interested in my project. Before taking his leave of us, the chief suggested that I return to the villa that evening when the weekly happy hour would take place. He added that I was welcome to bring my wife, as it was a family event. He then left me with the senior liaison officer. who explained the mission and organization of OGE and patiently decoded the many acronyms used at the observer group.

I returned by myself that evening. I was met by the senior liaison officer, who took great care to introduce me to his colleagues. About two hours into the evening, the chief called for everyone's attention. He welcomed two new UNMOs to the station and wished one departing UNMO farewell. Immediately after these hails and farewells, he introduced me to the assembled group as an anthropologist who would be writing a book about OGE, saying that they should expect to see me around the villa, and asking me to make a few remarks. There was considerable surprise about my interests, and there were lots of jokes about the primitive culture of military observers and me being there to see if they had evolved beyond Neanderthals.

Following that evening's introduction, my presence at the villa was legitimated. But it remained for me to negotiate my role with UNMOs of different nationalities, each of whom understood my work and interests in different ways. Since differences in perceptions about the role of conversations with me could be problematic, this heterogeneity of role definition was in itself a challenge.[23] My introduction was the start of a period of weeks that were critical to my project yet exceedingly frustrating.

During this time, that I was able to establish a basic rapport with the UNMOs at OGE that could foster deeper relations. It was frustrating because the building of this rapport and the negotiation of my role as a researcher had to be carried out in the context of a restricted range of action.

In 1959, Erving Goffman showed that people "perform" differently in public than they do in private.[24] In traditional anthropological work in a community, there are a variety of public spaces in which the researcher can observe and participate, even when he or she has not yet been permitted access to private spaces. Through work in multiple public settings, one can begin to discern systematic patterns by triangulating observations and experiences. One of the challenges faced by a researcher studying up in an institutional setting is that the vast majority of space is private and restricted because of security or other concerns.

Upon entering the OGE villa, one stepped into a round entrance hallway. To one's right was a set of stairs leading to the second floor, which was completely occupied by offices. In front of the entrance were two rooms, the duty officer in one and communications equipment in the other. To the left was a doorway that led to a room of about fifteen by twenty feet containing a bar and several tables. The bar was the only public space in the villa.

Because it was a unique, small space, one's presence in it was conspicuous. Yet, without an invitation into private areas it was the only place to which I had free access. In fact, even this access was controlled, since cash was not accepted at the bar. Instead, drinks were paid for with chits, purchased with US dollars and sold only to OGE staff or associate members of the villa.

For the first weeks of my fieldwork, I spent four or five hours, four days each week, in the bar. I was not an associate member of the villa and therefore I had no bar chits. UNMOs would come into the bar and talk to me for a few minutes. Some would buy me coffee or a drink. But having no bar chits meant I could neither reciprocate those gestures nor initiate conversation by inviting people to join me by offering them coffee or a drink. Moreover, nearly all were guarded in their speech and demeanor. Some, particularly the United States and Soviet UNMOs, either were suspicious of my intentions or construed my project ("writing a book about us") as a prelude to the publication of a best seller that would bring enormous monetary return, especially when I sold the movie rights.

During this period a kind of rapport began to develop between me and the UNMOs. First, they got used to seeing me at the villa. Second, in the bar and at the Friday happy hours we began to discover areas of common interest that did not bear on their operational responsibilities. Thus an interest in computers brought me into extended interaction with an Italian and a French UNMO. And an interest in guitar playing brought extended interaction with a Soviet and a United States UNMO.

As this initial period drew to a close, two things happened that solidified and deepened my rapport with the UNMOs. First, because of my knowledge about computers I was invited into one of the private offices for coffee and a discussion of communications programming. Second, I attended my first "big" happy hour, and I was accompanied for the first time by Sandy, my wife.

The happy hours at OGE had a standard ritual form (see chapter 5). Each month, one of the national contingents was responsible for arranging four Friday night happy hours. Two were known as "small" happy hours, one was a family barbecue, and one was a "big" happy hour with some kind of special event or entertainment.

This particular happy hour had a theme that required people to come dressed in a local costume. The observers and their families had been in the Middle East for some time, and there were many rich and culturally sensitive costumes. As part of the evening's entertainment, the Recreation and Welfare Committee had hired a belly dancer. The belly dancer arrived late, and when she finally did perform, she spent much of her time bringing various members of the audience to the stage to dance with her.

We were seated at a table with the chief of OGE, the UN senior liaison officer, the Egyptian general who was their contact, and with all of their wives. As the belly dancer wended her way toward us through the other tables, I calculated that of all the people at our table it would be me she pulled to the stage. I was sure that this would destroy any chance I had for further research at OGE. To my relief, she chose Sandy. I knew, but the belly dancer did not, that Sandy had studied belly dancing for three years in the United States and in Egypt, and had briefly danced professionally. The very next day, we were invited to become associate members of the Recreation and Welfare Committee, and for months afterward we heard compliments about her dancing that evening.

My long hours at the villa's bar and our attending that big happy hour marked my passage through another set of gate-keeping controls and the consolidation of a legitimate role at OGE. After a long beginning, it seemed that many of the UNMOs had decided that we were probably good people, despite our being anthropologists.

Deepening and Maintaining Rapport

There was no magical moment when I established lasting rapport with the UNMOs at OGE. Rather, our joining the Recreation and Welfare Committee began another phase. Over several months, I had the opportunity to consolidate my anthropological role and to deepen the rapport that had begun to form between the UNMOs, their families, and us.

The deepening of rapport and construction of legitimate and mutually comfortable roles were expressed in many ways, large and small. Rapport in anthropological fieldwork grows out of the reciprocity expressed in the day-to-day activities of living. Some of these are rather mundane; others have a high emotional charge. For us, they included our becoming associate members of the Recreation and Welfare Committee, thus establishing for me a role in the community that was legitimate and could be assimilated to the culture of the observer group. Importantly, this enabled me to purchase the bar chits that would allow me to reciprocate social interactions with UNMOs.

As I became more deeply familiar to the UNMOs, many of them took an interest, perhaps a self-interest, in my work. They read my professional papers on anthropology and international security and, although they didn't always like what they read, it established me as a bona fide scholar. This led to an American Marine lieutenant colonel insisting that we visit the museum dedicated to the Egyptian victory in the October 1973 war together. He and I spent a lively afternoon talking about the social construction of victory and about the symbolism and meaning of the placement of Egyptian and captured Israeli ordnance on display there. His informed and thoughtful discourse on these matters showed how wrong were the easy anthropological stereotypes of the military.

Sandy and I became integrated into the social life of the mission. We shared family dinners and exchanged favors. We marked life-cycle events, traveled, and vacationed together with members of the OGE community.

We conceived a child, and after five hopeful months lost him to an infection acquired in Egypt, which brought great interest and an outpouring of compassion—especially among the Soviet and American contingents, which had previously been the most difficult to reach. Tragic as this event was for us, it also opened a new avenue for exploration, because UNMOs and their family members began to talk with me about their own health concerns and challenges.

The deepening rapport opened doors for my research as well. I was invited to observation posts by UNMOs and rode with them on their patrols. During one trip, we were stuck in the desert sand for hours, and so I experienced what had been described to me as a rite of passage in the life of a UNMO at OGE.

When it was apparent that introducing a tape recorder and questionnaire to supplement my activities at the villa would not breech the developing rapport, I was able to begin my more systematic research. At this point, the leader of the Soviet contingent indicated that my research questions would need to be vetted by their embassy before his group could participate further in my study. After presenting my study to an embassy representative, I was given permission to interview members of the Soviet contingent. Four and a half months after I was first granted permission to do research at OGE, I was able to begin making formal, semistructured, recorded interviews with UNMOs. Toward the end of my research, I conducted an interview with a US lieutenant colonel. When we were done, I discovered that the batteries in my field recorder had died during our conversation. Although I had notes, I expressed my disappointment, whereupon the colonel placed on the table between us a small Dictaphone and urged me not to worry since I could copy his tape—which I did. This incident underscored for me the deep ambivalence with which my work continued to be regarded even as it was drawing to a close, for it indicated a level of discomfort with my work and a level of acceptance of it.

Fieldwork and Reciprocity

I completed my ethnographic fieldwork with UNTSO in 1992, after having collected materials about OGE and all of the other posts, including the headquarters in Jerusalem. Anthropologists have long honored the view that there should be some kind reciprocity between the researcher and the people with whom he or she works. That is part of the foundation upon which the rapport necessary for fieldwork is built. It is expressed in many ways when one is in the field, as my preceding description shows. And bonds of reciprocity continue after the researcher has left the field. This is true of traditional anthropological work.

In addition to research with UNTSO, when I was in Egypt I was also part of a team doing eye disease research in the Nile Delta. Sandy had been part of that team before me, and she had lived in one of the villages in which the team worked. One day, long after she had lived in the village, and even after my own work there was done, we answered a knock on our front door in Cairo to find a mother and her adult son from the village. Naturally, we invited them in and served them tea and food. Eventually, they told us that they had come to ask a favor: the son wished to get a visa to visit the United States, and they hoped we would help them. After all that these villagers had done for us, the bonds of reciprocity required that we do what we could. And in any event, our visitors were enacting a cultural institution by asking us to intercede on their behalf.[25] I spent the next day with them at the US embassy, helping them navigate their way through questions and answers, forms and interviews.

Fieldwork with UNTSO had been a mutually affecting process with lots of opportunities for reciprocities to develop. I developed deeply personal friendships with some of our "informants." My research about cultural aspects of peacekeeping led me to a dual focus on the culture of UNTSO and the importance for UNTSO of understanding the cultures of the people with whom it worked—including the local population and the staffs of the NGOs with which they cooperated.

When I returned from my UNTSO fieldwork, I had no serious intentions of engaging in training or institutional reform efforts. But my research with UNTSO placed me in an enduring web of reciprocal relations that demanded attention, and this changed my plans. Joan Ablon has written about how working in one's own society creates lasting bonds and "new and different opportunities for reciprocity."[26] For me, new opportunities came in the form of a metaphorical knock on the door, when some of my informants—from the military and from NGOs—asked me to help them think about culture and peace operations in a way that would support their training of mission personnel.

In order to respond to these requests, I had to do additional research. I discovered that this work was greatly facilitated by the relationships I had built up in the field. Anthropologists often work with a procedure called "snowball" or "network sampling." This involves following the connections of those people with whom the anthropologist has already worked. In the same way, in my further research, acquaintances from my original fieldwork created links for me.

Those links took me, literally and figuratively, to many continents and institutions and introduced me to military officers, international civil servants, NGO and agency personnel, and diplomats. Some of these places, like the United Nations Secretariat, were to be expected. But others, like war colleges and military bases, were unexpected for me, a peace activist and Vietnam War–era war resister. Yet all have advanced my research and deepened my understanding of peacekeeping and appreciation of variation within the military.

Anthropological fieldwork on peacekeeping is a form of studying up. It focuses on a social institution that is by nature multinational and transnational. All of the challenges of ethnographic fieldwork are present in this form of work, but some ethical and practical problems may be more present. In my UNTSO work, I found the initial stages of the fieldwork—gaining access and building rapport—to be among the most attenuated and difficult I had experienced in dozens of years of anthropological fieldwork. But persistent and open engagement with the peacekeepers at UNTSO and elsewhere has led to good working relationships. Like work in more traditional research contexts, fieldwork in this setting has proven to be an exchange that is deeply affecting. I have also been impressed by the enduring network of relationships peacekeepers enter into that facilitates ongoing research.

These relationships cross organizational lines and offer new perspectives on how peacekeeping missions operate. I began my research with a question about the role of culture in peacekeeping. Experience at UNTSO and in subsequent research taught me that there is no single role played by culture. Rather, culture affects peacekeeping operations in multiple interconnected ways, even as they appear discrete. In the chapters that follow, I discuss how these connections are manifest.

5

Symbolic Construction of Community and Cooperation

Traffic moved slowly but steadily as I drove from downtown Cairo to the what was then the suburb of Heliopolis on my way to OGE. It was midday. The road was clogged as always; cars, trucks, busses, and the occasional donkey cart all moving as though following some well-developed choreography. I headed north on the Corniche el-Nîl to the intersection for the Al-Gâla elevated roadway, built to relieve traffic congestion from the streets below. As I approached the turnoff to the Al-Gâla flyover, the traffic signal went from green to red. Despite this, and with no hesitation, the traffic around me continued through the intersection. I too made the turn without stopping, knowing now, as I had not a few months before, that drivers only stopped at this and other signs and signals when traffic police were present and presumably watching for those who did not obey the signals. My stopping now would only confuse those around me. Merging onto the Al-Gâla flyover it was nearly impossible to determine how many actual lanes were intended by the roadway's architect. Three, four, five, or six rows of vehicles—the number changed constantly. Lanes appeared and were reabsorbed as drivers edged forward along the road, beeping their horns to alert one another to their presence and position, or using hand gestures to inform nearby drivers of their intentions or to urge desired behavior from those drivers. Al-Gâla eventually came back down to Al-Ramsis Street, and from there I turned left onto Al-Urûba, the more swiftly moving road to the airport at the outer edge of the city. Despite the quicker pace, cars moved freely across lanes, horns and hands still in play. Eventually, I made a left turn onto Al-Thawra Street, where the OGE building was located.

Arriving at OGE, I reflected on how different my driving experience was here in Cairo from what it had been in Chicago or New York City. The traffic signals, hand gestures, and horns were all things that I had experienced at home. But in Cairo drivers understood them in completely different ways than would a driver in Chicago or New York City. Not understanding the meanings of these symbolic practices and the deeper assumptions about human social life to which they link could lead to frustration and conflict rather than to relatively smooth interaction. Not once in five years of driving in Cairo did I see an incident of road rage, even when I saw drivers do things that almost certainly would have led to clashes in cities in the United States. When through my own poor understanding of the rules of the road I entangled the bumper of my car in the wheel well of a military bus, while navigating traffic that was merging from Al-Urûba onto Al-Ramsis Street, I expected an angry confrontation as the soldiers poured out of the bus. Instead, to my surprise they simply helped to release my car from its embrace of the bus, all the while displaying the utmost courtesy and good humor.

Culture provides frames of reference that shape every aspect of human experience, even mundane aspects like driving through town. It fashions and is fashioned by repeated social practices, by what people do in their daily lives. Learning to interpret the symbols into which the various cultural meanings are encapsulated and knowing the appropriate practices to use to engage the desired meanings allows a person to interact successfully and cooperatively with others. Driving in Cairo, as elsewhere, requires that the driver anticipate and cooperate with people who they have never met and with whom they may never again interact.

In chapter 3, I showed that culture forms the basis for human social cooperation. In many ways, the challenges facing those in peace operations revolve around the need to understand how to cooperate effectively with others in the mission and with the local populations in the mission area. Thus, in addition to whatever technical knowledge they must master in order to be effective in peace operations, they also face the cultural challenge of learning the organizational culture of the particular peacekeeping institution to which they newly belong and may be part of for perhaps no more than six months or a year. And as I discuss in chapter 7, they must also be aware of the different organizational cultures of other institutions working in the mission area. Both of these circumstances involve the need to cooperate with people they may not have previously encountered and with whom they might not work again. In this sense, joining a peacekeeping mission is much like entering into the Cairo traffic.[1]

In this chapter, I discuss some of the ways that military observers at OGE learn to participate in the peacekeeping meaning system of that group and how this connects to the meaning system of UNTSO and peacekeeping generally.[2] To do this research, I used the tools of anthropological fieldwork—listening, observing, interviewing, and, at times, participating in the activities at OGE—which allowed me to learn about the group's system of implicit meanings. I was then able to understand how this system of meaning shaped, and was shaped by, everyday practices in OGE, and how participation in this system allowed mission members to see themselves as peacekeepers, which entailed certain constraints on their actions. As Robert LeVine points out, such "clarification [of culture] is only possible through ethnography."[3]

In addition to describing some of the symbolic material of peacekeeping, I describe some activities, especially rituals, that help shape social cognition in relation to peacekeeping and international affairs. Consistent with the larger proposition I advance in this book, I claim that the proper understanding of peacekeeping as a respected instrument of international action depends on recognizing that symbolism, and its everyday enactment, plays a crucial role in shaping political perceptions about peacekeeping, both within individual missions and generally. This claim rests on the understanding that the legitimacy of peacekeeping in general, and of its ability to play a role in mediating conflicts in particular, results from the symbolic transformation of the political contexts within which peacekeeping is carried out. In large measure, peacekeeping has attained its legitimacy by restructuring the context of political action by developing and manipulating symbolic representations of international consensus and joint action, and by elaborating and repeating ritual behavior that reinforces these representations.

There are many levels at which the use of symbols and ritualized behavior effects ideological shifts in relation to peacekeeping. These levels range from the effects on individuals to the understandings constructed by small groups to the emergence of peacekeeping in national and international consciousness. As described in preceding chapters, the system of meanings conceptually maps peacekeeping onto root metaphor in which the United Nations is a key symbol that signifies a world with new political space and social concern. In peacekeeping, this mapping happens, for example, when participants experience the attenuation of national sovereignty when troops from other nations are stationed in the receiving country's territory, when mission command and control functions are held by officers from another country, when information and daily duties are conducted jointly with troops from countries that are potential adversaries, or when military units renounce the use of force and pursue their ends through more pacific means. Through anthropological fieldwork, it is possible to show the meaningful links between such seemingly mundane daily activities and more macrosociological phenomena, including expansive policy concerns involved in constructing international order.

Symbol and Ritual in Peacekeeping

The most obvious evidence that symbols have invested legitimacy in peacekeeping is that the blue beret or blue helmet is now widely recognized as denoting United Nations peacekeeping troops. This was not always so. This most durable symbol of peacekeeping was constructed out of the hurried need to distinguish UN troops from those of the armed forces they were separating during the 1956 Suez crisis, when surplus World War II allied combat helmet liners were painted blue.[4] Following the ad hoc origin of this and other peace-keeping symbolism, such as the ubiquitous white UN vehicles used in peace-keeping missions, the legitimacy accorded to peacekeeping today has grown through sixty years of relatively ordinary symbolic representation and ritual repetition.

The substance of symbolic action in day-to-day transformations of political perceptions is often overlooked because it is not especially glamorous. Like-wise, it is easy to overlook the importance of symbols and rituals for legitimat-ing peacekeeping because they are individually unremarkable.[5] Yet it is not from the isolated symbols and rituals that the legitimacy of peacekeeping is constructed. Rather, the power of peacekeeping symbolism derives from the deployment of symbols and rituals in a variety of arenas and from the sym-bolic restructuring it entails.

In order to illustrate this, in this chapter I describe some of the symbols and rituals that have shaped and channeled perceptions of peacekeeping. In discussing the effect of peacekeeping on political relations (and of political relations on peacekeeping), it is hard to separate its material success from its symbolic success.[6] The descriptions of peacekeeping ritual and symbolism I discuss below draw mainly from my work with OGE, but they also draw selectively from other missions as well. I concentrate on UNTSO and on its several observer groups because of its unique role in United Nations peace-keeping. As noted in chapter 1, UNTSO was the first peacekeeping mission established by the United Nations, and, since it is still in operation, it is the longest continuously operating mission as well. UNTSO is also important because it has had a unique role in introducing both military and civilian per-sonnel to peacekeeping. Many peacekeepers, officers and civilians, cut their teeth by participating in UNTSO, going on later to other missions. Even more directly, at times UNTSO has provided the technical planning teams for new missions, and its personnel have formed the initial contingents deployed to those missions.[7]

As described in chapter 2, observer groups and peacekeeping forces dif-fer in their missions and in their formal organization, and these differences are important. Nevertheless, to a great degree both rely on overlapping sets of rituals and symbolism for their legitimacy and coherence. Indeed, much of the symbolism and ritual used by observer groups is drawn and adapted from those commonly found in military life.

A Note on Ritual

Human experience is profoundly shaped by our use of symbols, which enable us to place our actions in the context of the meanings that symbols make avail-able to us. Thus they help us make sense out of our day-to-day experiences.

Anthropological work leads repeatedly to the conclusion that our capacity for symbolizing is at the root of our experience as a species.[8] Symbolism saturates human experience; people use symbols in nearly every aspect of their lives. Part of this symbolic construction is the embedding of our sense of who we are and what we are doing in a symbolic matrix. That is, our identity is created by investing differences, sometimes small differences, with symbolic meanings that distinguish us from others.[9]

Not all symbols are equal in our experience. Some are generally more salient than others and have more crucial significance for how we think of ourselves and how we understand our world (see chapters 3 and 8). As well, the context in which symbolism is experienced can heighten and reinforce its cognitive and emotional effects. Ritual is such a context. For that reason, ritual plays an important role in human social life, and anthropologists have paid it considerable attention.

Within anthropology and related disciplines, discussions of ritual activity include a variety of ways of conceptualizing ritual. The merits of each perspective are passionately debated.[10] Rather than entering that debate here, I simply note that I find useful a definition of ritual that includes five features. Rituals are (1) conventionalized in that their performance adheres to some specific set of rules that cannot be easily breached; (2) repetitive, both in their performance and in their occurrence; (3) essentially social, involving groups of people thus evoking communal experience; (4) emotionally involving, because they shape participants' affective images of themselves and of others; and (5) conveyors of meanings on several levels simultaneously.[11] Of particular interest with regard to peacekeeping are rites of reversal. These are ritualized activities that induce ideological shifts so that the impossible or unthought-of becomes possible and acceptable, even valued and promoted (see chapter 3).

Ritual activity can have very powerful effects on those who participate in them, harmonizing the emotional and cognitive orientations of participants so that they share more fully in the sentiments at which the ritual is targeted. Rituals involve both "producing and controlling experience."[12] Rituals that mark the transition from one life status to another, commonly referred to as "rites of passage," which are among the types of ritual with which people are most familiar. University life in the United States, for instance, is bounded by convocation and commencement ceremonies, rituals that serve to mark transitions of young people into and out of the status of college student. Rites of passage, like other rituals, are structured activities. Writing early in the twentieth century, Arnold van Gennep identified three stages in rites of passage, when participants (1) are separated from general society, (2) receive special knowledge that assists their transition to a new life status, and (3) are reincorporated into society at large, now in their new status. The middle stage of rites of passage places participants in an ambiguous status, a liminal phase. There is sufficient variety in the structure of rituals so that not all of the stages must be equally well developed. Also, the liminal phase can involve other rites that are nested within it, duplicating all three stages of ritual structure.[13]

Because of its complexity, the liminal phase of ritual processes has been a particularly fascinating locus of anthropological work. In his pathbreaking studies of ritual among the Ndembu of northwestern Zambia, Victor Turner explored a number of the symbolic and social ways that ritual affected its participants and their society, focusing especially on the liminal period. In particular, he noted that during the liminal experience, ritual participants encounter a symbolically constructed space in which their ordinary relations to society and others undergoes radical transformation. Turner captures this radical restructuring of experience in the concept of *communitas*, which he says is a conception of "society as an unstructured . . . and relatively undifferentiated comitatus, community, or even a communion of equal individuals."[14] He lists twenty-six dimensions of contrast between the experience of the liminal phase and ordinary existence, including the following oppositions: homogeneity/heterogeneity, absence of rank/distinctions of rank, and simplicity/complexity.[15] Each of the contrasts Turner lists involves an inversion or reversal of mundane experience.

Ritual involves the particular constellation of social arrangements that bring about powerful cognitive and affective results, like the experience of communitas. But these effects are not merely ephemeral. Rituals involve universal elements, like the five characteristics noted in the definition above, and also elements that are specific to the content of a particular ritual.[16] When these are combined, they act as drivers that have observable physical effects on the participants' central nervous systems. These effects tune the central nervous systems of ritual participants to help them adopt common cognitive, emotional, and action orientations toward the world.[17] There is a long list of things that act as drivers during ritual, including "chanting, dancing, ingesting psychotropic drugs, fasting, and other forms of privation."[18] The autonomic tuning that facilitates and is facilitated by the ritual experience is also found in rituals that are more reflective in their local structure, such as ceremonial rituals like the Catholic Mass or Zen meditation.[19]

Ritual Symbolism in Peacekeeping

The ritual symbolism of peacekeeping is evident in the conventionalized actions through which peacekeeping missions are created, such as Security Council consultations and resolutions that authorize missions; tasks assigned to peacekeeping troops; uniforms, insignia, and accoutrements associated with peacekeeping in general and with particular missions; and social activities organized under the auspices of peacekeeping missions.[20]

Although many different kinds of people work in and around peacekeeping missions, one of the central symbolic aspects of peacekeeping is the establishing and maintaining of social order by military personnel using pacific means. The often expressed rationale for this is that by bringing together troops from many nations to work under one command, the deployment of a peacekeeping mission symbolizes international attention on a crisis area. This in turn is put into action when troops are selected for a mission. As Eyal Ben-Ari notes, "a civilian member of the UN heading logistics for UNTSO explained: 'the UN tries to have as many nationalities as possible so it clearly represents a global mixture of people, not a regional, not a national people.'"[21]

The deployment of a peacekeeping mission thus acts symbolically as a visible demonstration of international consensus and joint action. And this supports the root metaphor that structures the United Nations as an institution in service of a pacific world order that empowers the weak, feeds the hungry, conquers disease, and settles conflicts peacefully.

In fact, establishing a peacekeeping mission may mean many different things to different people, because each may have a different political understanding of the situation.[22] Some nations contribute troops for peacekeeping missions because of local political perceptions, and others have more instrumental ends in sight. For instance, Canada's participation in United Nations peacekeeping can be seen instrumentally as a way of pursuing its political objectives.[23] But in Canadian political culture, Canada's participation in peacekeeping derives from the national pride taken in the role that its Prime Minister Lester Pearson played in developing peacekeeping and in part from a sense of contribution to the international community.[24] Fiji, which has contributed troops to nearly all peacekeeping missions, is motivated in part by the economics involved in sending troops from the small island nation to participate in UN missions. For New Zealand, one incentive is that participation in peacekeeping operations allows its officers to gain joint and combined service experiences for which there is otherwise limited opportunity.[25] It is worth noting, however, that even the most seemingly pragmatic and instrumental motives are wrapped in cultural interpretations. So, while revenues from the United Nations paid for troop service or equipment rentals may be important, the rhetoric and reasoning deployed in relation to this activity is culturally determined.

These differences in national political perceptions can effect how troops are selected for missions. This leads to one source of cross-cultural conflict within missions when someone makes invidious comparisons that question the professionalism and competence of troops from other countries. Although there

were only a few instances when I saw these kinds of differences cause anything but small conflicts during my fieldwork, in my interviews UNMOs often
pointed to many ways, large and small, that other national contingents did not
display adequate levels of professionalism. The perceived failings ranged from
personal to operational aspects of their experience. For instance, one infor-
mant scoffed at a colleague's lack of professionalism and noted that when the
colleague arrived at UNTSO he did not know how to wear a uniform properly:
"When he first put on his battle dress uniform—the field uniform—in Jerusalem, he did not know how to blouse his pants. He did not know how to wear
a beret." Others pointed out that some colleagues didn't know how to perform
basic tasks: "One of the [other] officers set a kerosene heater on fire because he
did not know how to light one." "Some people have never been in a desert. They
don't know how much water to consume each day. They don't know how to dig
out sand." Also, some called into question the more general skills and training
their colleagues had prior to joining the mission: "Now the Scandinavians, the
Russians, the French, to a degree, have schooling prior to coming over here.
But I think it is more like how to get along in the organization rather than, 'this
is a sand dune, this is how you drive over it; this is a land mine.'" Differences
in perceptions of professionalism are common to most situations where troops
from different countries must work together. In a study reported in 2003, Efrat
Elron and her colleagues found that "a cause for some friction and uneasy feel-
ings by some of the study's participants was the gap in the levels of professionalism that existed between some of the armies."[26] To complicate this question,
some analysts draw a distinction between professionalism and competence.
They observe that one can be unprofessional but competent or professional but
not competent. The implication is that what matters is that a colleague be competent whether he or she is professional or not. In peace operations, this easy
distinction obscures the fact that acting professionally is part of being competent, since a great part of a mission's work involves human interaction.[27]

At the individual level, I found that UNMOs attached a wide variety of
meanings to their service with UNTSO. These included a personal commitment to a vision of global order based on universal principles of social justice;
an opportunity for financial gain; a chance to see the Holy Land; a strategy in
career advancement; an opportunity to improve skills as a foreign area officer; a chance to see how one would react under fire; and a chance to escape
an unfortunate posting.[28] This variety of individual meanings affects the individual motivations that peacekeepers bring to their task. I discuss how individual motivation, and its shaping, figures into a broad cultural understanding
of peacekeeping in the next chapter.

Peacekeeping operations also take place in the context of the daily lives of
multiple communities: diplomatic, military, NGO, and local. Each of these

embodies culturally constituted ways of behaving and understanding the objectives and practices of the operation. Sometimes the intersection of these cultural spheres is problematic (see chapter 7).

Medals and Ribbons

One of the most immediate problems facing the institution of peacekeeping is the need to integrate individuals with diverse backgrounds, understandings, and agendas into a quasicorporate entity, the mission, and help them adopt the identity of peacekeeper. In such situations, symbols can be extremely useful tools for coordinating perceptions. Since symbols represent and unify disparate meanings, they can be used to embody and bring together diverse ideas. Through symbolic representation, "these various ideas are not just simultaneously elicited but also interact with one another so that they become associated together in the individual's mind."[29]

UNMOs in UNTSO wear the blue beret and display the United Nations flag, as do members of other observer missions and peacekeeping forces. These symbols serve to integrate the local activity of the mission with higher levels of political organization. More locally, however, UNMOs share a number of symbols that serve to establish an individual's identification with the group. For instance, each wears on his or her uniform a badge unique to the mission, as illustrated in figure 5.1. These badges are designed specifically for the mission.[30] The badges, and the medals and ribbons that are subsequently awarded to commemorate service in the mission, are an important aspect of military life.

These badges help to integrate members from many different national services into the mission. All denote the international nature of the operation by including reference to the United Nations through its symbols or in

Figure 5.1: UNTSO Observer Group Egypt Medal
Photo by Robert A. Rubinstein.

words. Sometimes, the inte-
grative task is explicit, and
the badge includes symbols
of national identity as well.
Wearing these symbols of
the mission helps UNMOs
to be recognized as members
of the mission and integrates
them into it. For instance, in
1990, the People's Republic
of China began to contribute troops to UNTSO. Nine
officers joined the observer

Figure 5.2: UNTSO Observer Detachment
Damascus Badges
Photo by Robert A. Rubinstein.

groups. At one, Observer Detachment Damascus (ODD), the Chinese presence led to the redesign of the mission badge, as displayed in figure 5.2. Previously the ODD badge had shown the United Nations symbol as well as
elements of the French, Soviet, and American flags. To this was added the
Chinese flag.

Such symbols help to establish continuity in the mission despite changes in
the political environment or shifts in the purpose of the organization. Tanja
Hohe Chopra notes that in East Timor, UNMOs would exchange national
badges as well, which contributed to the breaking down of national barriers and
served to establish goodwill and common frameworks of understanding.[31]

The symbols and ceremonies used in peacekeeping are not original to
it. Rather, as peacekeeping has developed, well-known symbols from other
spheres of social life—especially from military organizations and some from
family and community life—have been appropriated and invested with new
meanings. This borrowing improves rather than diminishes the efficacy of
these symbols, because when encountering them people draw on their stock
of past experiences and associations with such symbols.[32]

At first I thought the idea that small tokens, like badges, medals, and ribbons, would make a difference to "military men" was improbable. As I interviewed UNMOs, however, I learned that UN medals were an extension of
military practices all around the world. Moreover, the ribbons and medals
worn by soldiers partially define who they are. They project and are received
as signs of identity. Indeed, one observer noted that medals and ribbons "are
the sacramentals of the military profession."[33]

Just as peacekeeping has appropriated symbols from other domains
of social life, so too it has appropriated rituals. Together with symbols
that signal group membership and organizational continuity, life in an
observer group is marked by activities that are ritually delineated. Indeed,

medals are bestowed upon their recipients in a solemn ritual called the "medal parade."

Medal Parades

The medal parade is a military ritual in which participants are separated from their peers, given praise and medals that acknowledge their experience, and then reintroduced to their group in a new status. Medals, especially those that denote participation in combat or uniquely dangerous or meritorious missions, can be highly sought after. In cases where a person is discovered to have falsely claimed the right to wear a medal, embarrassment can be extreme. Such falsification can end a career. In one extreme case, Admiral Jeremy M. Boorda committed suicide when he was discovered to be wearing combat ribbons to which he was not entitled.[34]

Military medals, ribbons, and award ceremonies laud service and achievements in the profession of arms.[35] Medal parades orient participants to a unit's collective combat prowess and the experience and readiness of its individual members. The United Nations also awards its medals at medal parades, which are a common feature of all peacekeeping missions. Thus, just as the symbols used by a particular peacekeeping mission connects its members to one another and to the larger peacekeeping community, so do its rituals. For instance, figure 5.3 shows medal parades from UN missions in Haiti, Burundi, and the United Nations headquarters.

During my fieldwork with UNTSO, I observed a number of medal parades. Some of these preceded a change of command ceremony, and some were just medal parades. All had the same internal structure: those who were to receive medals were separated from general society and formed into the parade, guests were seated, the UNTSO chief of staff inspected the parade, medals were presented, a speech was given, and the parade was dismissed. Immediately following the parade, the officers were reintroduced to general society at a reception. An important feature of these receptions, and of other social gatherings, is the sharing of food, sometimes prepared by the peacekeepers themselves.

The structure of the United Nations medal parades is much like those of other military medal parades. But in the same way that the military symbols adopted by peacekeeping are altered and invested with new meanings, so too are the rituals at peacekeeping missions. While the structure of these activities is the same despite differences in time and place, their content changes.[36] Thus, UN medal parade participants are praised for their contribution to the work of an institution that seeks to change the world for the better. Reflecting on the messages of a May 2000 UN medal parade in East Timor, an Australian peacekeeper reported that the substance of the messages of the ceremony were

Figure 5.3: United Nations Peacekeeping Medal Parades. From top: (1) United Nations Operation in Burundi. United Nations/Mario Rizzolio, 2006. Used with permission. (2) United Nations headquarters. United Nations/Mark Garten, 2006. Used with permission. (3) Port-au-Prince, Haiti. AP Photo Archive/Daniel Morel, 1996. Used with permission.

"also what a UN medal represents. It is about the gift of freedom, choice, safety and security. This is a gift to be given to those around the world that are suppressed, and oppressed. . . . [The force commander] let us know that we had been a part of the whole that had propped a new and fledgling nation."[37]

Observing and Patrolling

After the 1973 war, UNTSO deployed a group of observers to monitor the military situation in the Sinai. This Sinai Observer Group (SOG) worked with the second United Nations Emergency Force (UNEF II). Following the Camp David Accords, UNEF II had to withdraw. The Egyptian government asked that UNTSO maintain its presence in Egypt, and SOG was reorganized as OGE. The operational tasks assigned to OGE differed substantially from those of SOG, but the continuing presence of an observer group in the mission area projects an image of continuity of concern and purpose, locally and internationally.

Another symbolic means of establishing continuity for the mission as operational realities change is in the names used to describe revised duties. Although during my field research OGE members still went on patrol, and they did so from observation pots (OPs), as had members of SOG, but the OGE patrols had no significant military operational elements beyond their execution, and they originated from outposts rather than OPs.

Patrolling and staffing OPs are two activities that are shared with all other UNTSO observer groups, though in other groups, patrolling includes the operational responsibilities of inspecting troop concentrations, monitoring cease-fire agreements, and reporting on these. Observation often takes place from well-marked positions. Figure 5.4 shows observation posts in use in three missions from the late 1980s to 2006.

Patrols and OPs, like medals and medal parades, link the local activities of UNMOs and OGE with those of other groups, providing for a kind of internal continuity. Patrolling and observing are key activities of peacekeeping missions, including both observer groups and forces. In many ways, observation and the construction of OPs are quintessential aspects of peacekeeping. Reporting on the Canadian peacekeeping activities in the former Yugoslavia, one researcher noted: "It's almost routine by now. You take over a section of the line, you man the old observation posts, OPs, and you start building new ones. . . . You count the shots and report them. . . . If the OP is in a town you put chicken wire around it to stop grenades."[38]

It is through daily activities such as observation and patrolling that peacekeeping culture is shaped, and the repetition of this symbolism of peacekeeping increases its legitimacy and social capital.

Figure 5.4: United Nations Peacekeeping
Observation Posts. From top: (1) United Nations
Interim Force in Lebanon. United Nations/
Mark Garten, 2006. Used with permission.
(2) Finnish peacekeepers, Jabal Marun, Lebanon.
Photo by Marjatta Hinkkala, 1992. Used with
permission. (3) United Nations Truce Supervision
Organization, El Arish, Egypt. Photo by Robert A.
Rubinstein, 1991.

The Happy Hour Cycle

Military life is structured around a series of social rituals that organize members' activities and orient the ways they think and feel about their lives. Much of this military ritual activity is tied to very practical considerations such as maintaining clear lines of communication or knowing who is or is not a member of the unit. It is not an exaggeration to say that much of the activity of an observer group follows a ritual cycle that marks off various life events, like comings and goings and changes in status. It is a fact of life in an observer group that people are constantly arriving and departing. This is partially related to movement between the station headquarters and week-long OP duty. These kinds of arrivals and departures are marked off by regular events within the station including, before leaving, a general briefing and planning of logistics for the week, and, upon returning, debriefing and perhaps a free drink at the station bar. Interestingly, OP duties conform neatly to the steps of rites of passage: separation, transition, incorporation. Each of these rituals has powerful effects on those experiencing them, adjusting their cognitive and affective perceptions and integrating them into a corporate group.

In part, the constant movement also results from the varied six-month to three-year tours of duty for officers serving as UNMOs with UNTSO. Although the total length of UN service varies from country to country, in the Middle East UNMOs were usually required to spend half of their tour posted in an Arab country and half posted in Israel. Because of this, every week new UNMOs arrive and current members leave from each observer group. The way the military custom of hail and farewell has been appropriated in the ritual cycle of the observer groups is directed at incorporating UNMOs into the larger group at the station (not just into their country detachment).

The military custom acknowledging arriving and departing individuals in a public ritual has not, however, simply been transferred unchanged to the peacekeeping context. Rather, it has been reinterpreted and fitted into the ritual cycle of the group. At OGE, for instance, the hail and farewell was part of a weekly rite of intensification that served to reinforce identification with the group. Each Friday evening the observer group assembled for a happy hour, which was sponsored by one of the national contingents. These have a regular structure throughout the month, and each happy hour has a regular internal structure. The hail and farewell takes place in the context of this repetitive group activity. Not only are arriving and departing members identified, perceptions of the nature of OGE and UNTSO are structured and reinforced. For instance, in addition to providing information about arriving members, the happy hour is also an occasion where it is stressed that the UNMO is entering the OGE family or community. During farewells, there is nearly always explicit reference to the ways the departing UNMO contributed to dissolving the boundaries of nationality and service branch between him and others in the group. In addition to the very military activities and awards that are part of these rituals, at OGE humorous nonmilitary awards were also bestowed. These included the giving of international cooking awards and reminiscences about some of the cultural miscommunications and learning that the UNMO had experienced while at OGE. This latter emphasis was one way of instructing and reminding group members about some of the cross-cultural challenges they faced working in the peacekeeping mission.[39]

Metaphors of family and community are woven throughout these occasions and serve to focus perceptions of the group. Since local diplomatic and military personnel are frequent guests at these activities, their perceptions of OGE are also shaped by this shared experience.

The themes supported by the ritual cycle of the local group also link the activity at the station to the larger UNTSO organization. The magazine *UNTSO News*, for instance, which is distributed to UNMOs and a limited number of local diplomats and other military officers, repeatedly refers to the metaphoric peacekeeping family. The message redundantly delivered is that UNTSO is a stable organization with historical continuity that has bridged gaps in national understandings in order to provide neutral, nonpartisan observers of political situations in the Middle East and elsewhere.[40]

Traditional military rituals and symbols are appropriated and given new meanings in the context of peacekeeping. This allows the elaborating of a myth of stability, continuity, joint action, and neutrality for those who serve in the missions as well as for those outside it who interact with or hear about the mission. In addition to the structuring of perceptions that results from activities within peacekeeping missions, additional legitimacy arises from the cognitive restructuring entailed by peacekeeping missions collectively as rites of reversal. The use of unarmed military personnel for peacekeeping missions has certainly been logistically useful. But its effect has been much broader than simply meeting the labor needs of peacekeeping. Because authorizing and fielding peacekeeping missions, physically separating troops from national armed forces, and ceding command of them to the force commander (who is potentially from a different country) involve ritualized activity, the use of military personnel buttresses a system of cultural reversals. These reversals symbolically allay fears of domination and promote the restructuring of political perceptions in order to legitimate actions that would otherwise be unacceptable.[41] Through the use of symbols and rituals, the instrument of United Nations peacekeeping develops and maintains an authority and legitimacy it would otherwise lack. This makes it possible to incorporate a changing set of individuals, each of whom may hold a partisan view, into the position of peacekeeper.

Connecting Levels of Experience

I have spoken about peacekeeping symbolism and ritual to many groups, military and civilian. In nearly all of the military settings, their importance has been readily acknowledged, and it has been in some civilian settings as well. However, at some presentations I have been asked a few questions that were reminiscent of my own initial skepticism on this topic. These questions sounded something like: "Sure this is interesting, but does it *really* matter to peacekeepers, who surely have more important concerns in places where their safety is often at risk?" To these questions, I have responded by noting the corroborating responses of former peacekeepers in the audiences, whose testimony about these issues is personal and powerful.[42] An episode from my fieldwork at UNTSO adds to this testimony.

Well into my field research, one military observer shared with me a memorandum that had originated at one of the observer groups, made its way to the highest levels of UNTSO administration, and had presumably been forwarded to United Nations headquarters in New York. In that memorandum, the writer argued the importance of the United Nations sharing with individual peacekeepers the honor of the award of the Nobel Peace Prize by issuing an official medal to all who had served on peacekeeping missions prior to 1989. He noted that earlier efforts to make this happen had not brought a response from UN headquarters. The writer asserted that this lack of response was "offensive" to those who had been involved in peacekeeping. He went on to say that just as military peacekeepers should share this honor through the issuing of medals, appropriate acknowledgment should be made of civilian members of mission, though just what an appropriate equivalent to the military medals would be was outside of his knowledge.[43]

Peacekeeping engages people from all around the world and from all walks of life. The success of peacekeeping missions depends upon the technical skill of those involved in particular missions and upon the practical arrangements surrounding them. Such practical concerns include the adequacy of the resources made available to the mission, the quantity and quality of the personnel deployed to the mission, the material resource placed at the mission's disposal, and the terms on which the mission enters its area of operation. But in addition to these, another factor that can promote the effectiveness of a mission is how successful the mission is in getting people with diverse backgrounds and ways of looking at the world to identify with a common set of understandings about the mission, about who they are collectively, and about what they are doing. In other words, for peacekeeping to succeed it is important for mission members to be on the same page. Obvious though this may seem, it is not an easy thing to achieve.

In this chapter, I have reviewed some of the symbols and rituals that peacekeeping uses to coordinate the way that peacekeepers think about themselves and their mission. Peacekeeping ritual and symbolism help to shape the identities of those in the mission and to align the ways they think about their tasks. Like all human symbolism and ritual, they do this by coordinating how group members interpret, value, and act by drawing on our human cognitive and emotional endowments.

One result of peacekeeping symbolism and ritual is the construction of community, which eases coordination among them. But to understand how symbolism and ritual figure into a broad understanding of the role of culture in peacekeeping, it is necessary to look both below and above the level of the group. The former leads us to look at the individual in peacekeeping. Especially important at that level is the question of how the cultural inversions that support peacekeeping (and that peacekeeping in turn supports) are differentially realized in the actions of individual peacekeepers. In the next chapter, I look at the ways individual motivation is a factor in peace operations. To do this, I draw on the theory of psychological reversals to suggest how peacekeepers' motivational states matter.

Looking at the levels above the mission leads us to consider the interactions that mission members have beyond their own group. Thus, in chapter 7 I explore factors affecting the interaction of mission members with others in the area of operation. In that chapter, I examine, for instance, how culture affects the interactions of military peacekeepers with humanitarian nongovernmental and international governmental organizations. The kinds of issues I look at are sometimes approached as challenges to interoperability among these kinds of participants.

In addition to looking at the on-the-ground challenges of interoperability, a broad understanding of the way culture affects peacekeeping requires that we look at social organization of even greater scope. In addition to the factors mentioned above, peacekeeping success depends upon the strength of support for peacekeeping among national constituencies; the level of political support for the mission within the international community, as reflected at the United Nations and among various regional and intergovernmental organizations; and how the mission is received and understood by people who live where it takes place. All of these latter considerations involve using the symbolic capital accrued by peacekeeping in general.

Symbolic capital is created out of many small interactions that call upon various nonmaterial aspects of social life, such as perceptions of honor, wealth, expertise, prestige, and legitimacy, to affect the outcomes of those interactions. In general, these involve people relying on some aspect of their own or another's reputation in their decision to act in particular ways. Symbolic capital can be earned, and it can be spent. The amount of symbolic capital an individual or an institution has matters; it matters greatly to a collective enterprise like peacekeeping. This is the issue I take up in chapter 8.

Understanding the linkages among levels is particularly important for those planning a mission. The strategic scaffolding described earlier requires using knowledge of how each level of action relates to the others so as to plan for mission structures that are mutually supporting. Before moving to the broader levels of analysis presented in chapters 7 and 8, I turn to examining the individual in peacekeeping. In many ways, this is an excursion into the well-charted but, paradoxically, still unsettled area of social theory, which concerns the relative importance of social structure and agency in human life.

6

"You Will Have to Kill Me to Get By"
Individual Action and Peacekeeping

"You will have to kill me if you want to move past this point." This was what a peacekeeper said as he stood in front of an Israeli tank in order to stop it from moving into Lebanon in the early 1980s.[1] One of the key reversals in peacekeeping is that soldiers do things that they would not be able to do, or which would be unacceptable for them to do, in ordinary situations. This involves using tactics that would be unacceptable during conventional military activity and can include dramatic action, like placing one's body in the path of an oncoming tank. Similarly, during service in Bosnia Canadian peacekeepers reversed their ordinary practices. After clearing paths of mines, knowing that the newly safe paths would be used by one of the disputing parties to penetrate its adversary's territory, the Canadians set an ambush. When the intruders came near, they turned on bright lights pointed toward themselves.[2] Thus inverting the tactic of using surprise to overpower and subdue an enemy.

At other times, reversal is enacted through mundane tasks ranging from driving to cooking to standing watch. One UNMO described the experience of such an inversion. As an officer, he was used to having mundane tasks performed for him. In peacekeeping, he experienced a status inversion when those mundane tasks became his responsibility: "Down at my first OP . . . as I was scrubbing the toilet, I reflected on how far it was from being in charge of all training in [my national service] to scrubbing a toilet in South Lebanon. . . . You do all the small tasks that are done for you by enlisted men."

It would be wrong to surmise from these examples that inversions in observer missions involve only mundane tasks while inversions among peacekeeping forces involve military tactics. The lone peacekeeper blocking the Israeli tank was part of an observer mission; the Canadian ambush was part of a complex peacekeeping operation, and these involve mundane inversions as well. Reflecting on their mission in Bosnia, where they encountered a hospital, one Canadian peacekeeper noted: "There were people that were bedridden, starving to death, they couldn't get out of their beds. The Canadian government and the UN had to bring diapers in. It's not something that soldiers are trained to do, but it's just one of the jobs that we had to do because it's part of our mandate. The soldiers were actually changing the diapers of the bedridden patients."[3] This example also has elements of a gender reversal. Care for the ill is often viewed as so-called women's work and is performed by people in "feminized" professions such as nursing. The act of soldiers caring for patients thus also has a gendered aspect to it.[4]

The previous chapter showed how the symbols and rituals used by peacekeeping missions help to create a sense of shared identity and common purpose at the group level. They also link members of the mission to a larger institution that they do not directly experience. Peacekeeping is a large undertaking. At any time it may engage the efforts of hundreds of thousands of peacekeepers, logistical supporters, and coworkers in the field and at headquarters. Peacekeeping symbols and rituals may also facilitate cooperation and coordination by shaping individuals' dispositions so that their actions are consistent with, rather than antagonistic to, the goals of peacekeeping. One useful attribute of symbols and rituals is that they simultaneously engage a variety of meanings. This is one reason participants in a ritual can respond to their experience of it in a range of ways. The ability of symbols and ritual to evoke simultaneously a variety of meanings and emotions suggests that by themselves symbols and rituals are not sufficient for aligning the way peacekeepers think and feel and act.

Despite its broad scope, the essence of peacekeeping is in the many individual interactions taking place each day between peacekeepers and the people they are deployed to help, the interactions are the mechanism through which the control and prevention of violence must take place. These very human-scale encounters have immediate effects on the mission, and they have consequences that reverberate well beyond a particular mission. In this chapter, I turn to individual behavior in peacekeeping. The main work of this chapter is exploring one way of linking individual behavior to the culturally patterned behavior of peacekeeping as a whole.[5] This involves looking at models of how cultural processes link to individual action. To illuminate this area, I use psychological reversal theory. This leads to a consideration of how training might better prepare peacekeepers. Near the end of the chapter, I turn toward looking at the effects of individual action on peacekeeping at a broader level. This involves some comment on the link between agency and structure in social theory.[6]

Organizational Narratives and Motivation

Motivation is linked to culture through narrative. "Narrative shapes our motives by shaping our goals and the way we attain these goals, as well as our perceptions, and our ways of remembering and thinking and feeling."[7] Narratives construct frames we use to interpret our experience. These frames contribute to the development of more-or-less automatic ways of responding to the challenges we meet in our environment. When these are part of professional experience, they form a kind of trained intuition, but all people form response expectancies based on their experiences.[8] How well we are served by these expectations feeds back into the narrative in an iterative process. But because these are privileged response patterns, the feedback is not taken at face value and used to modify those schemas. Rather, the processes that lead to modification are more complex, involving a number of cognitive biases that lead us to see the merit in some experiences but not in others.[9] These biases make the modification of our cognitive schemata (response expectancies or intuitions) more problematic when data fed back from our experiences are given either greater weight than they deserve or dismissed inappropriately. Since each of us has several ways of responding to a particular situation, the one we use is shaped in part by our motivational state at the time. Narratives, like symbols and rituals (which are themselves a kind of narrative), can dispose people to respond in certain ways to things and events they encounter in their environment.

A Tale of Two Units

In July 2001, I went with Jim McCallum, my colleague from the United States Army Peacekeeping Institute, to Fort Drum in Watertown, New York, to help train two Army units that were to be deployed that November as peacekeepers in Kosovo. This was the start of their preparations for that mission. We worked with them on the negotiation skills they would use as they carried out the many tasks essential for maintaining order and civil society in their area of operation. Our plan for the two days was to spend the mornings doing didactic work and the afternoons conducting a number of practical exercises designed on the basis of debriefings with units that had already returned from duty in Kosovo. The practical exercises were to give the members of the unit a sense of the problems that they might encounter to solve through negotiation. Our schedule was to work with the units separately, one the first day and the other the next.

One of the practical exercises involved simulating a unit staffing a checkpoint on a road that joined the Serbian and Albanian parts of Kosovo. The simulation was structured as follows: It is Albania's national day. A car festooned with Albanian flags approaches the check point, seeking to drive into the Serbian sector. The driver, a leader in the Albanian Kosovar community, has been celebrating this event and wants to continue that celebration on the

Serb side. Since the status of Kosovo is vigorously contested, allowing the car to proceed, especially with the Albanian flags displayed, could cause an incident. The exercise was to prevent this incident.

During the practical training on the first afternoon, the person role-playing the driver was doing a particularly convincing job. He was not making it easy for the young soldier whose job it was to keep him from crossing the checkpoint. After a short but clearly frustrating set of interactions, the soldier exclaimed "I'm not going to talk to this guy, I'll just tell him what to do. I've got all the weapons!"

The following day, all of the members of the second unit who participated in the practical exercise went to great lengths to resolve the situation through negotiation. No one got shot.

To me, the differences in the atmosphere of the two units was palpable. Obviously, the reaction of the soldier that first afternoon was inconsistent with the message of the training we were providing. In seeking to account for these differences, I first looked at the symbols reflecting the organizational culture of each unit. The hallways of the headquarters of the first unit were filled with memorabilia of various battles in which the unit had engaged and in which they had particularly distinguished themselves. The walls and display cases were filled with commendations, photographs, historical accounts—all testimony of the unit's effectiveness in war fighting.

The second unit's headquarters was no more than a kilometer down the road from the first unit's. It too had a long and distinguished combat record, having fought in all of the same places as had the first unit. Despite this, the attitudinal distance between the two units was immense. The memorabilia that filled the second unit's walls and display cases also consisted of commendations, photographs, and historical accounts. But the theme of this unit's display was sacrifice in peace support operations. It celebrated service in support of peacekeeping missions in Somalia, Bosnia, Haiti, and elsewhere. Rather than celebrating its distinction in war fighting, the second unit chose to honor and display its achievements in humanitarian efforts. The contexts created by the two sets of displays, however, tell only part of the story. During the practical exercises, most people from both units strove to resolve the simulated conflict through negotiation. So the organizational cultures of the units play only a partial role in understanding the actions of the young soldier and of others who had less dramatically abandoned negotiation for force.

Broad National Narratives

During the course of my research, I found that UNMOs came to UNTSO for a wide variety of reasons and that this affected how they perceived and performed their duties.

When analyzing the interviews and my fieldnotes, I recognized that some of these were patterned differences that mapped onto how peacekeeping operations were viewed by the UNMOs' national militaries. These differences appeared to derive from broad national narratives concerning peacekeeping, which were linked to the way the mission assignments were conceptualized and carried out by the UNMOs.[10]

With only one exception, UNMOs from the United States, for example, reported that peacekeeping was seen very differently by their national services than it was by other militaries with which they had become familiar. The American UNMOs talked about peacekeeping as a despised activity that would gain them no credit with their services. They told me that being assigned to peacekeeping was the mark of a career gone awry. Hence, those who were at OGE were either close to retiring or they had run into trouble in their career and were using the assignment to UNTSO as a way to repair that damage. For example, one American UNMO described how he was using his assignment with UNTSO to advance an otherwise stalled career: "Coming to the end of my tour at Fort [. . .] it was time for me to be transferred. . . . I could not get a decent troop assignment. So what I did was, Major [. . .] knew about this assignment and gave me the phone number about it and said, 'You go to the Middle East for a year and then you go back to a troop post that you desire.' So I called based on that."

In contrast, UNMOs from countries other than the United States consistently told me that peacekeeping was a highly prized and valued assignment. They reported that their careers would be helped by their time with UNTSO. The following comment from an interview with an Australian UNMO was typical: "It's a very sought-after position. People want to come here and serve. Most people are aware of it. . . . It is a hands-on type job. . . . I was very keen to come here."

Both groups acknowledged that one result of this difference in narrative was the quality of professionals sent to the mission. In a characteristic comment, an Irish UNMO related: "The officers we send out here are not dodos. We don't send out dummies. They're usually—I won't say they're the best—average or above average. So, looking at that fact against the fact that we're aware that the Americans don't send their best. . . ."

Mission Assignment

Broad national narratives affected how the UNMOs framed their conception of the mission. For many of the Americans, the mission of UNTSO, and OGE in particular, was just a waste of time. They felt that their talents were not being put to good use and that there was no operational challenge for the mission. In contrast, non-Americans saw the mission as fulfilling an important political, and hence international security, role.

The contrasts among the three comments below illustrate this difference. The first two are from American UNMOs, and the third is from an Australian UNMO.

> The mission in Egypt is ridiculous. It's a show-the-flag-and-we're-present-only-because-Egypt-wants-us-here. It's a terrible waste of money and time. I'm getting paid lots of money to do nothing.

> Like I said earlier, I think they could do the same mission with probably ten people instead of fifty-some people. Use their manpower better. There are places in the world where people need it; right now this is not one of them.

> This is a real mission, but it is political in nature. And that's why sometimes UNMOs think it's symbolic. But I can't agree with that. . . . From a political stance, there is a third side in addition to the parties, which is watching the conflict, and this side has its own point of view, its own opinion, and this has been made known to the public, so it's not just a symbolic mission. . . . The professional challenge is that when you are manning the [observation post] and doing patrols in the desert, then you need your pure military experience.

Concept and Conduct of Duties

Broad national narratives and framings of the mission directly influence how UNMOs see what they are doing. Those whose narratives dispose them to see the UNTSO mission as unimportant carry this orientation into their work. Those who see the mission otherwise engage their duties with a distinctly different sense of purpose. This is reflected in the comments below. The first is from an American UNMO, and the second is from a Swedish UNMO.

> [Assignment to UNTSO] gets you out of the net for a while and lets you rest and recuperate and see strange and wonderful things, but it doesn't really do anything. I mean, the challenges of navigating the Sinai desert are met within the first day and then it's old hat, it doesn't do anything for you.

> It's very good for the future for yourself. After serving with officers from different countries, twenty-four hours a day for one week with each officer, you know him very well, and after one week you

are more and more open to each other. You can speak about many, many different things, and I think I know at least ten, twelve countries' systems . . . and how their officers are thinking and so on. I think I can use my knowledge in the future in my country when I am thinking about how the military works in different countries.

There are two inversions implied in the preceding quotes from UNMOs. The first is that since all of the tasks are done by officers, they take up chores that would ordinarily be done by enlisted personnel. The second is that the act of "showing the flag" is given a meaning completely reversed from what it ordinarily means. Showing the flag is a traditional military activity that is used to communicate a nation's military strength and its ability to project power. In the context of peace operations, the meaning assigned to showing the flag is reversed, indicating the presence of the United Nations and signaling not the projection of power but the provision of a space for conflict management.[11]

From Group Motivation to Individual Motivation

There are a few studies that examine the psychology of peacekeeping as it relates to larger forces shaping the orientations that peacekeepers bring to their assignments. These examine motives for participation, perceptions of the benefits of serving, stresses experienced by peacekeepers and their reactions to them, general effects of training on peacekeepers' attitudes and how organizational narratives affect how peacekeepers think and feel about participating in peace operations, as does my discussion above.[12]

For the most part, these studies have a limited focus on peacekeepers' performance in the field, perceptions of their tasks, and job satisfaction. The findings of these studies are consistent with the variation in general motivation I have described above for UNMOs at UNTSO. Some peacekeepers frame their mission as a valued and valiant one. Others deride participation in peace operations as something that does not challenge them and does not draw upon their professional military skills.

Liora Sion describes, based on her study with Dutch soldiers who had served in Kosovo and Bosnia, how Dutch soldiers prepared for their peacekeeping deployments by undertaking exercises that emphasized infantry combat skills.[13] She shows that this relates to high levels of dissatisfaction with participation in peacekeeping, because the work of the mission did not draw on those skills. The way soldiers responded to peacekeeping was also linked to their self-image. At the time of her study, the army in the Netherlands was viewed as ineffectual and "feminine." Training in combat before the peacekeeping mission helped soldiers construct a more robust self-image, which was then challenged by their peacekeeping experiences.

In an earlier study, Maren Tomforde identified how self-image plays a role in German soldiers' participation in peacekeeping. She discerns five distinct categories among German soldiers who served in Kosovo: (1) leader and educator, (2) martial adventurer, (3) careerist, (4) male warrior, and (5) helper in uniform.[14] Tomforde found that these categories related to the reasons that soldiers gave in favor of, or against, participating in other missions.

The peace operations studied by Sion and Tomforde are multidimensional, nontraditional missions that emerged in the 1990s. Yet, consistent with one of the themes of this book, the concerns they discovered among those peacekeepers directly reflect those found among peacekeepers in traditional missions. Just as issues of training and self-image were important among UNMOs serving at UNTSO, they affect the ways that soldiers everywhere approach peacekeeping.

The Problem of Individual Action

The many daily interactions that take place among peacekeepers and cooperating agencies and organizations, and between peacekeepers and local populations, have an effect on how the mission is perceived by those who participate in it and by outsiders. For that reason, it is important that peacekeepers' interactions with others be consistent with the image of the mission desired by the international community. Despite the general cultural orientations encoded in narratives, symbols, and rituals, a person may respond to the same situation differently at different times. Indeed, sometimes these responses can be diametrically opposed to one another. This is one reason that knowledge of culture does not allow the prediction of individual action. But recognizing this reality is not the same as saying that individual behaviors are random and arbitrary. Nor is acknowledging the potential for the same person to react differently to the same situation a reason to ignore the individual level of analysis. Indeed, there is increasing acknowledgment that the actions of ordinary soldiers have strategic importance.[15] Some peacekeeping missions have run into trouble as a result of individual actions. Among these are the torture and murder of a Somali teenager by members of a Canadian Airborne regiment (see chapter 1) and the recent widespread sexual abuse and exploitation of local women by peacekeepers in various missions.[16] In a real sense, these are all actions taken outside of the peacekeeping motivational framework. In situations where commanders have turned a blind eye to or actively accepted peacekeepers under their command having sexual liaisons with locals, the norm is most certainly

threatened. Other examples of disregard for peacekeeping norms and of negative interactions have also been documented in missions around the world,
like those in Kosovo, Cambodia, and East Timor.[17]

Yet with the notable exception of one study (of how Swedish peacekeepers
in Bosnia reacted to and performed in life-threatening situations), the peacekeeping literature has not examined the underlying mechanisms that illuminate how peacekeepers act in the event.[18] It is therefore important to sketch a
way of approaching the vital task of understanding the dynamics of individual
motivation and to do so in a way that reasonably connects this with the higher
levels of analysis that are the main concern of a broad cultural understanding
of peacekeeping.

Motivation: Psychological Reversal Theory

Psychological reversal theory is a useful way of approaching the question of
motivation in peacekeeping. In addition to being a very well-developed area
of research in its own right, it is a theoretical approach that links logically with
the ones I am using to look at social dynamics at the group level. Reversal
theory gives a specific account of the interaction between individuals and their
environments. It is a theory about dispositions, so just as culture theory directs
attention to dispositions for action at the group level, reversal theory directs
attention to dispositions for action (not determinants).[19] Also, reversal theory
recognizes that individual behavior may be characterized at different times by
different motivational states, in the same way that group action may be framed
by different cultural themes.[20] Finally, using reversal theory also directs attention to the conditions that support maintaining relatively persistent motivational dispositions, in the same way that looking at culture in peacekeeping
directs attention toward the mechanisms for maintaining cultural inversions
at the group level. These features of reversal theory make for a kind of theoretical scaffold between the individual and group levels of analysis, thus following
of the rule of minimal inclusion. Such a multilevel approach is particularly
important to motivation.[21]

Reversal theory suggests that an individual's motivational dispositions fall
into eight metamotivational states. These describe motivation as arising from
an individual who is: (1) goal oriented (telic) or (2) activity oriented (paratelic); (3) rule following (conformist) or (4) rule breaking (nonconformist);
(5) competitive with and objectifies others (mastery) or (6) caring toward and
experiences others as people (sympathy); (7) concerned with self (autocen-
tric); or (8) concerned with the well-being of others (allocentric). The combination of these states describes how a person relates at any particular time to
four domains of experience: (1) relationships, (2) transactions, (3) rules, and

(4) mean-ends.[22] Fundamental to reversal theory is the view that the meta-motivational state pairs are dichotomies; they are not continua. In addition, reversal theory treats motivational states as highly fluid, not stable personality traits. A person can move from one state to its opposite relatively rapidly, or she may maintain a motivational state for a longer period of time. Shifts in motivational state may be triggered by things and events in a person's environment. Equally, they maybe be triggered by a person's physiological processes.

For peace operations to be successful, there needs to be a fundamental alignment between motivational states and the root metaphor of cultural inversion represented by the operation. Table 6.1 presents a theoretical view of such an alignment.

Table 6.1 Motivation and Peacekeeping

Motivational States	
Traditional Military (TCMAu)	**Peacekeeping (PSCAL)**
Goal oriented, anxiety avoiding (Telic)	Activity oriented (Paratelic)
Rule following, cooperative, and compliant (Conformist)	Rule following, cooperative, and compliant (Conformist)
Competitive, seeks control, objectifies others (Mastery)	Caring toward, experiences people as people (Sympathy)
Concerned with self (Autocentric)	Concerned about others (Allocentric)

Adapted from Rubinstein 2006, 149.

The PSCAL (Paratelic, Conformist, Sympathy, Allocentric) constellation of motivational states works synergistically and leads peacekeepers to particular responses that are consistent with the broad cultural inversions that define the institution.[23]

How an individual reacts during the conduct of their duty—be it maintaining a checkpoint, patrolling a sector, interrogating a suspect, or interacting with the local population—depends in large measure upon their motivational state at the time of the encounter. I suggest that when peacekeepers act from a motivational state other than that described in the table, they are much more likely to act in ways that fall outside of the cultural inversion from which peacekeeping gains its legitimacy and social capital.

Since a shift in motivational state can be triggered by environmental factors, peace operations need ways to help their members move into appropriate motivational states. For example, stress can induce physiological and psychological arousal. How an individual handles that arousal depends on his set of motivational states (for instance, avoiding further arousal or seeking it) and on whether the arousal causes him to move from one set of motivational dispositions to another. In this context, the symbols, rituals, and discourse employed at the group level interact with an individual's experience to help maintain the alignment of motivational states. But, as Mary Foster pointed out, "not every individual will be moved either in the same way or to the same extent by a ritual, myth, or other cultural production."[24]

In peacekeeping, people are placed in paradoxical situations. One of the complaints raised by those who object to using soldiers as peacekeepers is that expectations for people trained as warriors and fighters are incompatible with expectations for those trained as police.[25] As I noted above, the standard operating procedures used in observer missions and peacekeeping forces may call on peacekeepers to do the opposite of what their military training might dictate. Among the environmental factors that can initiate a shift in motivational state is a situation in which a person feels themselves to be vulnerable.[26] Many situations encountered by peacekeepers put them in positions of vulnerability, where they may feel threatened. The perception of threat can trigger a change away from the constellation of motivational states appropriate to peacekeeping.[27]

Reversals may take place instantaneously and outside of awareness. For the peacekeeper, that shift can mean the difference between acting in ways consistent with the goals and imperatives of peacekeeping and acting in ways that undercut the endeavor. This suggests that it is important that peacekeepers learn to manage their motivational reversals. Since peacekeepers come from a wide variety of cultural backgrounds, training will need to provide both techniques for inducing reversals and culturally appropriate material for achieving the new motivational state.[28] Imagery is a particularly powerful tool for making psychological biases and states emerge into conscious experience.[29] Michael Apter, the originator of psychological reversal theory, and others have developed a number of techniques for helping people become aware of and manage motivational states. Several of these techniques involve the use of guided imagery exercises in which an individual is lead through a series of imaginary rooms and taught to link the experience of those rooms to their motivational states.[30] Such techniques help people become aware of their motivational frameworks and improve their ability to self-monitor those states. Adapting these techniques to peacekeepers' training can be an important step in stabilizing the linkages between the various levels of systemic organization that affect peacekeeping as an institution.

In the context of peacekeeping, troops have long been described as "soldier-diplomats." In their roles as diplomats, peacekeepers must negotiate constantly with other people within the mission and with local peoples. That is one reason that negotiation training, such as that I described in the early part of this chapter, is important for preparing for participation in peacekeeping.

How a peacekeeper understands and frames the matters to be negotiated is linked to his or her motivational state and draws on his or her understanding of the contextual and structural aspects of negotiation. Deborah Goodwin presents the most sophisticated analysis of negotiation in the context of peace operations.[31] She identifies some critical ways in which our standard academic models of negotiation must be amended for use in peacekeeping.[32] In doing so, she develops a set of suggestions about the kinds of training required for peacekeepers that also link to individual factors such as learning style, reactions to stress, and communicative competence.

Agency and Social Action

In his commentaries on the Roman civil war, Julius Caesar observed that "in war great events are the result of trivial causes."[33] Despite advances in military technology, this observation still rings true today. This is demonstrated by the recent acknowledgment of the role of the "strategic corporal," especially in operations other than war, which is the military category into which peacekeeping fits."[34] Because the essence of peacekeeping is human engagement, the effect of individual action on the larger institutional and structural context is substantial.

Modeling of the link between collective behavior and individual action is one of the most troublesome areas of social theory. As I discussed in chapter 3, conceptualizations of culture as a directive and homogenizing force were abandoned by anthropologists soon after the mid-twentieth century, largely because they did not account for the intracultural variation that ethnographers found during their fieldwork. The fact that knowing a person's culture does not allow one to predict precisely that person's actions thus becomes an important problem in anthropology, as it is in other social sciences. Attempts to link individual actions to collective behavior have led to some very interesting and productive theoretical developments, like those in cognitive linguistics, symbolic anthropology, and practice theory, which I use in this book. Although these theoretical efforts are very fruitful, they do not fully meet the challenge of linking individual action to collective behavior.

The partial disconnect between the individual and his or her group is one reason that cultural accounts of phenomena, like peacekeeping, meet with some skepticism. Cultural accounts are often characterized, incorrectly in my view, as soft, unscientific, or anecdotal.[35] Yet the underlying logic of cultural accounts is no different than the logic supporting accounts that derive from theories that use quantitative, statistical techniques to demonstrate their efficacy.[36] Concepts such as "consumer confidence" rely on statistically normative behaviors and also do not allow the prediction of individual actions. Even though such measures do not allow the prediction of individual economic actions with any greater facility than do cultural accounts, they form the basis for important public policy decisions.

As instruments of international diplomacy, peace operations take place on a grand stage. But the success of any mission depends upon the actions of individuals and small groups. Often these actions are judgments made on the fly and over seemingly mundane matters. How these matters are handled may go unnoticed, or it may cause an international incident.

How an individual responds to such a challenge depends upon many things. Among these is, of course, his or her training. A second thing that conditions his or her response is the social environment in which he or she acts. And a third element that shapes a peacekeeper's response is the personal motivation that he or she brings to the situation.

All individuals respond to their environments based on the cultural dispositions that define for them the range of permissible and appropriate actions. Which of the repertoire of permissible actions they enact depends in part on the motivation that energizes that action. One of the goals of training peacekeepers prior to their deployment is to locate them in a web of symbolic meanings and behavioral models so that the members of a mission will share basic intuitions about their work. This can align the general motivational orientations of the members of a mission in a more-or-less coherent way. The organizationally patterned language, symbolism, and ritual behavior all work together to support the cultural inversions involved in peacekeeping and create the potential for alignment between the individual and group levels.

The cultural technologies of symbolism and ritual operate on a general level and allow for the simultaneous embrace of a variety of culturally valid models and meanings. To enhance this capability, we need to develop training that allows peacekeepers to be aware of and to manage their motivational states so that these mesh with the basic symbolic inversions critical to peacekeeping. First, this would be training that develops appropriate narratives, so that consistent frames are derived from them. Those frames will shape response expectations, which together with factors in the environment will move individuals into appropriate motivational states and shape the actions they take. Second, training must equip peacekeepers with the skills necessary for them to identify the factors in the peacekeeping environment that may trigger motivational shifts in them. Once they can do this, training should, third, equip peacekeepers with the introspection skills needed to self-monitor their motivational states. Finally, training needs to teach peacekeepers to manage their own motivational states. The goal of this training is to foster the flexibility to move appropriately between states. Taking these steps from theory to practice will lead to more effective and sustainable peace operations.

Peacekeeping is a large-scale phenomenon. At any given time there are hundreds of thousands of military personnel, NGO staff, and international civil servants deployed in the field. Despite the broad scope of peacekeeping, individual actions play an important part in the success or failure of each mission. Because there are reciprocal and contingent relationships among the levels of organization expressed in peacekeeping, the overarching structure of peacekeeping helps to shape and direct individual actions. At the same time, individual actions are important to maintaining the overarching structure of peacekeeping, as discussed below.

Peacekeeping is a serious endeavor. It routinely addresses matters of life and death. These matters are not addressed simply by the abstract corporate entities that comprise the mission. Rather, these matters of life and death are faced everyday by individual peacekeepers—whether military, humanitarian, or civil servant—in real contexts. How these individuals respond to the challenges they meet determines not only the outcome of the specific encounter, but also contributes to maintaining the social capital of the particular mission and of peacekeeping generally. In this sense, peacekeeping is an emergent process in that what individuals do is shaped by the social structural constraints within which they work while at the same time their actions alter those social structural constraints in a pattern of repetitive, reciprocal structural coupling.[37]

The Need for Multilevel Analysis

It is not enough simply to investigate how members of a mission come to adopt a common identity, nor is it sufficient to understand how the political workings of the United Nations (or other institutional sponsors of peacekeeping) make legitimate decisions about peacekeeping. Likewise, an understanding of the financial and logistic challenges of peacekeeping alone will not give an adequate account of peacekeeping. Nor is it adequate to focus in isolation on the political incentives and disincentives for nations to contribute to particular missions. Rather, the mutually constitutive quality of individual action and social structure means that an adequate account of peacekeeping requires attention to multiple levels of systemic organization. Further, it is not sufficient that accounts at different levels of analysis merely be juxtaposed one to the other. Rather, they should be mutually implicative of one another. That is, they should form a theoretical scaffold that allows the interpreting analyst to move coherently among levels.[38]

The core of peacekeeping as an instrument of international action is the cultural inversion that allows otherwise unacceptable activities to be valorized. In addition to this general consideration, a multilevel approach is necessary especially when considering motivation. A person's motivation is affected by multiple factors, internal and external to the individual. Motivation may be affected by the cultural, social, and structural contexts of individual acts, or it may be affected by internal factors like hunger or fatigue. This chapter explored how inversion at the group level is transferred and supported at the level of the individual. To do this, I used reversal theory, a model of psychological motivation that is epistemologically and logically consistent with the dynamics of cultural inversions as they have been modeled by other theorists. The linking of the social and individual levels through these theoretical models is a step toward elucidating the mechanisms through which the dynamic tensions between structure and agency are managed. It helps as well to clarify how peacekeeping can be made a more effective instrument of collective action. In the next chapter, I return to the group level and examine the challenges of coordination and cooperation among peacekeepers and between them and the various other actors with whom they work in the mission area.

Organizational Cultures
and Peacekeeping

I was well into my second year of fieldwork at UNTSO, OGE when I began to hear grumbling from my informants about the present and previous leaders of both the observer group and of UNTSO. From a methodological perspective, it was not surprising that it had taken a long time for the military observers to warm up to me and to begin speaking candidly with me. It took considerable time to build rapport with members of a group, some of whose reactions upon meeting me, and learning that I would be doing an anthropological study among them, were suspicion and hostility thinly veiled by humor.

At the time that my informants began offering their complaints and critical assessments of their leaders, I was caught somewhat off guard. Not having a military background, and sharing in the general anthropological bias that allows our field to totalize and essentialize militaries in a way that would be unacceptable for other groups we study, I had the naïve belief that militaries participated in a common culture and that their similar structures implied common methods of acting.[1] As well, literature on military and diplomatic communities often downplayed the importance of culture for those participating in technical endeavors like diplomacy, military services, or multilateral institutions.

So I was surprised when one of my informants, a French captain, reflected on the differences he was experiencing in the way leadership was enacted in OGE compared to what he had experienced in his own army. He found the relationships between junior and senior officers in UNTSO to be much more relaxed and informal than in the French army. He worried that although he found this informality personally pleasant, making for a good social environment, it would make responding to a dangerous situation somewhat problematic. He suggested that "in case of emergency—and I mean if we are in danger to be shot at, to be bombed—those links among us would need to be tighter."

Another French officer observed that he too felt that the level of informality at UNTSO was greater than would be tolerated in the French army. He continued that although this offered no problem for him,

> If it had been reversed . . . probably, if the chief here would be
> French, I think some people, British, Anglo-Saxon people, Ameri-
> can people, would find some problem—relationship problems—
> with a French officer. For example, one thing is that it is very
> amazing for a French officer to be called by his first name. We are
> not used to that in the French army. No. . . . And it's quite interest-
> ing seeing the chief very close to us. We can talk to him. I don't
> want to say that in the French army we can't talk, but the relation-
> ship is very much: there's the chief, there's the other [hand gestures
> showing one above the other].

In fact, it was not long before his supposition was confirmed. An American military observer independently raised the topic of leadership during one
of our talks and described with considerable disappointment his experience
working in a unit that had been commanded by a French colonel. About that
colonel the military observer said,

> The French colonel had a different manner. He very consciously
> separated the French from the rest of us. . . . The French colonel
> was very much standoffish. And it was very hard to get them into
> any social activities at all, other than Friday night social affairs. The
> colonel had certain military expectations which maybe make sense
> for the French Army, and in particular the Foreign Legion, which
> was his background, but given the way the US army fills these slots
> these were unreasonable expectations. . . . He wanted me to know
> Arabic. He was very disappointed that I spoke no Arabic. He was
> disappointed that I didn't have a second language. . . . Even when
> he spoke to me the first time, he would lapse into French while he
> spoke to me. So, you knew automatically that I was a second-class
> citizen with him because I was neither a French speaker nor an
> Arabic expert.

As I heard more about these issues, I was tempted to think that they were
just an expression of the tensions that emerge periodically between the Fran-
cophone and Anglophone worlds. Just as I was beginning to think this was the
case, a Soviet military observer and I chatted over beers, and he expressed deep
exasperation about his experience with the chief of the observer group. He was
confused and upset and angry, he told me, because the chief had just chewed
him out about his use of a United Nations vehicle for personal purposes. He
acknowledged that this was an infraction of the rules but didn't understand
why the chief had taken him to task, because earlier in the week they had sat

together in the very bar where we were now speaking, addressed each other by first name, and discussed personal and family matters. It was very odd, he told me, that a friend should treat him like that.

Peace operations bring together diverse actors: military officers and enlisted personnel from different services, agents of NGOs of varying scope and size, international civil servants, and individual "citizen diplomats," all of whom have different national, institutional, and personal backgrounds. In any encounter that includes such diversity, tensions and conflicts can be expected to arise.[2] When the sources of these conflicts result from mismatches about, for example, expectations of what action is appropriate, the speed and directness with which responses should be made, or the motivations that guide action, it is likely that some component of these conflicts is the result of cultural differences.

In the same way, peace operations bring the actors in the heterogeneous mission into contact with local populations. These local populations often draw upon cultural backgrounds different from those of the operation and its members. The potential for culturally based misunderstanding and conflict are increased. Participants in peace operations must therefore be equally aware of the local cultures of the people with whom they deal.

In this chapter, I return the focus to the dynamics at the group level. I discuss especially how organizational cultures affect the interaction among actors in a mission. Drawing on my discussion of culture in chapter 3, I consider some ways that culture affects peacekeeping on the ground and look at how these considerations have been approached. An additional level of complication results from the fact that the perception and legitimacy of peace operations at the macrolevel are affected by how those operations are viewed by both local populations and the international community. These views are influenced by the local-level interactions between peacekeepers and local populations as well as interactions among the military and civilian components of peace operations (see chapter 8).

The challenge facing peace operations resulting from the cultural diversity that they embrace is so great that it has been the focus of considerable discussion. Military components of peace operations increasingly find that they must cooperate with NGOs, IGOs, and agencies of national governments that are also working in the mission area. Indeed, General Sir Michael Jackson, the chief of the General Staff of the British Army, asserts that success in peace operations depends upon the integration of military and civilian efforts: "Success in any stability operation depends on weaving the various civilian and military lines of effort together like strands of a rope."[3] The interactions among these different organizations has at times been quite problematic. As a result, some effort has been spent on preparing military peacekeepers for their encounters with the cultures of these other organizations.

One approach has been to list presumed cultural differences between military and nonmilitary organizations as dichotomies. For example, table 7.1 sets out some generalizations about organizational cultural differences between these groups as described by US Ambassador Richard Holbrooke. The distinctions in the table are intended to show the contrasts between how militaries do business and how NGOs and IGOs do business. They were offered in the context of training for military personnel about to embark on peacekeeping missions. In a similar but more extended effort, the United States Institute of Peace compiled two editions of a book of brief general descriptions of NGOs, IGOs, the military, and government agencies involved in peace operations. These books also include brief descriptions of the characteristics of individual agencies and organizations. And they contain brief descriptions of what they term the "culture" of these organizations. Both guides provide suggestions for additional resources, divided by subject area—for example, economics, governance, and peacemaking—but neither provides suggestions about where to find further information on organizational cultures.[4]

Table 7.1: Generalizations about Military and Civilian Organizational Cultural Differences

Military	IGOs/NGOs
• Closely controlled	• Independent or semi-independent
• Hierarchical	• Decentralized
• Well resourced	• Minimally staffed, under resourced
• Extensive doctrine/standard operating procedures	• Few standard practices
• Short term	• Long term
• Culturally insensitive	• Culturally aware
• Precise, predictable	• Creative, unpredictable
• Highly accountable	• Little accountability
• Expeditionary, quick	• May already be in the area of operation
• One constituency	• Multiple constituencies
• Comfortable with status quo	• Idealistic change agents
• Appreciate precise tasks	• Thrive on ambiguity
• "Carries the flag"—well-defined official status and national identity.	• IGOs usually have official status; NGOs usually have no official status.

Compiled from *Civil Military Relations: Working with NGOs* (video)
(Washington, DC: InterAction, 2002.

On first consideration, efforts such as these seem quite useful. They appear to move the discussion of culture away from the surface cultural elements that are the focus of the cross-cultural engagement found in travelers' advice (see chapter 1) to look at deeper aspects of culture. Unfortunately, these descriptions have the characteristics of stereotypes, and so treat culture as unchanging, shared by all members of a group, and determining behavior. This can have the untoward effect of giving people who use them a false sense of competence in dealing with members of other organizations. So, while descriptions like those offered by Ambassador Holbrooke and in the United States Institute of Peace handbooks initially seem helpful, when they are taken as accurate guides for dealing with individual members of IGOs and NGOs, they do not enable peacekeepers to generate culturally appropriate responses to novel situations.

Thus, even to the extent that having a handy catalog of information about some of the actors in peace operations is useful, it is inherently limited. Because the cast of characters in peace operations changes constantly, there is no way to develop an inventory of all of the actors involved in those operations.[5] Rather, even at this level the only really useful way to approach organizational cultural differences is an analysis that engages the dynamic, partially shared, dispositional nature of culture.

Cultural Styles and Dimensions

In their attempts to move beyond the surface manifestations of culture, researchers who study intercultural encounters have developed a number of approaches for diagnosing culture-based conflicts. As a result, there are many schemes for understanding how and why culture affects interactions among different groups. All of these frameworks seek to describe groups in terms of cultural styles or dimensions.[6] Importantly, each derives from empirical research: comparative analysis of ethnographies, organizational surveys, or psychological analysis. Five of these frameworks are commonly encountered in discussions of international affairs and widely applied to training for peacekeeping missions and other areas of professional military education: (1) narrative resources and verbal style, (2) culture and context, (3) thinking and reasoning styles, (4) information processing styles, and (5) management of power and social relations. I review these briefly here because they are an important but, as I discuss in the next chapter, still incomplete advance in understanding culture and peacekeeping.[7]

In the following discussion, the dimensions, and their presentation in tables displaying contrasts in styles, implies a kind of dualism among groups. The researchers who use these dimensions to discuss cultural differences often array groups along a continuum, the ends of which are represented by the cultural extremes. When this is done, the dimensions are still used to mark out static, homogeneous, patterns. However, as I discuss in the next section of this chapter, the dimensions can also be reframed so that they become analytic categories for interpreting observed behavior rather than categories for describing collectivities of people. This reframing allows the cultural dimensions to be put to the service of more dynamic understandings of culture.

Looking for culture-based differences in the narrative resources and verbal styles used by different cultural groups results from the observation that groups use language differently. Some groups place special value on verbal skill, using it as a unique element of a person's reputation, while other groups do not. Based largely on the theoretical work of anthropologist Edward Hall, researchers distinguish between two styles of speech; direct and indirect. Table 7.2 shows the contrasting characteristics associated with each style.

Table 7.2: Narrative Resources and Verbal Style

Indirect	Direct
• Tend to be silent more often	• Value self-expression
• Use ambiguous language	• Value verbal fluency
• Avoid saying "no" to others to maintain harmonious atmosphere	• Express opinions directly

Differences in language use are most often said to distinguish Western from non-Western speech habits. It is also possible to see such differences between military language and diplomatic language: the directness and "transparency" preferred by military planners contrasts with the diplomatic preference for ambiguity and more "flowery" presentation.

A second culture-based style difference often noted is variation in the importance cultures assign to context in social relations. This dimension interrelates with preferences for particular narrative styles. The distinction is drawn between high- and low-context cultural groups. Table 7.3 outlines the characteristics of each style.

Table 7.3: Culture and Context

High-Context	Low-Context
• Attend to nuance and nonverbal cues	• Explicit content of message primary
• Polychronic	• Monochronic
• Collectivist	• Individualistic
• Concern with maintaining or saving face	• Tell it like it is

High-context cultural groups promote collective interests over individual interests and striving for harmony and action through consensus as ultimate goals. As a result, great attention is paid to nonverbal cues and situational nuance; multiple activities and agendas are pursued at one time; and care is given to avoid embarrassing others. In contrast, low-context cultural groups privilege individual interests over those of the group, and efficient, effective action is more valued than is maintaining group harmony. The result is an expectation that people say what they mean and mean what they say, letting the chips fall where they may. This distinction is classically applied to cultural differences between Americans and Japanese or Egyptians, or between organizations that highly regard individual acts of initiative and those that seek consensus before proceeding.

A third, related, difference is said to be found in thinking and reasoning styles associated with cultural groups. Table 7.4 shows the extremes of the characteristics of thinking and reasoning styles.

Table 7.4: Thinking and Reasoning Styles

Nonlinear	Linear
• Reasoning process indirect • No search for measurement • No external truth	• Logic and rationality • Search for objective truth • Discovery of external truth

Differences in thinking and reasoning styles are used to account for a variety of cross-cultural misunderstandings. Persuasion is often an important feature of peace operations. Especially in concert with culturally conditioned expectations about verbal style, styles of thinking and reasoning contribute to the success or failure of persuasive efforts. For example, Americans are said to find accounts that provide a direct presentation of a logical argument bolstered by independently verifiable, objective measures to be most persuasive. In contrast, Arabic speakers report finding such arguments sparse and unconvincing, requiring in addition that their interlocutors' presentation display, through linguistic conventions, their personal commitment to (and belief in) what they are talking about. Anthropological linguist Barbara Johnstone Koch demonstrated that one characteristic of this Arabic persuasive style is repetition and presentation in slightly different ways of the claims that are being asserted.[8]

The danger of a mismatch in such an exchange is not simply that one party will fail to persuade the other of the correctness of its views; one or both may attribute to the other ill will, deceitful motivations, or lack of competence. Such attributions may chill relations between them and also between people who directly witness or otherwise hear about the encounter by affecting the ways that they characterize the interlocutors.

A fourth approach to cultural differences is to look at the way preferred information-processing styles handle uncertainty and ambiguity. Some cultural groups are described as highly valuing the ability of people to act even in situations that are ambiguous or have uncertain risks; to other cultural groups, such action is anathema. At one end of this dimension are groups that resist innovation and change, finding deviant ideas and ways of proceeding to be dangerous. At the other end are groups that tolerate or seek alternative ways of action. It is often supposed that groups that avoid uncertainty motivate by appealing to group members' sense of security, esteem, or belonging, while groups that tolerate ambiguity are thought to motivate by appealing to group members' sense of achievement and efficacy.

This dimension of cultural difference was described by organizational researcher Geert Hofstede as tolerating or avoiding ambiguity and uncertainty. The characteristics of this dimension are shown in table 7.5.

Table 7.5: Information, Uncertainty, and Ambiguity

Strong Ambiguity Avoidance	Weak Ambiguity Avoidance
• Vigilant to avoid uncertainty	• Uncertainty is a natural part of life
• Ambiguity is a challenge and is stressful	• Ambiguity does not provoke stress
• Different ways of doing things are dangerous	• Different ways of doing things are interesting
• Structure and rules are essential	• Structure and rules are kept to a minimum

A fifth cultural dimension, described by Hofstede and often used in analyzing organizational conflicts, considers how group members relate to differences in power and authority. According to this line of analysis, peoples differ in their understanding, for example, of the proper way powerful supervisors should relate to people who are less powerful and people they lead. This dimension would be used to interpret the conflict between the Soviet UNMO and the OGE chief of staff, described at the beginning of this chapter. It characterizes groups according to culture-based expectations about the extent to which the less powerful members of organizations within a cultural group expect power to be distributed unevenly. In this continuum, low and high extremes have the characteristics shown in table 7.6.

Table 7.6: Power and Social Relations

Large Power Distance	Small Power Distance
• Great dependence on supervisor	• Limited dependence on supervisor
• Great emotional distance	• Small emotional distance
• No collaboration in decision making	• Prefers collaborative decision making
• Subordinate cannot contradict supervisor, who is seen as separate and unapproachable	• Subordinate can approach and contradict supervisor

The analysis of cultural differences by reference to varying styles and dimensions is an advance over approaches that focus only on the surface differences between groups. Analyzing styles and dimensions can also be an improvement over approaches that treat culture as if it determined how members of a group act and as if it were shared equally by all members of a society, thus dealing with difference by asserting stereotyped caricatures of group differences. Despite offering overgeneralized descriptions of elements of a group's culture, and because dimensions and styles are described in terms of continua, they move attention away from the idea that cultural differences are absolute and toward the idea that they are relative. Thus, although cultural styles and dimensions can be used in the same static and homogenizing ways as travelers advice and stereotypes, they can also be used to embrace the idea that cultures are dynamic and heterogeneously shared.

Cultural Aspects of Military and Civilian Conflicts in Peace Operations

During peace operations, people from many kinds of organizations and different nations come together in the interest of maintaining collective security and promoting humanitarian ends. Obviously, cultural conflicts can occur between people from different national groups. Yet even among people from the same national group who participate in different organizations—military, relief, or international civil service—conflicts based on different organizational cultures may arise. Cultural models help people form expectations about the right way to proceed. They also provide the tools that people use to understand their experiences in a meaningful way.

In looking at specific cases, it is important to keep in mind that culture *informs* these processes; it does not determine them. Thus, even people from the same national group, serving in the same organization, may have differing understandings and expectations. Nonetheless, being aware of the role of cultural mechanisms, and the place of cultural styles, can help peacekeepers deal with cross-cultural conflicts and considerations.

There are several areas in which culturally based differences lead to conflicts in military and civilian expectations and understandings of peace operations. Not recognizing these may lead to difficulties in coordinating action. In general, such cultural considerations can be grouped into four areas: (1) management structures; (2) symbols, boundaries, and security; (3) media and information; and (4) context and legitimacy.

Management Structures

Just as there are different cultural styles in governing the relations between powerful supervisors and those whose work they direct, so military and civilian organizations in peace operations give different meanings to and have differing expectations of management structures.

At one extreme, for the military, a consistent theme in peace operations management structures is reflected in a command framework that has four essential characteristics: (1) there should be unity of command; (2) the chain of command should be structured so that it can respond quickly and promote fast and efficient decision making; (3) areas of responsibility should be clearly defined; and (4) areas of responsibility should be of manageable size. In terms of cultural styles, this view of command and control would be similar to the large power distance style identified by Hofstede.

At the other extreme, humanitarian organizations, especially smaller ones, view management very differently. Partly because of constraints of size and resources, but especially for reasons of cultural (and historical) development, humanitarian organizations may be characterized not as seeking unity of command but rather camaraderie of command. In contrast to a hierarchical structure that clearly defines the tasks and responsibilities of each bureaucratically nested individual, all are expected to contribute their efforts and expertise whenever and wherever these are needed, regardless of the structural definition of their position. This view of management is similar to the low power distance style.

Some of the larger humanitarian agencies, like the Red Cross, appear to have a commitment to a hierarchical management structure. In fact, these organizations are cultural hybrids; they have explicit structures that imply larger social distances between supervisors and staff, but the organizational ethos still demands consultation and smaller distance. The preferences expressed within each organization derive in part from their history and interactions with military organizations. For instance, the International Committee of the Red Cross has a long history of managing large organizational structures and interacting with (although maintaining independence from) the military.[9]

When management structures follow clearly separate styles, the potential for discord is great, but the source of the discord can be quickly identified. In settings where management structures are very similar, problems may still arise because members of different organizations interpret those arrangements differently. A frequent complaint about peace operations, for instance, is that although they have what appears to be a traditionally hierarchical command structure, in fact this structure is interpreted differently by different national militaries and by civilian organizations. The high value placed on consultation and participation by humanitarian organizations, even in the context of clear, hierarchical structural management arrangements, presents a challenge to coordinated action.

Symbols, Boundaries, and Security

In cross-cultural encounters, differing interpretations of the context for action and how to relate to that context may disrupt relations. Similarly, cross-cultural considerations are important to managing peace operations because they influence the ways elements of the mission conduct themselves on the ground, perhaps especially in relations with the local population. In their ideal form, these lead humanitarian organizations to act without regard for a political program. Rather than providing aid in order to forward a political outcome, aid is distributed impartially. This impartiality is enacted in the way humanitarian workers give aid and symbolized by the placement of operations in the midst of local populations. Few boundaries—physical, political, or symbolic—are placed between aid workers and the people they serve. Aid workers are in close daily contact with the local population.

In contrast, military units involved in peace operations symbolize and enact their missions by control and separation. Thus, even in the most uneventful peace observation missions, military personnel are physically separated from local populations. Buildings and observation post perimeters are secured, and entry into the compound is tightly controlled.

This indicates that people working in humanitarian and military organizational cultures expect and support different kinds and amounts of ambiguity in their operating environments, and that security is interpreted differently as well; security arrangements deemed appropriate by one organization can undermine safety and security according to the other.[10]

To some degree, conventional military units tend to be more consumed by force protection questions than special forces units are. This varies across national militaries as well, but variation does not change the broader point that, without the same infrastructure/superstructure supporting them, aid workers tend to live in much closer relationship with local populations than do uniformed personnel.[11]

Media and Information

Just as culturally based verbal and narrative styles can lead to conflict among individuals, different expectations about the roles of information and media may make military and civilian coordination in peace operations difficult. On one hand, humanitarian actors treat information and its public dissemination through the media as a mechanism for indicating the dimensions of the humanitarian crisis they face. Images of refugees displayed by the media—the starving and the ill—serve to raise popular public support, including money, for their efforts. The tragedy is newsworthy, and its display, at least initially, is helpful for mobilizing public support.

Particularly in the case of peace operations that involve the use of force, news coverage can generate both support for the military and protests against it. Images of civilian casualties from military actions in a peace operation may turn public support just as quickly as images of soldiers dead or captured. The media, then, is a contingency to be controlled and given just the information deemed appropriate by the mission.

The potential for misunderstanding, suspicion, and conflict in relation to media access to information exists between military and humanitarian organizations. This is complicated by the need to include the organizational cultures of the media.

Context and Legitimacy

When military peacekeepers deploy to a mission area, they do so only after their mission has been authorized by the Security Council and following extensive discussions and agreements between the United Nations and local governments. They derive their legitimacy from the legal framework within which they work.

Some of the civilian organizations present in the mission area will also have negotiated with the local governments agreements that define the scope of their actions. These agreements confer legitimacy on their work also in a legal sense. As well, some NGOs, especially humanitarian organizations, may locate their legitimacy in the fact that they are implementing the humanitarian imperative of providing aid to those in need regardless of their political or legal standing.

Whatever the legal basis for their formal legitimacy, all of the organizations and agencies in the mission area must develop substantive legitimacy through their relations with local populations. It is to the dimensions of those relations that I now turn.

Peace Operations and Local Populations

In order to be effective, peace operations must engage the local population's sense of credibility and potential. It is therefore essential that the mission operate with an understanding of the traditional local structures of legitimacy and an awareness of how conflict may have fissured and fragmented those structures. Understanding the cultural aspects of relations with local populations can be developed using the same tools described earlier. Collective action by local populations results in part from the enactment and elaboration of cultural models.

Since cultural models are open to modification by feedback derived from prior action, the meanings and significance of words and deeds may change over the life of the mission. The field of action is broad as well as variable. The following is a list of signposts that peacekeepers should be alert to during the life of the mission. Understanding the dynamics of these cultural domains prior to deployment will form the basis of a case-specific cultural knowledge briefing. Having this information will help in devising strategies for addressing culturally sensitive areas of action in ways that will enhance the efficacy of the operation and limit the negative effects of intervention.

Because peace operations enter a scene where social and cultural institutions already exist, the areas of potential concern to a peace operation are as varied as is social life, and attention to cultural domains may prove particularly important. These include four aspects of culture: (1) law, politics, and conflict; (2) social stratification; (3) gender roles; and (4) economic and subsistence practices. Not only is an understanding of these structures important for peacekeepers, military and civilian, who are working on-site, knowledge of these cultural features is essential for planners designing missions.

Law, Politics, and Conflict

All societies provide a context for managing competition over resources and resolving disputes over how those resources are acquired and used. These frameworks are often translated into various sets of rules, formal or informal. Norms—informal expectations about how people should behave—encode conceptions of appropriate or expected behavior. Such normative expectations include general, though perhaps ambiguous, guides, like "public officials ought not take bribes" or "people should be good to their parents" as well as specific behavioral directives, like "thou shalt not kill." A single society may hold contradictory norms.

When norms are systematized or elevated to a formal status, binding rules are created, which are laws. Laws encode the overall adaptive strategy of a society. Legal systems, as societies themselves, change over time. It is important to be aware of the sets of cultural norms that guide the behavioral expectations of both the local population and the members of the peace operation. It is also important to be aware of the legal system that guides the behavior of the local population and of how this system has changed over time.

Norms are based on cultural models, and both perform several different kinds of work within a society. Three aspects of normative expectations are particularly important for peace support operations. First, norms provide what might be called "reality assumptions," or general beliefs of what can be taken for granted in regard to actions that are thought to be meaningful within the local context. For example, the degree of intimacy required of friendships is often a normative behavior that is taken for granted. In some societies, people expect that their friendships involve intense and frequent interactions, and in other societies friendships may be maintained over great distance and with infrequent contact. Second, norms help people evaluate the actions of others. Such norms, which might be called "ranking norms," are evaluative and underlie the achievement of status within a society. The third type of norm includes those that form the underlying expectations for membership in a particular group or social stratum. Such "membership norms" can include expectations about behavior, the performance of tasks, adherence to specific guidelines about how to act, or the display of a certain kind of symbolic costume. In areas of conflict, membership norms may include manner of dress or use of symbolic forms of greetings.

Legal systems and social norms are dynamic. Both change in response to new social and environmental realities. Sometimes these changes fracture traditional attitudes and ways of acting, breaking down various sets of relationships and the normative order surrounding them. It is likely that such transformations will occur in situations where peace operations take place. So it is useful to try to understand traditional normative structures themselves and how these may have fissured prior to the deployment of the peace mission.

Understanding the current systems of laws and normative relations is important for many reasons, but one of the most important is that these undergird a social group's sense of its traditional moral system. A moral system is the matrix from which legitimacy derives. For peacekeeping missions to be successful, they must be viewed as legitimate throughout their entire life cycle—from authorization by the Security Council to withdrawal. In addition, we need to understand the nature of the norms and laws underlying political legitimacy at the time the mission is deployed and to keep a sense of how these change while the mission is on the ground.

Failing to pay attention to the changing nature of normative expectations and legal encounters in a local population can lead to some undesirable consequences. For example, a mission may be welcomed when it is deployed, but as normative expectations change, influenced in part by the actions of the peace support operation itself, that welcome may turn into rejection and hostility, as happened, for example, during the deployments in Somalia discussed in chapter 1. Anticipating such a change in the mission climate depends perhaps most importantly upon keeping an awareness of the changing norms of behaviors, expectations, and group affiliations within the local population. It is worth noting that when interventions introduce governance, legal, and other structures that do not grow from local norms, they are setting the mission up for failure.

Peace support operations are often called upon to manage conflicts among local populations and to resolve disputes. It is important, therefore, to understand the traditional, legal, and normative dispute resolution mechanisms available in a society. Again, the cultural models underlying disputing lead to norms and expectations about responsibility for actions, appropriate compensation, appropriate people for resolving disputes, and the like.

For instance, how do members of a society become part of a dispute? In some societies, responsibility for a dispute and its settlement rests only with those individuals who are involved in the creation of the point of contention. In other societies, inclusion in a dispute may result from a normative expectation that all members of a group—perhaps a kin group—are automatically included among the disputants simply because of their relationship to the original protagonists.

Working from a dispute resolution model that emphasizes the individual's responsibility, it is possible to transgress the normative expectations of a society that sees responsibility as lodged in kinship, corporate, or friendship groups. Transgressing such a boundary would make the mission appear partisan within the dispute, perhaps even escalating the critical events; yet to the unsuspecting member of the support operation, the action undertaken would appear neutral and nonpartisan. Hence, choosing the "wrong" local authority because of a lack of cultural knowledge can have far-reaching consequences for the mission, at all levels, from the safety of individual peacekeepers to the failure of the mission as a whole.

Authority—which is the right, rather than the ability, to make decisions, command obedience, and arrange for the settlement of disputes—reflects normative expectations about the proper boundaries of power. It is likely that different individuals will have authority over different domains of social life; thus, we need to understand the relationship between people who have authority in a household, for example, and people who have authority in the local community and in larger corporate contexts. Anthropologist Tanja Hohe describes how in East Timor the elections conducted under the auspices of the United Nations Transnational Administration in East Timor failed to account for local practices from which political authority derived. The result was that the state building intended by the international community was less effective than had been hoped. Similarly, Thant Myint-U and Elizabeth Sellwood describe the lack of local knowledge in the missions in Cambodia and Bosnia-Herzegovina. In all three of these missions, the international community was less effective in its intended state building because lack of cultural knowledge meant the missions proceeded as though they had a blank slate upon which to work.[12]

Law, politics, and conflict management systems are often encapsulated in terms of political symbols and traditions of behavior and action. An understanding of the meaning of such symbols and sensitivity to them is one way to avoid unintentionally behaving in ways that appear partisan in the overall conflict. Since these kinds of subtle symbolic communications can have major ramifications for the success of the mission, it is important early in the mission to try to articulate a set of potentially problematic political symbols.

Social Stratification

All societies make distinctions among people. These distinctions separate the in-group of the society from outsiders. Distinctions are also drawn within the society to classify people according to categories that are considered significant and distinct. This classification is based on selected perceived cultural, physical, or other differences. An important aspect of this process is that even things that strike an outside observer as being the same can be made significant in the process of group differentiation.[13]

How people speak, what they eat, the style of their clothing, or the design of their houses, for example, may all serve as markers for various group identities. These markers often form a cluster of symbols, some of which are considered to be essential for the definition of identity. Under ordinary circumstances, individuals may manipulate or deploy in strategic ways the various characteristics that are used to form identities. As resources become scare, or there is increased competition for political power and access to goods and societal benefits, identity can become a point of tension and conflict. Under such circumstances, it may become difficult for people to move back and forth among the various social identities in which they might otherwise participate. Boundaries between groups may at one time be relatively porous but in times of stress and conflict become quite solid.

It is important for members of a peacekeeping mission to understand the dimensions of stratification and how it is marked, symbolized, and enacted by local populations.

Gender Roles

Even when collective violence is experienced by an ethnic group without particular regard to gender, women generally suffer more than men do. In circumstances where organized fighting is taking place, men may leave their homes to join an organized or guerilla-fighting force. This frequently leaves women at home with increased responsibilities for child care and the maintenance of collective cultural identity—in a setting where resources are limited and they are exposed to manipulation and pressure from within and outside of their communities. Often, women are made to have special responsibility for maintaining their group's cultural identity. The assignment of identity preservation to women—by circumscribing the modes and range of their action, regulating their sexuality, or "nationalizing" reproduction—may be taken up voluntarily or forced upon them. In either case, the result is that women's individual reproductive acts come to symbolize the collective identity of the group. As a result, political violence against women becomes freighted with symbolic meanings that go beyond the physical consequences to individual women.[14]

Women remain especially vulnerable when peace support operations are deployed in postconflict situations. There are two ways that this vulnerability is manifest. In many peace operations, local staff are hired to support the work of the operation. When this happens, real opportunities are created for women as well as for men. Unfortunately, in practice when local people are hired in a professional capacity they are paid less well and given fewer benefits and privileges than their international counterparts. Moreover, women are less likely to be hired for those professional positions.[15] This creates a gender gap, with women finding employment in lower-paying, more menial jobs that serve the well-paid international personnel. Such positions include secretarial, housekeeping, hotel, restaurant, and other legitimate but low-paying service jobs. In addition to nonprofessional roles, women who are vulnerable in postconflict settings may become involved in sexual relationships with the more powerful and wealthy international civil servants who are suddenly in the area.[16]

Criminal activity, including drug sales, smuggling of goods and people, and prostitution, may flourish especially in the early stages of peace operations, when the rule of law has not been fully established because the police force and judiciary are not yet working smoothly. Elisabeth Rehn and Ellen Sirleaf note that, "perhaps most disturbing of everything we saw and learned was the association, in the vast majority of peacekeeping environments, between the arrival of peacekeeping personnel and increased prostitution, sexual exploitation and HIV/AIDS infection."[17] The relationship is reciprocal. One recent study showed that there was a direct and positive correlation between the length of troops' peacekeeping deployment and the prevalence of HIV infection among them.[18]

Those planning peace support operations should be alert to the distortions in gender roles that can result from the sudden influx of wealthy and powerful personnel to an area. Also, there is a great need for planners to structure the operation so that it avoids creating the conditions that allow women to be exploited through criminal activities.

Economic and Subsistence Practices

In societies where conflict is severe enough to merit multinational humanitarian intervention, traditional economic practices and subsistence patterns will undoubtedly be disrupted. In addition to understanding how those traditional patterns are reflected in the organization of disputing groups, peace support operations must be conducted with a self-conscious sense of how their presence distorts local practices.

Peace support operations introduce goods—like food supplies—that would be otherwise unavailable to local people, and they infuse the economy with currency resources that can distort local economies. In such a context, peacekeepers should be alert to the effects of this infusion. Care must be taken that the relative abundance of goods and money in the peace support operation does not become socially destructive. Profiteering, exploitation, and illegal activities are all likely to accompany such distortions.

Even under "normal" circumstances, in some societies business activities and patterns of reciprocity may be quite different from what members of peace operations are used to from their own societies. And distinguishing between damaging distortions and appropriate activities may present a challenge. It is therefore essential for people involved in peace operations to understand as fully as possible the normative local business and economic practices, so that care can be taken not to reproduce situations of dependency and partisanship.

Moving beyond Pattern to Meaning

Cultural factors come into play in many areas of peace operations. These influences may be subtle or unmistakable. Some of the conflicts that peace operations respond to will in fact be based on cultural factors. Within military and civilian organizations participating in peace operations, cultural factors will affect views of what to do, what is right and wrong, what goals should be pursued, and whether they are being accomplished quickly enough and at an acceptable cost. Differences in the way peacekeepers and local populations engage their shared experiences create points of tension among them as well. Being alert to the potential challenges and problems that these differences can create is an important step, as is developing tools for dealing with them. The analytic tools associated with attention to cultural styles and dimensions are important advances for understanding and addressing cultural differences in peacekeeping. But in spite of how helpful these tools can be, they are, unfortunately, inherently limiting.

The analysis of cultural styles and dimensions leads to characterizations of other organizations and communities that assume that the cultures of those groups are homogeneously shared. It also promotes the idea that once these organizations and communities are described, the patterns will always characterize the way people in them work. While there is nothing inherently wrong with seeking patterns, it is essential to recognize that these patterns are observed in specific settings and in reaction to specific situations. Failure to do this results in the fallacy of detachable cultural descriptions (see chapter 1).

All of our knowledge is partial and contingent. There are at least two sets of reasons for this view, which anthropologists have embraced at least since the early part of the twentieth century.[19] The first set results from the inherent limitations of the tools that researchers use to discover the processes from which social phenomena emerge. Every research strategy directs attention to some aspects of social life and away from others. Also, there is no way to know when our knowledge about the world is completely accurate, or that we are using all the levels of analysis needed to fully address the problem being investigated.[20]

In addition to these methodological and epistemological considerations, the dynamic aspects of cultural phenomena require that we recognize the partial and contingent nature of cultural descriptions. The symbolic foundations of culture are open and dynamic (see chapter 3). In a very real sense, culture is emergent; whatever characteristics are attributable to it in a particular case are dependent on the interaction of processes external to a group of people as well as those that derive from the particular constellation of symbolic meanings recognized and used by the group. While the cultural patterns that emerge may appear to be unchanged over relatively long stretches of time, they are actually in constant active tension.

This is true for peacekeeping missions as it is for all other aspects of social life and for social institutions in general. Dealing with the highly dynamic nature of deep culture requires approaches to cultural analysis that combine the tools of symbolic analysis with understandings of how experience derives from and then alters patterns of meaning.

In the following chapter, I turn to this more dynamic view of culture in peacekeeping by drawing on the analysis of cultural models. I also relate cultural models to developments in cognitive social science—a way of connecting the styles and dimensions discussed in this chapter to the processes from which they derive meaning, thus placing peacekeeping in a broader cultural context.

8

Peacekeeping Under Fire

Since the mid-1970s, the most widely used approaches to cultural difference have been those that analyze differences in terms of dimensions of culture, like the ones discussed in the preceding chapter. These approaches are much used in international business training, organizational psychology, and by people who introduce others to cross-cultural experiences. For example, the dimensional analysis of culture produces advice about how best to conduct cross-cultural negotiation, how to work with people from other cultures, and how to think about leadership in culturally diverse organizations.[1] Not only have these approaches been embraced in these professional settings, they have more recently been brought into international relations and conflict management. Political scientist Raymond Cohen has been a leader in applying these approaches to negotiation in international relations. He uses the associated schemes to organize his general discussion of international negotiation, and he puts them to good use in a detailed analysis of difficulties encountered in negotiations between Egyptians and Israelis.[2] Anthropologist Kevin Avruch concurs that those seeking to understand international negotiation "would do well to consult it [Hofstede's schema]."[3] As I indicated before, the dimensional analysis of culture is increasingly being applied to peacekeeping, especially in training for missions that integrate civilian and military components.

Despite the enthusiasm for dimensional approaches, many are skeptical about their value. A substantial critical literature has developed that challenges the methodological and analytical choices that researchers made as they developed the dimensional constructs, calling into question their validity and reliability.[4] Other writers question the applicability of dimensional approaches in contexts where there is great intragroup variation among the dimensions, pointing out that, for example, in every society there is tension between acting for individual self-interest or for the interests of the group.[5] Or they reject the basic theoretical assumptions upon which dimensional analysis rests. Much of the discussion is highly technical, revolving around issues of psychometrics, research design, and the applicability of the statistical techniques used to discover the factors from which the dimensions are composed.[6]

Despite their limitations, dimensional analyses of culture can be useful starting points for navigating cross-cultural encounters. *But they are only starting points.* They provide a useful descriptive vocabulary for talking about how people's observed behaviors and statements of preference differ from one another. Critically, dimensional analyses of culture do not give immutable truths about a group's culture or make it possible to predict in any meaningful way what actions will be appropriate in a particular setting. Also, they lack connections to the specific circumstances of actions and ignore issues of history, conceptions of identity, and patterns of power.

Cultural styles and dimensions, like surface artifacts, are not meaningful in themselves. Rather, they are the impermanent manifestations of deeper cultural models from which they derive meaning. While it may be helpful to know how to display culturally appropriate artifacts and behaviors, it is critically important to know *why* and *how* they matter. What does it mean in the experience of people from the other culture? For that, it is necessary to consider the dynamic models that manifest patterns of action.

Cultural Models and Cognitive Schema

At its most general level, culture can be characterized by cultural models that are inferred by observing the actions of members of a social group.[7] When these models are experienced and enacted, people learn how to conform to the culture of their social group. At the same time, the experience and enactment of these mechanisms affect the cultural model, allowing it to change, or creating variations among members of a social group.

Cultural models establish frames within which meaningful action is possible, and at the same time feedback from experience alters those frames and the cultural models themselves.[8] Cultural model-based frames create images of the world that provide people with a basis for: (1) having expectations about what motivates others, (2) learning the "correct" way of responding to challenges in their environment, and (3) developing emotional responses to their experiences. In brief, peoples' representational, directive, and affective frames of reference for dealing with the world around them derive from the cultural models available to them (see chapter 3).

These cultural models are composed of ways of thinking about the world that are shared by many people, what might technically be called intersubjectively shared cognitive schema.[9] People organize their activities in reference to these models. And many of them are given linguistic form in conceptual metaphors that map one area of experience onto what we know about another area of experience. Cultural models provide coherent, systematic arrangements of knowledge. As we saw in Bateson's discussion of the Iranian concept of the "good man," social groups may sustain multiple models that can be used to understand and act on their experience (see chapter 2). Which model is normative for a group at any particular time, and thus temporarily characterize that group, depends upon ecological factors and the circumstances facing the individual and the group.[10]

A culturally competent individual uses fundamental cultural themes as tools, choosing the ones that are appropriate for responding to their situation. Options for structuring their actions and creating solutions to problems are derived from past experience and culturally appropriate exemplars. At particular times, groups can be characterized by the themes that make up their normative cultural models. These may also distinguish one group from another. The process of becoming competent in a culture requires mastering vast amounts of cultural knowledge. People acquire their cultural knowledge through observation and activity; this acquisition is possible because information is assimilated to cultural themes. The cultural themes act as frames into which experience can be fitted and made sense of. Just as one cannot become a competent user of a language by studying word lists and phrases—because there is no frame into which to fit them—so too a culture cannot be learned by studying the discrete meanings of cultural features but requires using a frame to which to fit one's experiences.[11]

Culture is learned through practice—by doing. Cultural models are made manifest through group practices. Practice, in this sense, includes language, symbols, rituals, and behavioral models. This practice is reflected in the cultural styles and dimensions, which are only important because they are manifestations of cultural models. Since cultural models are open to change, the practices that derive from them can be modified by experience. The nature and pace of this change are dependent upon what is happening in the social and physical environments that affect how well the cultural models allow groups to act successfully.[12] Making these sets of relations even more complex is evidence that cultural models are developed, modified, and may be discarded through reciprocal social structural coupling (see chapter 3).[13]

Members of cultural groups share verbal and linguistic representations that they use to render behaviors comprehensible, plausible, justifiable, and socially acceptable. They also may mark a person's identity on the basis of such factors. For example, styles of speaking, such as different dialects, may mark, even through subtle differences, membership in separate social groups—such as social classes, ethnic identities, or place of origin.[14] Further, each style has a set of patterns of speaking with which it is associated. These rules influence such mundane but important speech events as turn taking, how direct a person can appropriately be, and with whom and how it is appropriate to speak.

Cultural models are also manifest in other kinds of symbols. These include pictures, emblems, and activities. Symbols prompt social action and define the individual's sense of self. They also are an important means for making sense of the political process, which largely presents itself to people in symbolic form. In peace operations, the most well-known symbols are the blue beret or blue helmet and the United Nations' flag, but badges, medals, patrols, and parades are important as well (see chapter 3). Like all symbols, these convey meanings that are recognized by those who share in a cultural tradition. Also, like all symbols, each of these has multiple meanings.

Just as culture is learned and maintained through practice, it is learned by watching and emulating people who are believed to embody characteristics that are highly prized in a culture. These behavioral models provide examples of proper ways of acting in various settings and legitimate actions and expectations. Such heroes need not be real persons—they may be characters drawn from literature, movies, or group lore. As such, the traits emulated may be exaggerated or embellished. Both military and civilian groups participating in peace operations have such models. Military examples are the account of the lone peace observer standing before the advancing tank or how peacekeepers' deaths are spoken about. For humanitarian workers, examples may be individuals noted for self-sacrifice in the delivery of aid and the conceptual metaphor of humanitarian space.

Underlying political and national cultural conflicts provide additional layers of complexity. Here, symbols take on particular meaning, and interpretation of them goes beyond just what peacekeepers bring to the field. In relation to the Sudan, for instance, Jok Madut Jok notes that during the long North-South war, peoples around the country have developed high levels of distrust of the armies and ordinary people not from their own region.

> To reconcile this mistrust, [interveners] have to pay attention to the power of symbols and symbolism. The question of Shari'a in Khartoum and the way non-Muslims have been treated will continue to give southerners a feeling of insecurity in what is supposedly their own country. Other symbols include the use of Islamic colors such as the color of the passport cover, or the names given to things and places such as the river the Arabs call Bahr-el-Arab and the Dinka call the Kiir. The use of these terms or applications of these colors may not have any ill intentions behind them, but they are usually read differently by different people. It is important to look for neutral symbols if all citizens of Sudan are to feel at home in every corner of the country.[15]

An understanding of the way symbolism connects to the cultural models at work here is critical to peacekeepers now in South Sudan. The following sections explore further the role cultural models play for peacekeeping.

Cultural Dimensions, Cultural Models, and Root Metaphors in Peacekeeping

In order to give a fuller sense of how peacekeeping is affected by cultural models, and how those cultural models are affected by practice, in this section I discuss four examples of these links. At the broadest level, I discuss the importance of Security Council actions in relation to the authorization of missions. I then look at the way in which humanitarian action depends upon the enactment of the conceptual metaphor of humanitarian space. Next, in a somewhat more restricted scope, I consider the interaction of humanitarian and military elements in peace operations. I next turn to the local level and look at the treatment of local hires and the criminal and exploitative actions of some peacekeepers, which have been called the "unintended consequences of peacekeeping." My intent here is to show how these actions link to, and affect, peacekeeping. I do not intend to give exhaustive accounts of these areas, each of which has been subjected to sustained analysis by others. As I have indicated before, however, those analyses have been conducted without attending to the broad cultural context in which they take place.[16]

The Security Council: Performance and Legitimacy

A lot has been written about the need for Security Council reform. By and large, this work focuses on the anachronistic makeup of the Council and on the need to expand it to include nations that have claims on Council membership that they did not have in 1948. These discussions focus on the important aspects of legal and political legitimacy. In addition, the substantive legitimacy of the Council's actions rests in major part on the meaning derived from the root metaphor, and the cultural models derived from them, central to the United Nations: that it is an institution in the service of a pacific world order that empowers the weak, feeds the hungry, conquers disease, and settles conflicts peacefully. As a fundamental instrument of the Council, the legitimacy of peacekeeping rests on the Council's functioning within a framework that supports the cultural inversion key to the United Nations itself. As peacekeeping developed in the sway of this root metaphor, traditional military activities were used to support this image of the world transformed. Traditional military ritual and symbolism were appropriated and given new meaning in the context of peacekeeping. Through this and the highly ritualized and symbolic actions of the Security Council, peacekeeping contributed to the elaboration of an image of an international community acting in a neutral, consensual manner to sustain a stable world community. The use of the military without weapons in the service of peace is a core image carried forward from the root metaphor of a pacific world order.

It is the cultural model that organizes the reversals inherent in peacekeeping (see chapter 3). These reversals work together to support the basic inversion captured by the root metaphor and structure orienting dispositions that lead to the development of both the frame of reference peacekeeping was conceived in by the international community, and the frame of reference local actors used to interpret it. These cultural inversions create a space for alternative political representations to develop. The inversions establish the symbolic world in which peacekeeping gains legitimacy, standing, and authority.

At the level of the international community, the discussions at the Security Council have changed in ways that limit both participation and discussion.

> As the Council has become more effective and powerful, it has become more secretive. Like a parliamentary matryoskhka (doll), it now contains ever-smaller "mini-Councils," each meeting behind closed doors without keeping records and each taking decisions secretly. Before the plenary Council meets in "consultation," in a special room assigned to it near the Security Council, the P-5 have met in "consultation" in a special room now assigned to them outside the Security Council; and before they meet, the P-3 composed of the United States, the United Kingdom and France, have met in "consultation" in one of their missions in New York. All of these meetings take place *in camera* and no common minutes are kept. After the fifteen members of the Council have consulted and reached their decision, they adjourn to the Council's chamber, where they go through the formal motions of voting and announcing their decisions. Decisions that appear to go further than at any time in the history of the United Nations are now ultimately being taken, it seems, by a small group of states separately meeting in secret.[17]

Prior to this change in the way Council deliberations take place, the Council acted on highly controversial items in conventionalized discussions. The resulting performance communicated that the plans that emerged were for consensual, joint action. The activity of the Council was itself important to creating the image of the United Nations as a moral force for a cooperative, pacific world. This new reality has the opposite effect.

Consensus building is a messy and time-consuming process, as is clear from studies and from observing societies that use consensus as the normative mechanism of decision making. There is lots of talk, even heated argument and disagreement. Iterative rounds of talk, side conversations, and other engagements characterize these processes. These activities lead some people involved in the process to change their positions and others to go along with the dominant position. Importantly, it is the performance that creates the image of a decision jointly arrived at and a sense of satisfaction with the procedure used to achieve it.[18]

The current practices of the Security Council, in contrast, create an image wherein self-interested power politics reemerges as the rule, breaking with the symbolic traditions of peacekeeping and altering the public perception and approval of peacekeeping. My claim here is about the image projected by the Council's contentious discussions during the Cold War. It is obvious that power politics, especially between East and West, operated during the Cold War. However, the practices of the council created the idea that the missions it authorized emerged from a truly consultative, consensual process.

Indeed, Brian Urquhart observes that public debate in the Security Council during the Cold War was an important process in symbolically legitimating the consensus of Security Council actions. He notes that, further, the two consultation rooms (one for the P-5, the other for the president of the council) were physically horrible—small, cramped, and hot. This helped to keep the debate in public because staying in the rooms was extremely uncomfortable. But renovations of the Council's consultation rooms made them more comfortable, moving consultation inside and away from public view and reinforcing this pattern of private consultation.[19]

The reintroduction of power politics to peacekeeping has also affected how peacekeepers experience the missions to which they are assigned. In the contemporary milieu, the practices that maintained legitimacy, standing, and authority are destabilized, first by the Security Council's actions and then by the actions of national governments. As a result, the basic inversions that support the symbolic capital of peacekeeping are undone, thus pushing peacekeeping outside the core frame of reference that supported it in the past. Not only the mission, but the entire institution is thus challenged.

Humanitarian Space and Military Coordination

The differences between military and humanitarian agency practices I discussed in the previous chapter are peacekeeping illustrations of how group cultural dimensions and surface features link to deeper cultural models. Recall from the preceding chapter that humanitarian agencies viewed their security and safety as turning on their ability to live among the populations they serve. In contrast, the military perception was that safety derives from separating from the local population and tightly controlling their area of operation. On the face of it, humanitarians' insistence on dropping as many boundaries as possible and close association may seem irrational in the context of highly volatile and violent environments. But its rationality and meaning come into focus when these practices are understood as deriving from the root metaphor of *humanitarian space*.

Humanitarian organizations, as a rule, determine the legitimacy of their actions by applying the principal that everyone who needs assistance has a right to it regardless of their politics, religion, or ethnicity. Based on a concept of humanitarian space aid workers are sometimes able to act in situations where national authorities cannot. Humanitarian space is the understanding that impartial humanitarian action creates both a metaphorical and an actual space that makes aid delivery possible.[20] Humanitarian space is a conceptual metaphor that enables agencies to act in one domain—crises situations—in accordance with what we know about the properties of the other—the use of space. Thus, for instance, space is something we can move around in relatively freely; it is undifferentiated and expansive. Applying this to how to act in crisis settings, humanitarians ought to be able to move around and expand their work. It is from working with people in an undifferentiated way (that is, acting impartially) and moving freely that humanitarian workers traditionally derive security.

In contrast, military actions in peace operations are made legitimate through the political process and by reference to international law. When peace operations are authorized by a Security Council mandate, they derive their legitimacy from the legal status of the United Nations. A mandate sets out what actions may and may not be legitimately taken by the mission. It is then operationalized through the articulation of rules of engagement. Thus, the scope and nature of legitimate action is highly specified.

The tension between seeing legitimate actions as those that accomplish what must be done and seeing legitimate actions as those that conform to the explicit mandate creates the possibility for culturally based discord between military and humanitarian organizations in peacekeeping. Although this discord is seen on the surface in cultural dimensional differences displayed by militaries and humanitarian agencies, these are merely the temporary manifestations of cultural models from which those actions derive meaning.

Throughout the second half of the twentieth century, humanitarian workers were able to operate in relative safety, even in intensely dangerous conflict situations. As militaries involved in peace support operations have tried increasingly to coordinate with humanitarians, this situation appears to be changing.

Militaries escort humanitarian convoys and participate in "quick impact projects" intended to win the good faith of local populations. When peacekeepers engage in these kinds of activities, they create the potential for confusion. Local populations see humanitarians and troops doing some of the same things, and in situations of active conflict this may lead the local population to see the humanitarians as taking sides. Indeed, in some conflicts, as Béatrice Pouligny notes, local actors have been eager to see peacekeeping missions and humanitarians as allies rather than neutral interveners.[21] The resulting confusion has worried some humanitarians, who see the identification of their organizations with the military as a threat to their ability to maintain humanitarian space.[22]

Image and Reality in Civil Military Relations

Despite whatever reservations they may have about working with the military, many in humanitarian aid agencies see cooperation as an inevitable fact of life. They argue, therefore, that steps should be taken to make that cooperation work as smoothly as possible.[23] The underlying assumption in these efforts is that there is a basic parity in the engagement between militaries and aid organizations. They seek to create coordination mechanisms that allow militaries and humanitarians to be equal partners. These efforts are reflected in prescriptions offered by the aid agencies that try to discuss coordination in terms of their understandings of humanitarian response, seeking to preserve humanitarian space. They do this by laying out principles that set the terms of the military-civilian engagement. For instance, they suggest prohibiting militaries from engaging in humanitarian activities, defining what information aid workers can legitimately share with militaries (and vice versa), and limiting the military presence out of respect for humanitarian principles, as opposed to strategic concerns.[24]

Militaries too approach this engagement with openness to humanitarians' concerns and professing equality in the partnership. In part, these commitments are embodied in attempts to understand humanitarian agency culture. The result has been a tremendous effort to "work the problem" in discussions with humanitarian agencies and develop joint training opportunities. The profusion of training materials in this area is proof of good intentions.

In practice, the engagements turn out to be more one-sided than the rhetoric would suggest. Colleagues and I have elsewhere described the structure of the conversations we have observed between military and humanitarian representatives.[25] Here it is sufficient to note that they soon move from open engagement to frustration as the military asserts that things must proceed as they would have it and the humanitarian representatives express frustration at not being understood or taken seriously.[26] Yet this breakdown is not surprising if one looks at the way militaries define coordination and at the training materials used to promote it.

The training video narrated by Ambassador Richard Holbrooke is an example of many such activities (see chapter 7). It serves as well as any of the others as a lens through which to look at this issue. There are two things of note in these interactions. First, militaries focus on the dimensions of difference between their organizations and humanitarian agencies—*how* things actually get done. In contrast, humanitarian agencies focus on the cultural models that frame their actions—on *why* things get done. At the initial encounter, and for some time afterward, the context of goodwill defining the encounter means that this difference does not result in conflict. But when the conversation moves to practicalities, the differences mean that military and humanitarian personnel are, quite literally, talking past one another.

Second, in conversations about implementing coordination, the cultural terms of discussion are set by characterizations of dimensions of difference, like those rehearsed by Ambassador Holbrooke. Even humanitarian agencies accept these terms, although they are highly disadvantageous to them. For example, the African Civil Military Coordination Programme of the African Centre for Constructive Dispute Resolution recommends the Holbrooke materials.[27]

The reason this is problematic is that in each of the cultural oppositions presented by Holbrooke (and others) does more than describe differences in practice. Perhaps without meaning to, they also smuggle in evaluations of those practices, and it is always the NGOs' practices that are marked as poor, inadequate, or unwieldy.[28]

The differential valuing of humanitarian and military roles is reinforced in the definitions of civilian-military coordination used by militaries. As Stuart Gordon points out, NATO's definition presupposes the primacy of the military mission over the humanitarian mission.[29]

One result of this is that humanitarian agencies become, at best, junior partners. More often they are seen as clients of the military who must conform to military imperatives for planning and strategically based decision making.[30] This role shift is not lost on members of humanitarian agencies, who experience a range of reactions from frustration to anger. In short, the reality does not often match the image, and this proves problematic.

Engaging Local Populations

Inconsistencies between image and reality undermine the message of consensual action in the case of Security Council deliberations and spoils cooperation between humanitarian aid workers and their military counterparts. In the same way, the actions of military and civilian peacekeepers in relation to the local population can undermine mission effectiveness. There is a broad range of activities individual peacekeepers participate in while they are on a mission that undercut what the mission is sent to accomplish, diminishing the symbolic capital of the institution as a whole.

From the very beginning, peacekeeping missions have had consequences for people in the deployment locations. These involve, for example, changes in patterns of social relations, as described by Marianne Heiberg in southern Lebanon and the elevation of land and rental prices, which benefits some members of society but hurts others, as took place in Nicaragua, Kosovo, Cairo, and in nearly every other mission.[31] Some of these effects are unfortunate or ill advised but do not necessarily affect the core of peacekeeping.

Other practices are frankly illegal and self-evidently harm both the people in the mission area and the institution of peacekeeping. They include cooperating with organized crime, trafficking people, the promotion of prostitution and sexual abuse, economic malfeasance, and careerism. Many of these activities have been discussed by others under the rubric of unintended consequences of peace operations. Especially since these activities are the focus of sustained analysis elsewhere, and because they are so blatantly outside of the frames that are entailed by the cultural model of peacekeeping, they are not the focus of my discussion here.[32] Rather, I will look at less clear-cut examples of the ways that peacekeeping missions interact with local peoples.

Missions that deploy to postconflict settings can take a variety of forms. They may involve a very small UN presence, or the may involve the United Nations assuming responsibility for all aspects of an interim administration, what is colloquially called "painting the country blue." United Nations involvement may fall anywhere along this spectrum.[33] Regardless of how deeply implicated the United Nations is in the transitional activities, the image of what the United Nations is doing rests on the perception that it will provide assistance to help reestablish local control and governance. Indeed, this is the way the international community talks about missions, and this is the image that pervades local expectations about what a mission will do.

Regardless of how extensive the United Nations presence is intended to be, the strategic intention is that the mission will support and enhance local capacities for self-government and self-determination.[34] This means engaging members of the local community and involving them in the work of postconflict reconstruction. Conflicts change societies in predictable and unpredictable ways. Among the predictable changes is the demolishing of the local economies, which leaves people with little work and few options for supporting themselves and their families. Often, many educated members of the community, and those who have experience in local governance, will have fled the conflict or been killed in it. Despite this, when peacekeeping missions enter an area they find highly capable individuals who have remained behind and who are dedicated to repairing their societies.

How the mission engages these people is critical to its ultimate success. The United Nations' projection of its root metaphor through its symbolic repertoire, represented in mission statements, mandates, and other activities, encourages people to see the peacekeeping missions as supporting self-determination and local action. As a result, local populations meet peacekeeping missions with high expectations. Those expectations lead them to see themselves as full partners with the United Nations and to assume that they will have significant roles in the reconstruction of their communities. In addition to decreases in violence that often accompany the introduction of peacekeeping missions to a conflict, this is one of the reasons that local populations often initially welcome peacekeepers enthusiastically.

Unfortunately, the track record of the international community in engaging local populations has not lived up to this promise. As a result, the initial enthusiasm that greeted nearly every peacekeeping mission turned to ambivalence, and at times outright hostility. Certainly, this trajectory of response can be observed in missions like those in Somalia, Kosovo, and East Timor.[35]

Just as the Holbrooke narrative of military-humanitarian cultural differences served as a lens for that domain, here I draw mainly on my interviews with staff from Kosovo to illustrate these areas. I recommend as well Katarina Ammitzboell's study of the economic consequences for local populations of peace operations and Jarat Chopra's account of the East Timor mission as places to further explore these issues.[36]

The deployment of the United Nations Mission in Kosovo (UNMIK) and the influx of other international agencies created demand for space, which distorted the property market in Kosovo. One of my interviewees explained that she paid nearly $1,000 a month for a one-bedroom apartment in Priština, three to five times the pre-intervention rates. This rent inflation exacerbated the housing shortage that had been created by the war. She observed that the rental market was so distorted that local families could not afford the rent and moved from the city. Others who owned homes chose to rent them for profit and live in extremely crowded conditions with relatives or to leave the city. Thus, even though they were living on the local economy the effect was to separate internationals from the local population. I think of this as an unfortunate consequence of postconflict realities.[37]

But the peacekeeping mission and other international agencies create a demand for local staff. To hire this staff, they offer salaries that are much larger than found in the local economy. This creates a much skewed set of incentives; professionals leave the local economy to work in nonprofessional roles for the peacekeeping mission. Doctors and professors, for example, take jobs as translators, drivers, and cleaners. As one interviewee put it, "Anyone who knew English and how to use a computer tries to be absorbed by the giant international machinery. There, a chauffeur earns a salary ten times higher than a university professor."

Although they benefit from the higher income thus generated, the local staff are placed into subordinate roles.[38] This creates at least three difficulties. First, there is a kind of internal brain drain, where accomplished members of the local community who might take leadership roles in the reestablishment of governance are placed outside of the consultative processes where they might make a contribution. This leads to the perception that self-determination is given mere lip service.

Second, not long after the first flush of relief at having a good income, local staff realize that in relation to their international colleagues, they are rather poorly compensated in salary and benefits. This creates a sense that they are second-class citizens, indeed as one interviewee put it, "the biggest source of irritation is the drastic difference in pay between local and international staff." Their sense of irrelevance is reinforced when they see that many of the international so-called experts brought into their community know very little about the local situation. This leads to the perception that "UNMIK is imposing foreign values on their political system, and they resent that the changes are not being generated from within their own society."

Third, they observe the divide between themselves and internationals plays out in every context. Where at roadblocks "UN and NGO vehicles drive to the front of the line to be waved through," locals are made to wait, sometimes for hours. My interviewees reported further that locals and internationals were treated differently in stores, restaurants, and all other venues.

Rather than changing the logic of political behavior, this contributes to reinforcing the belief that "power begins with control over economic assets, including opportunities for patronage through allocation of jobs." In other words, rather than being seen as delivering on the promises of the root metaphor that frames peacekeeping, the mission comes to be seen as a continuation of older and despised political patterns. And, as another interviewee put it, "there is a deep sentiment that the UN and INGOs [international nongovernmental organizations] form a secondary occupying force," hardly an image consistent with the strategic intent of the mission.

Earlier I described the importance of aligning individual motivation in peacekeeping with the root metaphor of the institution as implemented at the strategic level. I suggested that achieving this means that peacekeepers should act from a particular constellation of motivational states. Strategically aligned actions in peacekeeping derive from motivational states that are caring, other-focused, and active. This motivational stance links to larger strategic concerns derived from the root metaphor that frames the United Nations in general, and peacekeeping in particular. In engaging local populations, this stance would necessarily lead to structures and practices other than the ones now commonly seen in peacekeeping missions. Also, those practices lead local populations to question the interpretive frame that the cultural model of peacekeeping establishes.

From Peacekeeping to Peace Enforcement and Back Again

With the end of the Cold War, many local conflicts erupted that had been kept under control by the patronage of the United States or the Soviet Union, like those in the former Yugoslavia and in Somalia (see chapter 1). Several of these conflicts led to humanitarian crises or threatened to undermine regional security. With the idea that peacekeeping could take a more active role in addressing these conflicts, peacekeeping missions were authorized by the Security Council at a much faster pace than before. In addition to increasing its pace, the Council became more willing to authorize Chapter 7 missions, which allowed for the use of force to bring an end to a conflict.

Thus, the 1990s saw peace operations deployed more frequently than they were in the prior forty years. These missions are often described as more complex than earlier interpositional peacekeeping operations. Yet many of the complexities faced by recent peace operations can be seen in earlier operations.[39] The existence of these complexities was masked by the apparent simplicity of those missions and by a relative lack of attention being paid by the international security community to local-level concerns.[40] Contemporary peacekeeping involves a variety of activities, although as I have shown in this book, these activities are not new to the institution. They include interpositional peacekeeping, using various degrees of force to bring parties to a ceasefire (peace enforcement), delivering humanitarian aid, and intervening in collapsed states to help administer society.

Within these kinds of efforts is the need to manage multiple "pillars" of peacekeeping, which include the development of political authority and civil administration, the establishment of policing capabilities and judicial systems, economic development, and the ensuring of security. These pillars had traditionally been relatively disconnected from one another, but beginning in the 1990s there were concerted efforts to design systems for managing them in a coherent way. The push for civil-military relations, discussed above, is one result of those efforts; a variety of policy studies on harmonization and peace maintenance are other manifestations of these efforts, as is the current discussion of integrated missions.[41]

Other results of these activities were interventions in failed states. These interventions involved military force to end fighting or to support the delivery of humanitarian aid. The missions undertaken in Somalia, Rwanda, Yugoslavia, and East Timor are emblematic of these new missions. As well as using force, sometimes the peacekeeping forces were asked to transition from Chapter 7 to Chapter 6 kinds of missions. This shift was often difficult, even more so when the missions had to return to Chapter 7 status.

As a result, more recent interventions have had mixed results, and there has been a lot of study given to why they have been disappointing, as the United Nations, national governments, and NGOs have conducted lessons-learned analyses. Accounts include a combination of various considerations: lack of political will, under-financing of missions, insufficient force, poor logistics and coordination, and mission creep, to name a few. Each of these plays a role in creating conditions under which peace operations do not work as well as they might.[42]

However, in my view, to fully understand why these blended missions are often disappointing requires an appreciation of how these operations have lost much of their culturally constituted and symbolically achieved power. Simply put, the cultural inversions that peacekeeping depends on have been destabilized.

Legitimacy and Cultural Inversion in Peacekeeping

The development of peacekeeping as cultural practices, symbols, and other cultural materials was entailed by, and in turn supported by, root metaphors about a new, cooperative, pacific world order. Symbols and metaphors are ambiguous, in that they support many meanings. Symbols, rituals, and metaphors are all examples of polysemic cultural phenomena. However, while they support many meanings, they will not support *any* meaning. I think that an important reason why peacekeeping is in trouble is that new missions have too often worked outside of the core meanings of the symbols of peacekeeping. They have come close to, if not crossed, the edge of what the root metaphor can support.

Drawing again on the model of reversals in peacekeeping developed in chapter 3, table 8.1 (see p. 138) describes the current situation.

These destabilizing actions collapse the space for alternative political representation by allowing cultural inversions and psychological reversals to revert to more usual states. In this confused environment, peace operations may create the opportunity for various business-as-usual practices to develop. These include various economic distortions (like the development of a two-tiered economy where internationals live extravagantly while local populations struggle financially), crime and prostitution, and the closing of humanitarian space.[43]

Table 8.1: Destabilized Cultural Inversions of Peacekeeping

Traditional Military: Business as Usual	Contemporary Peacekeeping: Confusion Reigns
No foreign troops on sovereign soil	Other countries' troops on sovereign soil
Separate from potential adversaries	Fight against and work with potential adversaries
Retain national command of troops	Commanding officer from other country, but also command by national capitals
Stealth and surprise	Stealth and surprise with occasional transparency of action
No contact with civilians	Contact with some but not other civilians; unclear lines of cooperation with civilian organizations
Use of war-fighting skills	Use of war-fighting and negotiation skills
Victory through force	Use of force and pacific means
Strictly observe prerogatives of rank	Unity of command stressed

Adapted from Rubinstein 2005, 537.

Destabilization of the cultural inversions upon which peacekeeping depends affects every level of organization—from the broad macrolevel to the local level, where it is particularly important. In addition to shifting peace-keepers' motivational energy, and the local populations notice the disconnect between image and reality. As with my earlier description of how important small symbolic differences were to military peacekeepers, the objection might be made that local populations do not really distinguish among peacekeepers. I described how in Kosovo the local population reacted negatively to the international presence as a result of this disconnect. Addressing the importance of how components of a mission act, Lews Sida noted that in their reactions to international work that "many [Liberians] had an idea of the work of NGOs and the UN and often made sophisticated distinctions."[44] Similarly, Mersiades observed that the fortunes of the United Nations' missions in Cambodia and Somalia depended upon local perceptions of legitimacy.[45]

My claim in this book is that cultural considerations affect all levels of peacekeeping, including the most microlevel interactions on the ground and the most macrolevel interactions in the international community. By applying anthropological methods and analyses, we have seen how interactions of relatively limited scope at each level of organization have started to destabilize the basic cultural inversion from which peacekeeping developed its legitimacy and accrued its symbolic capital. This destabilization has contributed to a further difficulty for United Nations peacekeeping. Throughout the early decades of its organizational life, the United Nations was identified with the drive to promote self-determination among peoples who were living under colonial rule at the end of World War II. The United Nations led the decolonization effort, which was in most cases directly against the self-interests of the major powers. Thus, the decolonization work was consistent with and reinforced the root metaphor upon which the United Nations' moral legitimacy depended.

An additional challenge is introduced when the changes within the Security Council and the organization itself following the Cold War intersect with the increase in the number of missions in which the United Nations is charged with administering and rebuilding nations. The rhetoric of self-determination is still powerful and valued. A normative response has been to try to establish Western-style governance institutions in societies devastated by conflict. These governance structures include free and fair elections, judical and policing systems, and standards for economic development, for instance.

The result of this is that postconflict societies are treated as though they are blank slates upon which the international community can inscribe these Western-style governance structures. But approaching a society as though its traditional understandings of how people should interact with one another and the structures that they view as legitimate for governing their collectivities either no longer exist or are no longer important does not make it so. In fact, as I pointed out earlier in this book, traditional understandings persist, and inconsistency between these and the governance structures that peacekeeping missions are implementing undermines the mission. An illustration of this comes from the East Timor, where UNAMET had extensive responsibilities for administering the country. In its efforts to establish a judicial system, UNAMET applied a Western-style legal system. Engagement with the already existing indigenous conception of justice was ad hoc at best. In relation to one area where the indigenous and imported systems clashed, Hohe notes: "In western criminal law, the perpetrator is accused by the state, and the prosecutor acts on behalf of the population. Here a victim becomes a pure witness. In the indigenous law, however, offenses are a matter between the families involved (except for the theft of public goods). The victim is on one side of the conflict and expects to be reimbursed."[46] The differences between these conceptions of justice have implications for the kinds of resolutions accepted as legitimate by the local population (reconciliation versus punishment), the nature of legal interpreters (impartial judges versus elders of the socially implicated families), and even what counts as an offense requiring state intervention.

The effect is more than just the undermining of the work of a particular mission. The privileging of Western-style governance structures and of Western understandings of political authority and legitimacy over those of local populations reproduces the earlier colonial relations that the United Nations did so much to end. This cultural imperialism presents a challenge for those whose job it is to plan missions, since to ignore it is to reproduce patterns of dominance and disenfranchisement that undermine not only particular missions but the United Nations in general. In their planning they need to highlight how a mission will seriously and respectfully engage local structures and understandings. This needs to be done even before a mission is deployed, or that engagement will be ad hoc and inadequate. These are issues of power and identity that communicate to local populations, and more broadly they are the kinds of issues with which anthropological analyses of culture can be uniquely helpful.[47]

To see that culture, as a symbolic system of meaning and extension of root metaphors, is at play in contemporary peace operations, one needs only to listen to the voices of those people creating, implementing, and experiencing peacekeeping. In that listening, we discover that much of what is communicated is inconsistent with the basic metaphor that allowed peacekeeping's symbolic capital to accrue. Once that frame has been broken by a peacekeeping mission, local populations reinterpret the way they understand the mission. Abandoning the frame of a possible new world of pacific relations for the more traditional power politics frame allows local populations to move the mission from a welcome agent of the world community to an unwelcome colonial agent.[48] In short, destabilizing the long-standing peacekeeping root metaphor damages the institution at all levels of social organization.

9

Intervention as Cultural Practice

The founding of the United Nations at the end of World War II was, among other things, an act of idealism. That idealism was given concrete form in the organization's charter, and soon thereafter in the Universal Declaration of Human Rights. Despite the rift that soon developed between the East and the West, the United Nations continued to embody that idealism through the decades following its establishment. United Nations specialized agencies and programs gave concrete form to this idealism. The World Health Organization made tremendous strides in improving the health of all people, greatly reducing—and in the case of smallpox, eliminating—the threat of infectious diseases, which had before the war condemned millions of people to a lifetime of crippling disfigurement or death. The United Nations International Children's Emergency Fund—established in 1946 and made permanent in 1953—led the world in promoting children's health, education, and well-being. The United Nations also played a critical role in promoting self-determination and decolonization.

The United Nations gained considerable moral authority as it put into practice through international cooperation the vision of a world freed from war and pestilence. Although this altruistic image was never the full story, the influence of the United Nations expanded, and the organization accrued considerable symbolic capital. Its work embodied a wide-reaching cultural inversion and formed the root metaphor organizing the institution's activities. Its flag, the blue color associated with it, the UNICEF donation box, and other symbols, each associated with a part of the institution, came to represent the United Nations as a whole.

Peacekeeping was introduced in this climate of world opinion. The use of military personnel to carry out nonmilitary functions became one of its hallmarks. Military personnel were called upon because they were available, not by design. As well, many of the ways peacekeepers carried out their tasks developed more by accident than by design. Nonetheless, as these ways of doing things were repeated by different peacekeepers taking up their assignments in different places, these patterns of activity took on meanings independent of their origins. They became cultural practices, and like all cultural practice they came to symbolize a deeper web of meanings.

Most of the practices incorporated symbols and activities from other domains of military and political life, but the meanings attached to those symbols and activities were extended and altered. Soon, when used in the context of United Nations peacekeeping, the traditional military symbols and activities came to represent setting aside politics as usual and allowing peacekeepers to do things that they ordinarily would not. Thus, almost by accident, the cultural practice of peacekeeping became linked to the root metaphor, making it manifest in the many cultural inversions that reinforced peacekeeping's moral authority.

From its very beginning, peacekeeping engaged the efforts of more than just military personnel. Various practical difficulties arose in the interactions that took place among military peacekeepers, international civil servants, and NGO personnel, but these were submerged under the general image of peacekeeping as being a soldier's duty. This image was reinforced by assertions like this one, by Dag Hammarskjöld: "Peacekeeping is not a job for soldiers, but only a soldier can do it."[1]

This assertion was often interpreted as meaning that peacekeeping requires certain kinds of technical knowledge and combat-related skills that only military personnel have. For instance, impartially and accurately identifying the source of shelling, the kinds of munitions being used, and troop movements all require such technical expertise. But, in principle, there is no reason that civilians could not be trained to competently deal with the practicalities of the job of peacekeeping. Yet, as W. H. Auden observed in his foreword to Hammarskjöld's posthumously published journals, Hammarskjöld was a deeply spiritual individual attuned to the symbolic and religious aspects of life.[2] It is not too much to think that in making his famous pronouncement that Hammarskjöld was also sensitive to and referencing the power of the cultural inversion of using soldiers for nonmilitary purposes.

In any event, the more peacekeeping missions were deployed, the stronger this image became, and their symbolic capital also multiplied. Prior to the 1990s, some aspects of particular missions were out of harmony with the inversion, as when UN forces became embroiled in fighting in the Congo and when the UNEF's withdrawal precipitated war between Israel and Egypt and their neighbors. At these times, peacekeeping's symbolic capital diminished somewhat, but, like the stock market, the general trend was dependably upward. So it was that in 1988 their symbolic capital was so high that peace operations were collectively awarded the Nobel Peace Prize.

From the 1990s forward, peacekeeping has been used much more frequently than it had been before. Some of the tensions that had always been present in peacekeeping, but had been enacted out of public view, soon moved to the forefront. As a result, images of peacekeeping stretched, and soon this instrument of international action was contorted into a nearly unrecognizable shape.

Peacekeeping is an act of intervention, and like all interventions it involves claims about legitimacy, standing, and authority that are socially constructed and culturally mediated. In peace operations, the intervention maintains a perspective on the conflict—most often, an interest in stopping violence, establishing a climate of human rights, and facilitating self-determination. Throughout a mission, and at all levels of action, there will be assertions of legitimacy (what actions are appropriate); standing (who has the appropriate status to carry out those actions); and authority (who has the power to intervene). These are based on international law or other international instruments. But also they are supported by less formal, culturally guided understandings, about which anthropological analysis can be quite illuminating. This is true within the operation and for the interaction of a mission with local populations. Cultural considerations must be a priority for peacekeeping to be effective.

Cultural considerations involve more than looking at the surface aspects of cultural difference. Image, expectation, and reputation play important roles in all intervention. As Marshal Sahlins put it, "In all its dimensions, including the social and the material, human existence is symbolically constituted, which is to say, culturally ordered."[3]

This is especially true for peacekeeping, which depends heavily on cultural inversions for the maintenance of its core meanings. Lack of attention to culture and meaning in peacekeeping is both unwise and dangerous. As I indicated earlier, resistance to incorporating cultural processes in international affairs analysis has a long history. In part, this is because culture and cultural processes are frustratingly impermanent and contingent. Yet in other areas of social life we are not so reticent about basing judgments on such nontangible and contingent considerations. In estimating economic cycles, for instance, much credence is given to consumer confidence as a basis for economic actions. This is not because it is an empirical indicator of the strength of an economy but because it has become a symbolic artifact that translates into real actions on the part of consumers and investors.

In the same way, "peacekeeping confidence" translates into real actions on the ground by local populations and by mission participants. To ensure that this confidence develops and is well placed, there must be consistency between the high-level strategic goals of peacekeeping missions and their enactment at every level, including interactions between individual peacekeepers and others in the area of operation. The strategic scaffolding is important for both the practice of peacekeeping and the maintenance of its symbolic capital. For these reasons, we must develop processes for ensuring that an understanding of culture as a dynamic meaning-producing system is incorporated into the planning and implementation of future peacekeeping missions. This requires recognizing that missions must be organized to support the inversions that link them to the root metaphor from which peacekeeping derives its standing, legitimacy, and authority. In situations where this link cannot be made, operations should be clearly designated and marked as something other than peacekeeping.

The implications of this position are far-reaching, and they reinforce some of those arrived at by other avenues of analysis. The need for international intervention is not likely to diminish in the foreseeable future. Indeed, high-level study panels reinforce the international community's commitment to intervening in crises in which civilian populations are threatened by violence or humanitarian need.[4] That many of these crises take place within states rather than between them is also a feature that is likely to endure well into the century.

Effective interventions in these contexts must take cultural forms that are meaningful and legitimate. There are at least two reasons for this, the first having to do with the violation of sovereignty, the second with the need to create the conditions necessary for peacekeepers and humanitarian actors to work effectively.

International interventions that use force and take place without the consent of the sovereign states within which they are deployed will continue to be a feature of international life. As envisioned in the United Nations Charter, some war-making activities undertaken with the consent of the international community may be necessary. Yet, because such intervention can easily be driven by political self-interests on the part of the interveners, great care has to be taken that the interventions be vested with the legitimacy that results only from United Nations auspices. Because of the dominance of US military power, and because Security Council veto power is held by an anachronistic selection of nations, simply having the United Nations imprimatur on an action is not enough. Rather, confidence needs to be renewed that the Council's actions result from real consensual processes.

Certainly, rebalancing the membership of the Security Council could play an important role in achieving this. But there are few observers who are very sanguine about the possibility that Security Council membership will change significantly any time soon. Also, as I have shown, a change in Council membership will not itself assure the popular perception that Council actions really are joint and consensual. For that, there needs to be a revision in the cultural practices of the Council so that each of its acts renews the popular embrace of its authority. This can only be done by performing its consultations in ways that are more public and recognizable by all as acts of consensus building.

In this sense, the renewal of the Council and, by extension, the legitimacy of peacekeeping depends on recognizing the ritual aspects of the United Nations. As well, it means being vigilant that the actions of the Secretariat and UN specialized agencies and programs comport with the root metaphors on which the organization is built. In short, it requires a re-embrace of the understanding that the legitimacy of UN actions, peacekeeping included, derive from the moral power invested in the organization.[5]

Without such a renewal of respect for the moral and performative dimensions of the United Nations, peacekeeping can too easily be seen as a cynical political exercise controlled by the United States and other world powers. The power of cultural practice to constitute such a renewal is critical.[6]

A high priority must be placed on restabilizing the cultural inversions that support peacekeeping so that missions do not continue to founder and peacekeepers do not continue to be placed in greater risk than they would be otherwise. This is because, like humanitarian space, the actions of peacekeepers are wrapped in the moral authority that the cultural inversions create. Peacekeeping will lose its meaning if image and reality in peace operations continue to diverge. Since some interventions undertaken by the United Nations will require the use of force, it becomes important too that those interventions be marked and symbolized to differentiate them from peacekeeping operations. These expeditionary forces ought not use the same symbolic artifacts as do peacekeeping forces. These artifacts must be strikingly different than those used by peacekeepers.

In thinking about this claim, I often return to the analogy between peacekeeping and policing. Police who patrol a beat are uniformed and outfitted differently than are their colleagues who participate in special weapons and tactics (SWAT) teams. Everyone recognizes the differences between them, both in terms of what they do and in terms of their standing authority and legitimacy. In the same way, peacekeeping forces and observer groups should be demarcated from expeditionary forces by the use of distinct symbolism.

Although arriving at them through different avenues, various studies, such as the *Report of the Panel on United Nations Peace Operations*, have proposed ways of revising peacekeeping practices that would make such desirable symbolic revisions possible.[7] Similarly, work done in the 1990s to design harmonized missions and efforts now underway to figure out how to make integrated missions possible can contribute to this process of symbolic revision. Thus, for instance, the conclusion that in integrated missions control is best vested in civilian authorities.[8]

In a sense, since peacekeeping is just one aspect of the organization, many of the challenges facing it are a subset of those facing the United Nations as a whole. As in any group, people hold competing and conflicting cultural models of it. One identifies the United Nations as serving merely as an extension of national political self-interest. The other identifies it as the embodiment of international interdependence. This tension is not new. In 1960, Dag Hammarskjöld called attention to these two models, which entail distinctly different futures for the United Nations and for the world community. He clearly preferred the model in which the United Nations actively moves the world community toward acknowledging, engaging, and enacting its interdependence.

Throughout the early history of peacekeeping this was the normatively embraced model of the United Nations. Peacekeeping practices developed as ways of enacting this model, and they derived legitimacy from it. I have not argued in this book that peacekeeping should be only a matter of observation and postconflict separation of forces, although these surely will continue to have a role in peace operations. Rather, I have endeavored to show that individual actions in peace operations and symbolism matter. There is considerable wisdom in the view that the ways we accomplish our goals matter, as do the goals themselves. As David Last has suggested, the boundary between peacekeeping and imperial policing is thin and permeable.[9] Many of the activities of the former are seen in the latter, so part of what distinguishes them from one another is the strategic vision they serve. This is why strategic scaffolding, a linkage and consistency between levels of action, is so important. For this reason, altering peacekeeping so that expeditionary force becomes one of its main features is likely to continue to diminish it as an instrument of international action. In relation to attaining peace, it is worth recalling Ralph Bunche's observation that war is not a true avenue to peace: "To suggest that war can prevent war is a base play on words and a despicable form of warmongering. The objective of any who sincerely believe in peace clearly must be to exhaust every honourable recourse in the effort to save the peace. The world has had ample evidence that war begets only conditions which beget further war."[10]

People are more sensitive to subtle symbolic differences than is often acknowledged in discussions of international affairs. It is essential that peacekeeping be recognized as cultural practice. That recognition should be an adjunct to ordinary considerations of politics, economics, and logistics, and it should focus on the broad cultural context in which peacekeeping is embedded. Only then will peacekeeping be able to fulfill its promise as a significant and meaningful instrument of international action.

Notes

Chapter 1

1. In this respect, the box was a particular kind of symbol in which one part of a thing represents the whole and evokes the totality from which it derives. It also evokes a complex set of cognitive and affective understandings. National flags are a good example of this class of political symbols. For a discussion of political symbolism, see Kertzer 1988 *Ritual, Politics, and Power*.

2. See accounts of this jockeying, and the geopolitical considerations in the formation of the United Nations, in Schlesinger 2003 *Act of Creation: The Founding of the United Nations: A Story of Superpowers, Secret Agents, Wartime Allies and Enemies, and Their Quest for a Peaceful World*; Urquhart 1987 *A Life in Peace and War*; and Urquhart 1993 *Ralph Bunche: An American Odyssey*.

3. Shortly after the United Nations was founded, the Cold War brought politics-as-usual back into play. The organization of the Secretariat and of the UN agencies rapidly got caught up in the Cold War. Many have suggested that this diminished the UN's capacity for action during its first forty or so years. I suggest later that the apparently negative aspects of this competition actually promoted the UN's work, at least in relation to peacekeeping.

4. Concerning WHO efforts on the eradication of smallpox, see Fenner 1989 *Smallpox and Its Eradication*; and Hopkins 1989 *The Eradication of Smallpox: Organizational Learning and Innovation in International Health*.

5. See Aarvik 1997 "The Nobel Peace Prize 1988, presentation speech by Egil Aarvik."

6. Of course, the UNICEF box still exists and is promoted by the agency. Information about the boxes can be found at http://www.unicefusa.org. I do not think that my experience of the disappearing UNICEF box is unique. An informal survey among colleagues and random "people on the street" suggests that it is widely shared.

7. Whitman 1998 "The UN specialized agencies, peacekeeping and the enactment of values," *International Peacekeeping*, 120.

8. For instance, see George W. Bush's statements in the debates during the presidential race in 2000, transcripts of which are available from the Commission on Presidential Debates, http://www.debates.org/index.html. See also, Rothschild 2003 "Bush trashes the United Nations."

147

9. See, for example, Bateson 1988 "Compromise and the rhetoric of good and evil."

10. See, for example, McClelland 1960 *The United Nations: The Continuing Debate*.

11. For more on the Somali situation and the international community's response to it, consult Hirsch and Oakley 1995 *Somalia and Operation Restore Hope: Reflections on Peacemaking and Peacekeeping*; Makinda 1993 *Seeking Peace from Chaos: Humanitarian Intervention in Somalia*; Sahnoun 1994 *Somalia: The Missed Opportunities*; and Simons 1995 *Networks of Dissolution: Somalia Undone*.

12. See, for example, the assessment in Urquhart 1989 *Decolonization and World Peace*.

13. Boutros-Ghali 1992 *An Agenda for Peace: Preventive Diplomacy, Peacemaking and Peace-Keeping*.

14. The term "failed state" is itself problematic as it raises a variety of ethnocentric and neocolonial issues. It is noteworthy that the term was articulated by the "developed world" as a way of describing places that did not conform to what it expected of them. Indeed, critics of the term suggest that the discourse of failed states is a cynical rhetoric that privileges power and allows the promotion of imperialist adventures, especially on the part of the West. See, for example, Chomsky 2006 *Failed States: The Abuse of Power and the Assault on Democracy*. Others have used the term to develop systematic indices of the relative standing of countries as failed states, thus creating a political tool for holding all states, including developed ones, to a common set of standards. See the Failed States Index, published by *Foreign Policy* magazine, http://www.fundforpeace.org/web.

15. Sahnoun 1994.

16. For documentary materials relating to the Somalia missions, see United Nations 1996b *United Nations and Somalia, 1992–1996*.

17. Durch 1996 "Introduction to anarchy: humanitarian intervention and 'state-building' in Somalia."

18. Not all analysts agree that the Somalia engagement was a failure. While some see in it missed opportunities, others view it as relatively successful, under the circumstances. See Hirsch and Oakley 1995, Sahnoun 1994.

19. Potential difficulties and challenges presented by such "dual command" affect all combined and joint military operations and have been evident in nearly all peacekeeping operations.

20. Bercuson 1996 *Significant Incident: Canada's Army, the Airborne, and the Murder in Somalia*.

21. The argument of these analysts is not limited to the events in Somalia, but treats the entire enterprise of peacekeeping as a kind of racist new imperialism. See, for instance, Razack 2004 *Dark Threats and White Knights: The Somalia Affair, Peacekeeping and the New Imperialism*.

22. The Commission's report was published in Somalia Commission of Inquiry 1997 *Dishonoured Legacy: The Lessons of the Somalia Affair. Final Report of the Commission of Inquiry into the Deployment of Canadian Forces to Somalia*, http://www.dnd.ca/somalia/somaliae.htm.

23. For example, Bercuson 1996, Winslow 1997 *The Canadian Airborne Regiment in Somalia: A Socio-cultural Inquiry*.

24. Details of this mission can be found in Bowden 1999 *Black Hawk Down: A Story of Modern War.*

25. Secretary Christopher's remarks were reported in Richburg 1993 "Somalia battle killed 12 Americans, wounded 78."

26. See, Mackinlay and Chopra 1993 *A Draft Concept of Second Generation Multinational Operations.*

27. On the use of force in UN operations, see Findlay 2002 *The Use of Force in UN Peace Operations*; Goulding 1996 "The use of force by the United Nations"; Picco 1994 "The U.N. and the use of force: leave the secretary general out of it"; Pugh 1996 *The UN, Peace and Force*; and Sanderson 1998 "The incalculable dynamic of using force."

28. On financing, see McDermott 1999 "Japan's financial contribution to the UN system: in pursuit of acceptance and standing"; Schoettle 1993 "Financing UN peacekeeping."

29. On law and order, see Chandler 2004 "Imposing the 'rule of law': the lessons of BiH for peacebuilding in Iraq"; Costa 1995 "The United Nations and reform of the police in El Salvador"; Holm and Eide 2000 *Peacebuilding and Police Reform*; Oakley, Dziedzic, and Goldberg 1998 *Policing the New World Disorder: Peace Operations and Public Security*; Perito 2004 *Where Is the Lone Ranger When We Need Him? America's Search for a Postconflict Stability Force*; and Plunkett 1998 "Reestablishing law and order in peace-maintenance."

30. On coordination, see Abiew and Keating 1999 "NGOs and UN peacekeeping operations: strange bedfellows"; Donini 1996 "Asserting humanitarianism in peace-maintenance"; Eide, Kaspersen, Kent, and von Hipple 2005 *Report on Integrated Missions: Practical Perspectives and Recommendations. Independent Study of the Expanded UN ECHA Core Group*; Joint Warfighting Center 1997 *Joint Task Force Commander's Handbook for Peace Operations*; Rubinstein 2003a "Cross-cultural considerations in complex peace operations"; Slim 1996 "The stretcher and the drum: civil-military relations in peace support operations"; and Weiss 1995 "Military-civilian humanitarianism: the 'age of innocence' is over."

31. On information campaigns, see Avruch, Narel, and Siegel 1999 *Information Campaigns for Peace Operations*; Lehmann 1999 *Peacekeeping and Public Information*; and Lindley 2004 "Untapped power? the status of UN information operations."

32. On the United Nations, see Chayes, Chayes, and Raach 1997 "Beyond reform: restructuring for more effective conflict intervention"; Ciechanski 1994 "Restructuring the UN Security Council"; Eide, Kaspersen, Kent and von Hipple 2005; and Thakur 2003 "Reforming the United Nations."

33. For an example, see Donald 2002 "Neutrality, impartiality and UN peacekeeping at the beginning of the 21st century."

34. On conflict resolution, see Druckman, Wall, and Diehl 1999 "Conflict resolution roles in international peacekeeping missions"; Leeds 2001 "Culture, conflict resolution, peacekeeper training and the D mediator"; and Woodhouse and Ramsbotham 2000 *Peacekeeping and Conflict Resolution.*

35. On sovereignty, see Heiberg 1994 *Subduing Sovereignty: Sovereignty and the Right to Intervene*, and International Commission on Intervention and State Sovereignty 2001 *The Responsibility to Protect: Report of the International Commission on Intervention and State Sovereignty.*

36. Heiberg 1990 "Peacekeepers and local populations: some comments on UNI-FIL"; Heiberg and Holst 1986 "Peacekeeping in Lebanon: comparing UNIFIL and the MNF"; Rubinstein 1989 "Culture, international affairs and peacekeeping: confusing process and pattern"; Rubinstein 1993 "Cultural aspects of peacekeeping: notes on the substance of symbols."

37. See, for instance, Chopra 2000 "The UN's kingdom of East Timor"; Chopra and Hohe 2004 "Participatory intervention"; Duffey 2000 "Cultural issues in contemporary peacekeeping"; and Hohe 2002a "Clash of paradigms: international administration and local political legitimacy in East Timor."

38. A sampling of this activity can be found in Hajjar 2006 "The Army's new TRA-DOC Culture Center"; McFarland 2005 "Military cultural education"; Selmeski 1997 *Military Cross-Cultural Competence: Core Concepts and Individual Development*; Varhola 2004 "The US military in Iraq: are we our own worst enemy?"; and Varhola and Varhola 2006 "Avoiding the cookie-cutter approach to culture: lessons learned from operations in East Africa."

39. For instance, Spicer 1967 *Human Problems in Technological Change.*

40. Winslow 1997, Duffey 2000.

41. Ghosh 1994 "The global reservation: notes toward an ethnography of international peacekeeping."

42. Segal 2001 "Is a peacekeeping culture emerging among American infantry in the Sinai MFO?," and Segal and Segal 1993 *Peacekeepers and Their Wives: American Participation in the Multinational Force and Observers.*

43. Information regarding the "Iraq Culture Smart Card" is available from the Marine Corps Intelligence Activity, Quality and Dissemination Branch, 3300 Russell Road, Suite 250, Quantico, VA 22134-5011. Regarding the Japanese advice, see Yamaguchi 2004 "Japan urges soldiers in Iraq to grow mustaches, bans pork and alcohol."

44. The importance of a multilevel view of human activity is demonstrated in Rubinstein, Laughlin, and McManus 1984 *Science as Cognitive Process: Toward an Empirical Philosophy of Science*, 93, where it is called the "rule of minimal inclusion."

45. I have discussed theoretical scaffolding elsewhere as well. See, for instance, Rubinstein, Laughlin, and McManus 1984; Rubinstein and Tax 1985 "Power, powerlessness, and the failure of 'political realism.'"

46. See Rubinstein 1992 "Culture and negotiation."

47. See, for example, Rubinstein 1986 "The collapse of strategy: understanding ideological bias in policy decisions"; Rubinstein 1988 "Cultural analysis and international security"; Rubinstein and Tax 1985.

48. In a sense, this book is an answer to the observation that much of the peacekeeping literature is too focused on solving immediate practical or policy problems and is thus divorced from larger discussions in international relations. See Paris 2000 "Broadening the study of peace operations."

49. I discuss symbolic inversion in greater detail in chapter 3. Here it is sufficient to note that a symbolic or cultural inversion involves a reversal in which doing or saying things that would ordinarily not be permitted in a society are not only allowed but positively valued. In the United States, the holiday of Halloween is such

an inversion. Normally children who disguised their identity and extorted goods (treats) from people by threatening to do them harm (tricks) would be subject to arrest. However, during Halloween such behavior is allowed and even promoted.

Chapter 2

1. Participation in the truce was induced by the Security Council's reference to the United Nations Charter Chapter VII that provides for the possibility of the use of military force to enforce the peace. See Security Council Resolution 50, 29 May 1948, S/801, http://www.un.org/documents/sc/res/1948/scres48.htm. As well, some trace the origins of United Nations peacekeeping to the 1947 United Nations Special Commission on the Balkans. The Commission, however, while a form of peace observation, differed in many ways, and significantly, from the pattern of United Nations peacekeeping missions. These differences range from the manner in which the Commission was established and staffed to its methods of operation in the field. See Nachmani 1990 *International Intervention in the Greek Civil War: The United Nations Special Committee on the Balkans, 1947–1953* and Rikhye, Harbottle, and Bjorn 1974 *The Thin Blue Line: International Peacekeeping and Its Future.* For that reason, UNTSO is conventionally accepted as the first United Nations peacekeeping mission.

2. Urquhart 1987 *A Life in Peace and War,* 115. In fact, from 1920 to 1936 the League of Nations had sponsored about a dozen missions that could be said to fall into the category of peace observation. See Wainhouse 1966 *International Peace Observation: A History and Forecast.* So the instrument developed by the United Nations had some antecedents in international politics.

3. Urquhart 1993 *Ralph Bunche: An American Odyssey.*

4. See, for example, Chopra 1999 *Peace-Maintenance: The Evolution of International Political Authority*; Durch 1996 "Introduction to anarchy: humanitarian intervention and 'state-building' in Somalia"; Durch 2007 *Twenty-first-Century Peace Operations*; Fetherston 1994 *Towards a Theory of United Nations Peacekeeping*; Harbottle 1970 *The Impartial Soldier*; Hillen 1998 *Blue Helmets: The Strategy of UN Military Operations*; International Peace Academy 1984 *Peacekeeper's Handbook*; Rikhye 1984 *The Theory and Practice of Peacekeeping*; Rikhye, Harbottle, and Bjorn 1974; Urquhart 1987; Urquhart 1993; Verrier 1981 *International Peacekeeping: United Nations Forces in a Troubled World.*

5. Rikhye 1984, 1–2. This was also the definition adopted by the Joint Nordic Committee for Military UN Matters 1986 *Nordic UN Stand-by Forces.* The focus of the International Peace Academy has broadened since the 1990s. The current mission statement on the IPA's website (http://www.ipacademy.org/) says, "IPA is an independent, international institution dedicated to promoting the prevention and settlement of armed conflicts between and within states through policy research and development."

6. United Nations 1996a *The Blue Helmets. A Review of United Nations Peace-Keeping,* v–vi.

7. United Nations 1996a.

8. United Nations 1996a, 173–99; Rikhye 1984, 81–89.

9. See Urquhart 1987 and O'Brien 1962 *To Katanga and Back: A UN Case History* for somewhat contrasting descriptions of the ONUC mission and its problems.

10. On the evolution of the use of force in peacekeeping operations, see Findlay 2002 *The Use of Force in UN Peace Operations*.

11. The Congo episode, including the murder of Patrice Lumumba, is a complex one. The narrative given here is not intended to describe the situation and its complexity. It is rather to highlight in summary fashion the difficulties that this situation presented for peacekeeping. For fuller accounts of the Congo's colonial history and independence, see Dayal 1976 *Mission for Hammarskjöld: The Congo Crisis*; Hochschild 1998 *King Leopold's Ghost: A Story of Greed, Terror, and Heroism in Colonial Africa*; and Nzongola-Ntalaja 2002 *The Congo from Leopold to Kabila: A People's History*.

12. For example, see Urquhart 1987, 153.

13. DeWitte 2001 *The Assassination of Lumumba*.

14. Urquhart 1993.

15. The Congo mission also affected the United Nations as a whole. Swedish diplomat Dag Hammarskjöld had been elected secretary-general of the United Nations in 1953, a post to which he was reelected in 1957. Hammarskjöld was dedicated to the international ideals of the United Nations and to the idea of an international civil service following the principles of independence, integrity, and impartiality. And he was a skilled and accomplished negotiator who proved enormously effective in shaping the United Nations. In September 1961, Hammarskjöld died in a plane crash in the Congo as he was traveling from Leopoldville to Katanga for a meeting to address fighting involving UN troops. For his selfless service to humanity and his shaping of the United Nations, Hammarskjöld was posthumously awarded the 1961 Nobel Peace Prize. The biographical statement accompanying his award notes that he developed "procedures and tactics new to the UN—the use of the UNEF, employment of a UN 'presence' in world trouble spots and a steadily growing tendency to make the Secretary-General the executive for operations for peace," http://nobelprize.org/nobel_prizes/peace/laureates/1961/hammarskjold-bio.html.

16. On the history and development of UNEF see, Rikhye 1978 *The Sinai Blunder: Withdrawal of the United Nations Emergency Force Leading to the Six Day War, June 1967*; Rikhye, Harbottle, and Bjorn 1974; Urquhart 1987; and Urquhart 1993.

17. I use the terms "symbolic capital" and "political capital" after Bourdieu, but my use of these terms does not conform strictly to his development of them. See especially chapter 7 of Bourdieu 1990 *The Logic of Practice*.

18. Burmese diplomat U Thant was appointed by the unanimous vote of the General Assembly as acting secretary-general to fill the time remaining in Dag Hammarskjöld's term. He was subsequently elected to two full terms as secretary-general.

19. Rikhye, Harbottle, and Bjorn 1974, 47–70.

20. Many others disagreed with this course of action, and it was a matter of public debate and derision. As discussed in Rikhye 1978, those who held the counterview that international forces could not be deployed at the pleasure of a national government cited an aide-mémoire written by Dag Hammarskjöld that they argued recorded that President Nasser had agreed that the force would remain until its

mission was accomplished, and thus had effectively ceded Egypt's right to dismiss the force. U Thant disagreed with that interpretation.

21. On the timing of the Sinai withdrawal and the diplomatic maneuvering surrounding it, see Rikhye 1978, especially chapters 2–6.

22. Rikhye 1978.

23. See Rikhye 1978 and Urquhart 1987, 209–16.

24. See Pelcovits 1984 *Peacekeeping on the Arab-Israeli Fronts: Lessons from Sinai and Lebanon*, 5.

25. Urquhart 1990 "Reflections by the chairman," 18.

26. See International Peace Academy 1984; Joint Nordic Committee for Military UN Matters 1986.

27. For instance, see O'Brien 1962, and Dayal 1976 concerning the mission in the Congo, Rikhye 1978 regarding the withdrawal of UNEF I from the Sinai in 1967, and Erskine 1989 *Mission with UNIFIL: An African Soldier's Reflections* about the peace-keeping force in Lebanon.

28. For example, see Harbottle 1970 *The Impartial Soldier*; Houghton and Trinka 1984 *Multinational Peacekeeping in the Middle East*; Rikhye 1984; Rikhye, Harbottle, and Bjorn 1974; Verrier 1981.

29. For general discussions of the principles of successful peacekeeping circulating in the mid-1980s—what I call the received view of peacekeeping—see Goulding 1993 "The evolution of United Nations peacekeeping"; International Peace Academy 1984; Joint Nordic Committee for Military UN Matters 1986; Rikhye 1984; Urquhart 1987; Urquhart 1993.

30. William Zartman is credited with developing the theory of ripeness in conflict resolution. See Zartman 1985 *Ripe for Resolution: Conflict and Intervention in Africa*. Although a widely used element of conflict resolution analysis, ripeness is also subject to critical debate that focuses on a variety of shortcomings, especially that it, like "political will," is identified after rather than before the fact. For various critiques of ripeness theory, see Greig 2001 "Recognizing conditions of ripeness for international mediation between enduring rivals"; Kleiboer 1994 "Ripeness of conflict: a fruitful notion?"; Pruitt 1997 "Ripeness theory and the Oslo Talks"; and Rubin 1991 "The timing of ripeness and the ripeness of timing."

31. This war is referred to as the Yom Kippur War by Israelis or as the Ramadan War by Arabs. Syria attacked Israeli positions in the Golan Heights at the same time. Israel had also taken the Golan during the 1967 fighting. See Blum 2003 *The Eve of Destruction: The Untold Story of the Yom Kippur War*; Heikal 1976 *The Road to Rama-dan*; Sobel 1974 *Israel and the Arabs: The October 1973 War*; Urquhart 1987.

32. In this event, the war was effective in restoring a sense of Egyptian national pride, as evidenced by the October War Museum in Heliopolis.

33. See Article VI of Annex 1, Protocol Concerning Israeli Withdrawal and Security Arrangements to the Treaty of Peace between the Arab Republic of Egypt and the State of Israel, http://www.mfo.org/files/Treaty.pdf.

34. Treaty of Peace between the Arab Republic of Egypt and the State of Israel, Article IV.2, http://www.mfo.org/files/Treaty.pdf. Ordinarily, a resolution can pass the

Security Council if veto powers abstain, thus making this a more stringent criterion for consent.

35. Urquhart 1987, 300–301.

36. Tabory 1986 *The Multinational Force and Observers in the Sinai: Organization, Structure, and Function*, 11–16.

37. Hillen 1998, Rikhye 1984.

38. Ben-Ari 2001 "Blue helmets and white armor: multi-nationalism and multi-culturalism among UN peacekeeping forces," 276–77, quoting a UNDOF commander.

39. For this reason troops from the superpowers and countries with a colonial past were typically not part of peacekeeping missions before 1991.

40. For instance, Urquhart 1987, 110.

41. Graves 2006 "Who can keep the peace?"

42. Skjelsbaek 1990 "UN Peacekeeping: expectations, limitations and results: forty years of mixed experiences."

43. Heiberg 1990 "Peacekeepers and local populations: some comments on UNIFIL," 148.

44. Kalb 1982 "The U.N.'s Embattled Peacekeeper," 59. See also Skogmo 1989 *UNIFIL: International Peacekeeping in Lebanon, 1978–1988*, 54–58.

45. Author's fieldnotes, 30 May 1989.

46. Laughlin and Brady 1978 *Extinction and Survival in Human Populations*.

47. See Bateson "Compromise and the rhetoric of good and evil." Bateson's analysis suggests that one way to track the relative strength of these particular normative views within Iranian society was through the analysis of film.

48. Fetherston 1994, 46–59; Rikhye 1984, 89–100; United Nations 1996a, 147–70.

49. Rikhye 1984, 48. According to the United Nations Charter, the Security Council has responsibility for maintaining peace and international security. In 1950, facing the Korea conflict, the General Assembly passed the "Uniting for Peace" resolution. This resolution allows the General Assembly to act on matters of peace and international security should the Security Council fail "to exercise its primary responsibility for the maintenance of international peace and security in any case where there appears to be a threat to the peace, breach of the peace or act of aggression." See General Assembly Resolution 377, 3 November 1950. Also, under this resolution an emergency special session of the General Assembly can be convened with twenty-four-hour notice. Between 1956 and 2000, ten such sessions were called.

50. Rikhye 1984, 83–84.

51. See, for example, Urquhart 1989 *Decolonization and World Peace*.

52. Boutros-Ghali 1992 *An Agenda for Peace: Preventive Diplomacy, Peacemaking and Peace-Keeping*.

53. The following definitions appear in paragraphs 20 and 21 of Boutros-Ghali 1992 (italics added):

"*Preventive diplomacy* is action to prevent disputes from arising between parties, to prevent existing disputes from escalating into conflicts and to limit the spread of the latter when they occur."

"*Peacemaking* is action to bring hostile parties to agreement, essentially through such peaceful means as those foreseen in Chapter VI of the Charter of the United Nations."

"*Peace-keeping* is the deployment of a United Nations presence in the field, hitherto with the consent of all the parties concerned, normally involving United Nations military and/or police personnel and frequently civilians as well. Peace-keeping is a technique that expands the possibilities for both the prevention of conflict and the making of peace."

"*[P]ost-conflict peace-building* [is] action to identify and support structures which will tend to strengthen and solidify peace in order to avoid a relapse into conflict."

54. UNIFIL's mandate and mission in southern Lebanon have changed several times during its operational life. On its role in postconflict peacebuilding in the late twentieth century, see Heiberg 1990, and Heiberg and Holst 1986. Following the war between Israel and Hezbollah, in 2006 UNIFIL's mandate was expanded and made more robust in Security Council Resolution 1701.

55. See, for instance, Paris 2000 "Broadening the study of peace operations"; Houghton and Trinka 1984; International Peace Academy 1984; Joint Nordic Committee for Military UN Matters 1986; Pelcovits 1984; Rikhye 1984; Rikhye, Harbottle, and Bjorn 1974; Verrier 1981.

Chapter 3

1. This event is described in Urquhart 1987 *A Life in Peace and War*, 136.

2. Operation Restore Hope was the second phase of United Nations authorized efforts in Somalia. The details of the Wanwaylen incident are straightforwardly described with admirable self-awareness by Stanton 1994 "A riot in Wanwaylen: lessons learned," and Stanton 2001 *Somalia on $5.00 a Day: A Soldier's Story*. It is also possible that beyond not understanding the cultural differences, they did not stop to think that someone could react differently to the same situation.

3. Duffey 2000 "Cultural issues in contemporary peacekeeping," for example, details a number of ways in which lack of cultural understanding was damaging to the missions in Somalia.

4. Personal communication, January 2004.

5. This incident was given wide publicity. A brief contemporaneous account of it can be found in Sengupta 2003 "The Iraq conflict: US says flag incident was a 'coincidence.'" A subsequent account describing the military's ham-fisted attempt to stage the scene is reported in Zucchino 2004 "Army stage-managed fall of Hussein statue."

6. For example, see Hohe 2002a "Clash of paradigms: international administration and local political legitimacy in East Timor"; Hohe 2002b "Totem polls: indigenous concepts of 'free and fair' elections in East Timor"; Hohe 2003 "Justice without judiciary in East Timor."

7. This description is from my interview notes. See also Rubinstein 2003a "Crosscultural considerations in complex peace operations."

8. Personal communication, 23 April 2001.

9. Dallaire 2004 *Shake Hands with the Devil: The Failure of Humanity in Rwanda*.

10. See, for examples, Avruch 1999 "Civilian perspectives on the analysis of civil military interactions: introductory remarks"; Rubinstein 2003a; Saner and Yiu 2002 "Porous boundary and power politics: contextual constraints on organisation development

change projects in United Nations organisations"; Seiple 1996 *The U.S. Military/NGO Relationship in Humanitarian Interventions*; Slim 1996 "The stretcher and the drum: civil-military relations in peace support operations"; Weiss 1999 *Military-Civilian Interactions: Intervening in Humanitarian Crises.*

11. Hohe 2002a "Clash of paradigms: international administration and local political legitimacy in East Timor," and Hohe 2002b "Totem polls: indigenous concepts of 'free and fair' elections in East Timor" show how international efforts in East Timor were less successful than they could have been because of a lack of cultural understanding.

12. On the emergence within the international community of free and fair elections as a normative measure of success see, for example, Paris 2003 "Peacekeeping and the constraints of global culture" and Reisman 1999 "Sovereignty and human rights in contemporary international law." On Cambodia, see Myint-U and Sellwood 2000 *Knowledge and Multilateral Interventions: The UN's Experience in Cambodia and Bosnia-Herzegovina.*

13. On the development of free and fair elections in the East Timor context and the difficulties with that mission, see Chopra 2000 "The UN's kingdom of East Timor" and Hohe 2002b.

14. For more on this critique, see, for example, Paris 1997 "Peacebuilding and the limits of liberal internationalism" and Paris 2002 "International peacebuilding and the 'mission civilisatrice.'"

15. For further information on Namibia, see United Nations 1996a *The Blue Helmets. A Review of United Nations Peace-Keeping*, 203–29; Saxena 1978 *Namibia: Challenge to the United Nations*; and Dobbins, Jones, Crane, Rathmell, Steele, Teltschik, and Timilsina 2004 *The UN's Role in Nation-Building: From the Congo to Iraq*, 29–44.

16. See chapter 2 above for a description of the roles of hurtful stalemates and reputation-linked considerations in peacekeeping.·

17. From the United Nations Department of Peacekeeping, "Namibia—UNTAG, Facts and Figures," http://www.un.org/Depts/dpko/dpko/co_mission/untag.htm.

18. United Nations 1996, 203–29.

19. Two of the most useful are Duffey 2000 and Hohe 2002a.

20. Examples include Ben-Ari 2001 "Blue helmets and white armor: multi-nationalism and multi-culturalism among UN peacekeeping forces"; Heiberg and Holst 1986 "Peacekeeping in Lebanon: comparing UNIFIL and the MNF"; Rubinstein 1993 "Cultural aspects of peacekeeping: notes on the substance of symbols"; and Sion 2006 "Too sweet and innocent for war? Dutch peacekeepers and the use of violence."

21. I say *relatively stable* because activities may be more or less fully institutionalized. The process of institutionalization for peacekeeping took place over a long period. On institutions and institutionalization see, for example, Wallis 1985 "Institutions," 400, who notes that "institutions are simply patterns of behaviour which persist and crystallize in the course of time and to which people become attached as a result of their role in the formation of identity or through investments of energy or social interests. Thus social activities or patterns of behaviour are *more or less* institutionalized, that is, involve greater or lesser degrees of formalization."

22. See Benedict 1934 *Patterns of Culture*; Benedict 1946 *The Chrysanthemum and the Sword*; Mead 1942 *And Keep Your Powder Dry: An Anthropologist Looks at America*. The history of anthropological attempts to understand culture is fascinating. For useful accounts of the history of these developments, see Erickson and Murphy 2003 *A History of Anthropological Theory*; Harris 2001 *The Rise of Anthropological Theory: A History of Theories of Culture*; and Hatch 1973 *Theories of Man and Culture*.

23. To be fair, some anthropologists did conclude that culture would not serve anthropology as an explanatory principle, but they generally did so for reasons other than those taken up by people outside of the discipline. See, for example, Kuper 1999 *Culture: The Anthropologists' Account*.

24. Kroeber and Kluckhohn 1952 *Culture: A Critical Review of Concepts and Definitions*.

25. I present this writer for no particular reason. This statement is just one example among hundreds of similar ones. The quote is from Lovell 1990 "The United States as ally and adversary in East Asia: reflections on culture and foreign policy," 90.

26. I have given a more technical account of these developments in Rubinstein 1989 "Culture, international affairs and peacekeeping: confusing process and pattern."

27. The concept of cultural lag was introduced into the sociological literature in the early twentieth century by Ogburn 1922 *Social Change*, 201, where he presents it in the following way: "Where one part of culture changes first, through some discovery or invention, and occasions changes in some part of culture dependent upon it, there frequently is a delay in the changes occasioned in the dependent part of culture, during which time there may be said to be a maladjustment." Herman 1937 "An answer to criticisms of the lag concept" puts it as follows: "(1) the various parts of culture are changing, some parts because of invention or discovery changing more rapidly than others; (2) because these parts are interrelated, a change in one part necessitates ('occasions') similar changes in other parts; and (3) the delay of those parts that change slowly in making the adjustment to those that change more rapidly is lag." And Worsley 1997 "Images of the other," 75, presents the concept in a more modern idiom as follows: "unevenness in the rate of change between different social institutions, different cultural domains, and popular perceptions of these social and cultural changes, have been designated by some anthropologists 'culture lag.'"

28. Maturana and Varela 1988 *The Tree of Knowledge: The Biological Roots of Human Understanding*, 75.

29. Maturana and Varela 1998, 193, call this "reciprocal structural coupling."

30. On this process, see Schön 1983 *The Reflective Practitioner: How Professionals Think in Action*.

31. Laughlin and d'Aquili 1974 *Biogenetic Structuralism*; Laughlin, McManus, and d'Aquili 1990 *Brain, Symbol and Experience: Toward a Neurophenomenology of Human Consciousness*.

32. Foster and Brandes 1980 *Symbol as Sense: New Approaches to the Analysis of Meaning*.

33. This discussion of the properties of symbols condenses a very large and complex literature. It is intended only to identify key features of symbolism so as to facilitate the argument advanced here. For general treatments of symbolism and ritual in political

life, see Cohen 1974 *Two Dimensional Man: An Essay on the Anthropology of Power and Symbolism in Complex Society*; and Kertzer 1988 *Ritual, Politics, and Power*.

34. Laughlin, McManus, and d'Aquili 1990.

35. See Hofstede 1991 *Culture and Organizations, Software of the Mind: Intercultural Cooperation and Its Importance for Survival*.

36. d'Andrade 1984 "Cultural meaning systems," 116.

37. I take this to be the basic insight conveyed by Pierre Bourdieu's influential concept of habitus (see Bourdieu 1990 *The Logic of Practice*). Although habitus is often seen strictly as a theory of social reproduction (e.g., Nordquist 1997 *Pierre Bourdieu: A Bibliography*; and McLeod 1987 *Ain't No Makin' It: Leveled Aspirations in a Low-Income Neighborhood*) Bourdieu stresses that the concept accounts for both conservation and change: "Habitus is what you have to posit to account for the fact that, without being rational, social agents are *reasonable*. . . . In short the ongoing dialectic of subjective hopes and objective chances, which is at work throughout the social world, can yield a variety of outcomes ranging from mutual fit (when people come to desire that to which they are objectively destined) to radical disjunction" (Bourdieu and Wacquant 1992 *An Invitation to Reflexive Sociology*, 129–30). It is also consistent with Whitehead's principle of conformation ("There can be no useful aspect of anything unless we admit the principle of conformation, whereby what is already made becomes a determinant of what is in the making" [Whitehead 1927 *Symbolism: Its Meaning and Effect*, 46]), with Bidney's view on free will ("The issue, then, is not whether man's 'will' is free, in the sense of being undetermined or causeless, but whether man as a whole is or is not to a limited extent the active agent and efficient cause of the cultural process and whether culture, if its historical conditions are understood, is subject to human control in the interests of human well-being. I maintain that human freedom and causal determinism are quite compatible and that no irreconcilable conflict is involved" [Bidney 1967 *Theoretical Anthropology*]), and Laughlin and d'Aquili's concept of the empirical modification cycle (1974, 84–86).

38. Stephen Pepper developed root metaphor theory as part of his study (1942 *World Hypotheses: A Study in Evidence*). Sherry Ortner developed the concept of key symbols (1973 "On key symbols").

39. Cohen 1974; d'Aquili, Laughlin, and McManus 1979 *The Spectrum of Ritual: A Biogenetic Structural Analysis*; Foster 1994 "Symbolism: the foundation of culture"; Kertzer 1988; Laughlin, McManus, and d'Aquili 1990.

40. Lakoff and Johnson 1980 *Metaphors We Live By*; Weiner 1994 "Myth and metaphor."

41. See d'Aquili and Laughlin 1979 "The neurobiology of myth and ritual"; Laughlin, McManus, and d'Aquili 1990; Schechner 1994 "Ritual and performance." This tuning is observed in effective rituals.

42. The metaphor and quotation are from Schauber 2002 *Working with Differences in Communities: A Handbook for Those Who Care about Creating Inclusive Communities*, chapter 2.

43. Babcock 1978a "Introduction," 14. Because I am taking a culture as symbolic meaning system approach, I use cultural inversion and symbolic inversion interchangeably.

44. Once one becomes attuned to them, symbolic inversions appear everywhere. For example, the popular television advertisement for Las Vegas tourism asserts, "What happens in Vegas stays in Vegas," thus underscoring that it is a place that contains and supports such reversals. For the technical literature on cultural inversions, see Babcock 1978b *The Reversible World: Symbolic Inversion in Art and Society*; Kertzer 1988; Turner 1967 *The Forest of Symbols*; and Turner 1969 *The Ritual Process: Structure and Anti-Structure*.

45. See, O'Brien and Topolski 1968 *The United Nations: Sacred Drama*, especially 1–77.

46. Catherine Lutz points out that that the first inversion in the table, "no foreign troops on sovereign soil," rests on a presumption of "the colonialist exceptionalism of the United States and to a lesser degree other Northern militaries who have had thousands of bases on foreign soil." See also the arguments made by Chopra 2000 "The UN's kingdom of East Timor"; Debrix 1999 *Re-Envisioning Peacekeeping: The United Nations and the Mobilization of Ideology*; Hohe 2003 "Justice without judiciary in East Timor"; Razack 2004 *Dark Threats and White Knights: The Somalia Affair, Peacekeeping and the New Imperialism*. They explore the ways in which peacekeeping can represent a new imperialism.

47. Indeed, the specific interpretations given to United Nations symbolism by local populations and by different nationals can vary significantly.

48. See Wallace 1970 *Culture and Personality*, 27–34, for his discussion of the organization of diversity within cultural systems.

49. In this view, missions are designed around structures developed by technical experts, and technical knowledge is taken to be acultural in nature. Thus, it is not necessary, in this view, to take account of information about the local cultural practices and governance structures where a mission is deployed. See, for instance, Myint-U and Sellwood 2000 *Knowledge and Multilateral Interventions: The UN's Experience in Cambodia and Bosnia-Herzegovina*, 33–34.

50. Saxe 1878 "The Blind Men and the Elephant."

Chapter 4

1. The Doomsday Clock used by the *Bulletin of the Atomic Scientists* to graphically represent the level of nuclear danger was set at three minutes to midnight in 1981. In contrast, in 2008 the Doomsday Clock is set at five minutes to midnight. Anthropological critique of those policies can be found in Beeman 1986 "Conflict and belief in American foreign policy"; Gonzalez 1986 "Ethnic targeting as a defense strategy"; and Rubinstein 1988 "Cultural analysis and international security."

2. The results of those symposia are published in Foster and Rubinstein 1986 *Peace and War: Cross-Cultural Perspectives*. These meetings also led to the establishing of the Commission on the Anthropology of Peace under the auspices of the International Union of Anthropological and Ethnological Sciences.

3. Nader 1969 "Up the anthropologist—perspectives gained from studying up," 303; Gusterson 1993 "Exploding anthropology's canon in the world of the bomb: ethnographic writing on militarism."

4. Nader 1969, 292.

5. Portions of the rest of this chapter are revised or reprinted, with the permission of the publisher, from Robert A. Rubinstein, "Methodological challenges in the ethnographic study of multilateral peacekeeping," *PoLAR: Political and Legal Anthropology Review* 21, no. 1 (1998): 138–49.

6. For more on the nature and essential importance of multilevel explanation, see Rubinstein and Laughlin 1977 "Bridging levels of systemic organization"; and Rubinstein, Laughlin, and McManus 1984 *Science as Cognitive Process: Toward an Empirical Philosophy of Science*.

7. Beginning in the early 1960s, two secret projects in which anthropologists had been involved came to light. The first was Project Camelot in Chile. The second involved anthropological input into counterinsurgency work in Southeast Asia. In both cases, anthropologists were actively involved in secret work, which many saw as violating the discipline's ethics. First, their work was used in ways that harmed informants and communities that had invested trust in anthropologists. Second, conducting secret work under the cover of anthropology put all anthropologists in danger, because its revelation gave fuel to those who saw anthropologists as agents of Western imperialism. Nearly all anthropologists whom I have asked have told me that at some point in their fieldwork, they were suspected by the local population of being agents of the CIA. This was my experience during fieldwork in Belize in the 1970s. In addition to the debates these episodes engendered, they resurrected earlier debates within the discipline concerning the proper relationship between the science of anthropology and the politics and policies of governments. See, for instance, Boas 1919 "Scientists as spies"; McFate 2005 "Anthropology and counterinsurgency: the strange story of their curious relationship"; and Wolf and Jorgensen 1970 "Anthropology on the warpath in Thailand."

8. For historical examples of work on war and militaries, see Brasset 1997 "Values and the exercise of power: military elites"; Katz 1990 "Emotional metaphors, socialization, and roles of drill sergeants"; Malinowski 1941 "An anthropological analysis of war"; Otterbein 1970 *The Evolution of War: A Cross-Cultural Study*; Pulliam 1997 "Achieving social competence in the navy community"; Randall 1986 "The culture of United States military enclaves"; and Tax 1967 *The Draft: A Handbook of Facts and Alternatives*. A number of very good studies have appeared more recently as well. See, for example, Ben-Ari 1998 *Mastering Soldiers: Conflict, Emotions and the Enemy in an Israeli Military Unit*; Hawkins 2001 *Army of Hope, Army of Alienation: Culture and Contradiction in the American Army Communities of Cold War Germany*; Lutz 2001 *Homefront: A Military City and the American Twentieth Century*; Simons 1997 *The Company They Keep: Life inside the U.S. Army Special Forces*; and Winslow 1997 *The Canadian Airborne Regiment in Somalia: A Socio-Cultural Inquiry*.

9. See Rubinstein 2001a *Doing Fieldwork: The Correspondence of Robert Redfield and Sol Tax*; Wilcox 2004 *Robert Redfield and the Development of American Anthropology*.

10. Examples of this methodological and conceptual shift are found in Gusterson 1997 "Studying up revisited," and Hannerz 1996 *Transnational Connections: Culture, People, Places*.

11. For example, in the early 1990s Robert Fernea of the University of Texas told me that he had returned to Egypt to do a restudy in Nubia, but permissions were taking so long that he could not do the work he had planned.

12. In the United States, any research with "human subjects" conducted with federal funding must be approved by an institutional review board (IRB), the composition and authority of which is regulated by statute. Over the years, the requirement for IRB approval of human subject research has become more widespread and has been made mandatory by universities, private sector companies, and journals. Researchers must also meet local requirements. For instance James Trostle notes that doing his ethnographic work on epilepsy at the Mayo Clinic required navigating a bureaucracy seven committees deep (2005 *Epidemiology and Culture*, xv).

13. For a sensitive discussion of these dynamics in a traditional anthropological setting, see Abu-Lughod 1986 *Veiled Sentiments: Honor and Poetry in a Bedouin Society*, 9–24.

14. Chagnon 1968 *Yanomamo: The Fierce People*; Malinowski 1961 [1922] *Argonauts of the Western Pacific: An Account of Native Enterprise and Adventure in the Archipelagoes of Melanesian New Guinea*.

15. Rubinstein 2001a.

16. Nordstrom and Robben 1996 *Fieldwork Under Fire: Contemporary Studies of Violence and Survival*; Sluka 1997 "Loyal citizens of the republic: morality, violence, and popular support for the IRA and INLA in a Northern Irish ghetto."

17. Brasset 1997, Simons 1997.

18. It is worth pointing out that this transience is also a difficulty for peacekeeping missions as organizations because there is, as a result of this movement, periodic and substantial loss of institutional memory. The symbolism and rituals described in chapter 5 are one way in which this memory loss is addressed.

19. Vadset 1988 "UNTSO and the future: reflections by the COS."

20. Abu-Lughod 1986, Brasset 1997, Chagnon 1968, Nordstrom and Robben 1996, Simons 1997.

21. I was moving to Cairo because my wife was to begin a position as a program officer in the Ford Foundation's Cairo Office.

22. Indeed, once through the underpass, there were several mosques that would have qualified as appropriate.

23. Briggs 1986 *Learning How to Ask: A Sociolinguistic Appraisal of the Role of the Interview in Social Science Research*.

24. Goffman 1959 *The Presentation of Self in Everyday Life*.

25. This is the social institution known as *wasta*, which is widespread in Egypt and elsewhere in the Middle East and legitimates working through the intercession of well-connected others to accomplish one's goals. See Cunningham and Sarayrah 1993 *Wasta: The Hidden Force in Middle Eastern Society*; Palmer, Leila, and Yassin 1988 *The Egyptian Bureaucracy*.

26. Ablon 1977 "Field methods in working with middle class Americans: new issues of values, personality, and reciprocity," 71.

Chapter 5

1. The challenge of driving in Cairo, and its usefulness as a metaphor for the cross-cultural challenges of peacekeeping, was underscored in an interview with one of my informants, who said about better pre-deployment training that "It would have to [include instruction from UNMOs who had experienced driving in Cairo]. It would be for people who have already experienced this, who had gone through what you are about to, because to have somebody give you a seminar who has only driven in Canada or New York and has not gone through this, he does not know how to drive here. He does not. He can read a hundred books, and it is not going to come through. What you need is someone who has the experience that you are about to have."

2. Portions of this chapter are revised and expanded or reprinted, with the permission of the publisher, from Robert A. Rubinstein, "Cultural aspects of peacekeeping: notes on the substance of symbols," *Millennium: Journal of International Studies* 22 (1993): 547–62.

3. LeVine 1984 "Properties of culture," 67.

4. Urquhart 1987 *A Life in Peace and War*, 134.

5. This is equally true whether considering the construction of legitimacy for local populations, or diplomats, or the international community generally, or peacekeeping troops themselves. For discussions of the importance of symbol and ritual in international diplomacy and political life, see Kertzer 1988 *Ritual, Politics, and Power*; and Rubinstein 1988 "Cultural analysis and international security."

6. This works in both directions. Peacekeeping failures can also be invested with symbolic power. See, for instance, Debrix 1999 *Re-Envisioning Peacekeeping: The United Nations and the Mobilization of Ideology*.

7. For instance, while I was participating in the International Peace Academy's 1988 Vienna Seminar, the UNTSO chief of staff was called away to lead a technical mission to support the planning of the United Nations Iran-Iraq Military Observer Group. Subsequently, the initial detachment of observers in that mission were seconded from UNTSO.

8. There is an extensive literature about the importance of the symbolic capacity to the human experience and especially to the development of culture. See Dolgin, Kemnitzer, and Schneider 1977 *Symbolic Anthropology: A Reader in the Study of Symbols and Meanings*; Foster 1994 "Symbolism: the foundation of culture," Kertzer 1988; Laughlin and d'Aquili 1974 *Biogenetic Structuralism*; Laughlin, McManus, and d'Aquili 1990 *Brain, Symbol and Experience: Toward a Neurophenomenology of Human Consciousness*; Ortner 1973 "On key symbols"; Sahlins 1999 "Two or three things that I know about culture"; White 1949 *The Science of Culture*

9. For discussion of the processes underlying the symbolic construction of difference among people, see, for instance, Barth 1969 "Introduction," and Zerubavel 1991 *The Fine Line: Making Distinctions in Everyday Life*.

10. The literature exploring ritual is large. I am drawing from it some aspects of analysis that are particularly useful for illuminating the role of ritual in peace operations. For discussions of ritual per se, see Bell 1997 *Ritual: Perspectives and Dimensions*; d'Aquili, Laughlin, and McManus 1979 *The Spectrum of Ritual: A Biogenetic Structural*

Analysis; Kertzer 1988; Laughlin, McManus, and d'Aquili 1990; Laughlin, McManus, Rubinstein, and Shearer 1986 "The ritual transformation of experience"; and Turner 1969 *The Ritual Process: Structure and Anti-Structure*.

11. For discussions of the nature of ritual symbolism congenial with this perspective, see d'Aquili, Laughlin, and McManus 1979; Kertzer 1988; Laughlin, McManus, Rubinstein, and Shearer 1986.

12. Laughlin, McManus, and d'Aquili 1990, 214.

13. Van Gennep says, "although a complete scheme of rites of passage theoretically includes preliminal rites (rites of separation), liminal rites (rites of transition), and postliminal rites (rites of incorporation), in specific instances these three types are not always equally important or equally elaborated" (1960 [1909] *The Rites of Passage*, 11.

14. Turner 1969, 96.

15. Turner 1969, 106–7.

16. Goldschmidt 1990 *The Human Career: The Self in the Symbolic World*, 174.

17. The best guide to the neuro-psychological basis of ritual action is found in d'Aquili, Laughlin, and McManus 1979; Laughlin, McManus, and d'Aquili 1990; and especially Lex 1979 "Neurobiology of ritual trance." "Tuning" as used in this setting differs somewhat from other uses of the term in cognitive science. That additional meaning references the process whereby cognitive schemata are adjusted to bring them into closer alignment with the experienced world. For this use of "tuning," see, for example, Rumelhart 1980 "Schemata: the building blocks of cognition." This use of tuning corresponds to what I call the empirical modification cycle, following Laughlin and d'Aquili, 1974.

18. Laughlin, McManus, and d'Aquili 1990, 146.

19. For an analysis of the Catholic Mass, see Murphy 1979 "A ceremonial ritual: the Mass." On meditation ritual see Austin 2001 *Zen and the Brain: Toward an Understanding of Meditation and Consciousness*; Laughlin, McManus, and d'Aquili 1990; Laughlin, McManus, Rubinstein, and Shearer 1986.

20. Rubinstein 1989.

21. Ben-Ari 2001 "Blue helmets and white armor: multi-nationalism and multi-culturalism among UN peacekeeping forces," 276.

22. For instance, see Rubinstein 2003b "Politics and peacekeepers: experience and political representation among United States military officers."

23. See Maloney 2002 *Canada and UN Peacekeeping: Cold War by Other Means 1945–1970*.

24. This sense of national pride in participating in United Nations peacekeeping is displayed in a 1995 film series produced under the auspices of the Film Board of Canada, entitled *Protection Force*. The series, which include three films, *Caught in the Crossfire*, *In God's Command*, and *The Price of Duty*, celebrated Canadian contributions to and sacrifices for United Nations peacekeeping.

25. Colonel P. Purushottaman of the Centre for United Nations Peacekeeping in New Delhi expressed a similar motivation when he noted that "the opportunities in terms of international training exposure, interoperability with multinational forces and cross-cultural exchanges make definite improvement in the professional outlook

of the peacekeepers," Murthy 2007 "Unintended consequences of peace operations for troop-contributing countries from South Asia," 166.

26. Elron, Halevy, Ben-Ari, and Shamir 2003 "Cooperation and coordination across cultures in the peacekeeping forces: individual and organizational integrating mechanism," 265.

27. As a result, peacekeeping missions, like other joint and combined missions, have to sort through different cultural expectations of what counts as proper professional behavior.

28. These examples are drawn from my notes from interviews at UNTSO.

29. Kertzer 1988, 11.

30. I purchased a small collection of badges for OGE and for other UN missions in a store in downtown Cairo. That the badges are available for sale outside of official channels is of little consequence. What is noteworthy are the meanings and the importance of those meanings for members of peacekeeping missions.

31. Personal communication, 2 September 2007.

32. Kertzer 1988, 45.

33. Trainor 1996 "Suicide over a medal? an ex-general's view," 6.

34. Trainor 1996.

35. See Boatner 1956 *Military Customs and Traditions*; United States Office of the Assistant Secretary of Defense 1996 *Manual of Military Decorations and Awards*.

36. For a discussion of the importance of distinguishing structure and content in anthropological analyses, see Rubinstein, Laughlin, and McManus 1984 *Science as Cognitive Process: Toward an Empirical Philosophy of Science*, especially 37–38 and 98.

37. Bartlett 2000 "UN medal parade," http://www.diggerz.org/~adaa/unm.htm.

38. See Pritchard 1995 "Caught in the crossfire."

39. Similar observations about the elaboration of ritual and about the use of explicit discussion of cultural differences as integrating mechanisms in peacekeeping missions are given by Ben-Ari 2001, and Elron, Halevy, Ben-Ari and Shamir 2003.

40. *UNTSO News* also includes the discussion of cultural differences, sometimes in a humorous context, thus providing another level of linking with the individual observer groups. For instance, *UNTSO News* 15, no. 4 (1994) contained many reflections on cultural differences in cooking and cleaning, such as one article titled, "Looking, Cooking and Cleaning on the Golan Heights."

41. See the discussion in chapter 3 above and Foster 1993 "Reversal theory and the institutionalization of war," 67–74, and Kertzer 1988, 132.

42. Related to how these little things mean a lot to troops is the brouhaha created when the US Army changed its headgear to the black beret. Lots of impassioned discussion about this change can be found in *Army Times* throughout 2000 and 2001.

43. I have characterized rather than quoted the memorandum to preserve the privacy of its author.

Chapter 6

1. "An American captain, attempting to enforce his understanding of where the line lies, said to an Israeli tank commander that if he wanted to pass, 'You will have to kill me'" (Washington Post 1983 "The Sharon-Weinberger Factor").

2. Pritchard 1995 "Caught in the crossfire."

3. Sergeant Ward, speaking in Pritchard 1995.

4. My thanks to Catherine Lutz for calling the gendered aspect of this example to my attention.

5. Although peacekeeping operations have been the subject of considerable research, analysis, and reflection, the literature that focuses on the individual in peace operations is relatively small. Much of this work is collected in Britt and Adler 2003 *The Psychology of the Peacekeeper*, and Langholtz 1998 *The Psychology of Peacekeeping*.

6. Some material in this chapter is revised and expanded or reprinted, with the permission of the publishers, from Robert A. Rubinstein, "Politics and peacekeepers: experience and political representation among United States military officers," in *Anthropology and the United States Military: Coming of Age in the Twenty-first Century*, ed. P. R. Frese and M. C. Harrell, 15–27, New York: Palgrave Macmillan, 2003; and Robert A. Rubinstein, "Motivation et maintien de la paix: elaboration d'un lien entre agir et structure," *Anthropologie el Société* 30, no. 1 (2006): 137–55.

7. Munro 1997 "Levels and processes in motivation and culture," xi. See also Kashima 1997 "Culture, narrative, and human motivation."

8. Rubinstein, Laughlin, and McManus 1984 *Science as Cognitive Process: Toward an Empirical Philosophy of Science*, 26; Kirsch 1999 "Response expectancy: an introduction."

9. Tversky and Kahneman 1982 "Judgment under uncertainty: heuristics and biases"; Rubinstein, Laughlin, and McManus 1984.

10. The UNMOs in OGE self-identified into four groups; those from the United States (about 25 percent of those interviewed), Soviets (33 percent), French (19 percent), and those from the rest of the world (about 21 percent). The latter group included UNMOs from Canada, Sweden, Denmark, Ireland, Italy, Norway, New Zealand, and Australia.

11. For instance, Kinzer describes the role that showing the flag played in the transition of the United States from a basically regional to a world power (2006 *Overthrow: America's Century of Regime Change from Hawaii to Iraq*, 78–80).

12. See, for example, the papers in Britt and Adler 2003 and Langholtz 1998.

13. Sion "Too sweet and innocent for war?: Dutch peacekeepers and the use of violence."

14. Tomforde 2005 "Motivation and self-image among German peacekeepers," 584.

15. Currently, for instance, there is considerable attention being given to the "strategic corporal" in operations other than war (of which peacekeeping is an example). "A strategic corporal is a soldier that possesses technical mastery in the skill of arms while being aware that his judgment, decision-making and action can all have strategic and political consequences that can affect the outcome of a given mission and the reputation of his country" (Liddy 2005 "The strategic corporal: some requirements in training and education," 140).

16. Rehn and Sirleaf 2002 *Women, War, and Peace*.

17. Chopra "The UN's kingdom of East Timor"; Ghosh "The global reservation: notes toward an ethnography of international peacekeeping."

18. Wallenius, Johansson, and Larsson 2002 "Reactions and performance of Swedish peacekeepers in life-threatening situations."

19. Bourdieu 1990 *The Logic of Practice.*

20. Apter 2007 *Reversal Theory: The Dynamics of Motivation, Emotion and Personality*; Apter, Fontana, and Murgatroyd 1985 *Reversal Theory: Applications and Developments*; Bateson 1988 "Compromise and the rhetoric of good and evil."

21. Munro 1997 "Levels and processes in motivation and culture," x.

22. Apter 2001 "An introduction to Reversal Theory"; 12. Apter 2007.

23. Apter 2005 *Personality Dynamics: Key Concepts in Reversal Theory*, 67–75.

24. Foster 1988 "Cultural triggering of psychological reversals," 67.

25. See, for instance, the discussion of this reluctance in Perito 2004 *Where Is the Lone Ranger When We Need Him? America's Search for a Postconflict Stability Force.*

26. Eidelson 2003 *Modeling Crowd Behavior: The Core Beliefs of Crowd Members and Control Force Agents.*

27. Apter 2005, 28.

28. Apter 2007, 163; Foster 1988.

29. Rubinstein, Laughlin, and McManus 1984, 155–59.

30. Apter 2007, 241–46.

31. Goodwin 2005 *The Military and Negotiation: The Role of the Soldier-Diplomat.*

32. In particular, Goodwin amends the standard model of principled negotiation (most popularly presented by Roger Fisher and William Ury in their book *Getting to Yes*) so that it is more realistic in the context of military negotiations where coercion is an ever-present option.

33. This English translation is from James Moorwood 1998 *A Dictionary of Latin Words and Phrases*, 83. The Latin reads, "*In bello parvis momentis magni casus intercederent,*" Caesaris 1881 *Commentarii de bello civili*, 43.

34. Krulak 1999 "The strategic corporal: leadership in the three block war"; and Liddy 2005.

35. See, Rubinstein, Laughlin, and McManus 1984, xvii–xxv.

36. This point about the underlying logic of inquiry is also made by, among others, Glasser and Strauss, in their classic work, 1967 *The Discovery of Grounded Theory: Strategies for Qualitative Research.*

37. Maturana and Varela 1988.

38. My multilevel model of peacekeeping is a direct application of the rule of minimal inclusion, which specifies that any adequate analysis of behavior must bridge levels and include data from the relevant levels of organization implicated in that behavior and consideration of the environment of that behavior. Rubinstein, Laughlin, and McManus 1984, 93.

Chapter 7

1. See my discussion of this asymmetry in Rubinstein 2003b "Politics and peacekeepers: experience and political representation among United States military officers."

2. Some material in this chapter is revised and expanded or reprinted with permission from my 2003 "Cross-cultural considerations in complex peace operations," *Negotiation Journal* 19:29–49.

3. General Sir Michael Jackson, chief of the General Staff, British Army. Remarks endorsing Jock Covey, Michael J. Dziedzic, and Leonard R. Hawley *The Quest for Viable Peace: International Intervention and Strategies for Conflict Transformation*, (Washington, DC: United States Institute of Peace Press, 2005), back cover.

4. Aall, Miltenberger, and Weiss 2000 *Guide to IGOs, NGOs, and the Military in Peace and Relief Operations*; Perito 2007 *Guide to Participants in Peace, Stability, and Relief Operations*.

5. This is noted by Richard Solomon and George Oliver in their introduction to Aall, Miltenberger, and Weiss 2000.

6. For more on cultural styles and dimensions, and their application, see, for example, Cohen 1997 *Negotiating across Cultures*; Fisher 1988 *Mindsets: The Role of Culture and Perception in International Relations*; Hall 1967 *Beyond Culture*; Hofstede 1991 *Culture and Organizations, Software of the Mind: Intercultural Cooperation and Its Importance for Survival*; and Kochman 1981 *Black and White Styles in Conflict*.

7. Much of the description and the tables in this section are drawn from Rubinstein 2003a "Cross-cultural considerations in complex peace operations."

8. Koch 1983 "Presentation as proof: the language of Arabic rhetoric"; Kim and Sherman 2007 "Express your self: culture and the effect of self-expression choice."

9. On various NGOs and IGOs, see Perito 2007.

10. In response to reading this, Tanja Hohe Chopra related (personal communication, 2 September 2007):

> I think of my work in Maliana, a border district in East Timor. We civilian staff and UNMOs lived out there every day, exposed to possible incursions of militias from West Timor. The American army (as usual not under UN command) was only stationed in Dili, as the rest of the country was considered dangerous. In their "humanitarian week," they decided that people in Maliana needed a dentist. So they flew in a dentist by helicopter from Dili, who operated in the Maliana hospital, while the hospital was surrounded by a whole platoon of American soldiers, heavily armed, guarding the dentist. We drove by and could not believe it. Needless to say, nobody from the community came, as they were scared they would be shot.

11. Personal communication, Anna Simons, 28 December 2000.

12. See Hohe 2002a "Clash of paradigms: international administration and local political legitimacy in East Timor"; Hohe 2002b "Totem polls: indigenous concepts of 'free and fair' elections in East Timor"; Myint-U and Sellwood 2000 *Knowledge and Multilateral Interventions: The UN's Experience in Cambodia and Bosnia-Herzegovina*.

13. For an exploration of the cognitive and social dynamics of the drawing of such distinctions, see Zerubavel 1991 *The Fine Line: Making Distinctions in Everyday Life*.

14. See Rubinstein and Lane 2000 "Population, identity and political violence"; Fábos 2008 *"Brothers" or Others: Muslim Arab Sudanese in Egypt*; and Jok 1998. *Militarization, Gender and Reproductive Health in South Sudan*.

15. Gender disparities are also observed within the international organizations working among the local populations. In situations where a peacekeeping mission seeks to make local institutions it is creating or supporting conform to internationally mandated gender equity quotas, locals often comment on the gender disparities in the organizations, and in some of the countries from which the interveners come. They may interpret this as a lack of sincerity on the part of the international community.

16. See Kent 2007 "Protecting civilians from UN peacekeepers and humanitarian workers: sexual exploitation and abuse," and Donika Kaçinari, personal communication, 12 January 2001.

17. Rehn and Sirleaf 2002 *Women, War, and Peace*, 61. Also, personal communication, Elizabeth Callendar, 1 June 2002.

18. Aning 2007 "Unintended consequences of peace operations for troop-contributing countries for West Africa: the case of Ghana."

19. Rubinstein 2001b "Reflection and reflexivity in anthropology." This is true of all knowledge, not just anthropological knowledge, although it is often unacknowledged.

20. Rubinstein, Laughlin, and McManus 1984 *Science as Cognitive Process: Toward an Empirical Philosophy of Science*, especially chapters 5 and 7.

Chapter 8

1. On the application of dimensional analysis to negotiation, see Brett 2001 *Negotiating Globally: How to Negotiate Deals, Resolve Disputes, and Make Decisions Across Cultures*. On general cross-cultural encounters, see Peterson 2004 *Cultural Intelligence: A Guide to Working with People from Other Cultures*. House, Hanges, Javidan, Dorfman, and Gupta 2004 *Culture, Leadership, and Organizations: The GLOBE Study of 62 Societies* uses the dimensional model of culture to address issues of organizational leadership.

2. Cohen 1997 *Negotiating Across Culture*; Cohen 1990 *Culture and Conflict in Egyptian-Israeli Affairs: A Dialogue of the Deaf*.

3. Avruch makes this comment specifically in relation to the understanding of negotiation between Israel and Arab countries (1998 *Culture and Conflict Resolution*, 124). I used Hall's high- versus low-context dimension to analyze negotiations between Palestinians and Israelis in my 1992 "Culture and negotiation."

4. See Bond 2002 "Reclaiming the individual from Hofstede's ecological analysis—a 20-year odyssey: comment on Oyserman et al. (2002)"; Fiske 2002 "Using individualism and collectivism to compare cultures—a critique of the validity of measurement of the constructs: comment on Oyserman et al. (2002)"; Oyserman, Coon, and Kemmelmeir 2002 "Rethinking individualism and collectivism: evaluation of theoretical assumptions and meta-analyses."

5. See Goldschmidt *The Human Career: The Self in the Symbolic World*. Nicholas Humphrey puts this as follows: "In a complex society . . . there are benefits to be gained for each individual member both from preserving the overall structure of the group and at the same time from exploiting and out-manoeuvring others within it" (1984 *Consciousness Regained: Chapters in the Development of Mind*, 20).

6. An example of this is the debate about the GLOBE study of culture and leadership in organizations. Earley 2006 "Leading cultural research in the future: a matter of

paradigms and taste"; Hofstede 2006 "What did GLOBE really measure? Researchers' minds versus respondents' minds"; Javidan, House, Dorfman, Hanges, and de Luque 2006 "Conceptualizing and measuring cultures and their consequences: a comparative review of GLOBE's and Hofstede's approaches"; Smith 2006 "When elephants fight, the grass gets trampled: the GLOBE and Hofstede projects." Technical anthropological debates about culture often lead to its being popularly dismissed as an incoherent or useless concept (as discussed in chapter 3). Curiously, similar technical debates about cultural dimensions models do not lead to their dismissal. I suspect that there is a certain amount of scientism involved. Whereas anthropological debates embrace qualitative materials, the technical debates about the culture dimension approach often rest on quantitative modeling, which may be less accessible to the general public.

7. Some of the material in this chapter is revised and expanded or reprinted with permission from my 2005 "Intervention and culture: an anthropological approach," *Security Dialogue* 36(4):527–44.

8. Laughlin and his collaborators describe this feedback relationship as the empirical modification cycle (Laughlin and d'Aquili 1974 *Biogenetic Structuralism*; Laughlin, McManus, and d'Aquili 1990 *Brain, Symbol and Experience: Toward a Neurophenomenology of Human Consciousness*; Rubinstein, Laughlin, and McManus 1984 *Science as Cognitive Process: Toward an Empirical Philosophy of Science*). Other researchers treat it under the category of cognitive tuning; for example, see Rumelhart 1980 "Schemata: the building blocks of cognition."

9. This definition follows d'Andrade 1990 "Cultural cognition," 809.

10. See the discussion of conceptual metaphor in chapter 3 above. There is a considerable literature on cultural models, schemata, and what has been called "cognitive social science." Useful introductions to this subject are found in Holland and Quinn 1987 *Cultural Models in Language and Thought*; Shore 1996 *Culture in Mind: Cognition, Culture and the Problem of Meaning*; Laughlin, McManus, and d'Aquili 1990; Ungerer and Schmid 1997 *An Introduction to Cognitive Linguistics*; Fauconnier and Turner 2002 *The Way We Think: Conceptual Blending and the Mind's Hidden Complexities*; Turner 2001 *Cognitive Dimensions of Social Science*; and Lakoff and Johnson 1980 *Metaphors We Live By*.

11. In a sense, cultural models play a role similar to the deep structure of a language: its syntax and its semantics and pragmatics.

12. By "successfully" I mean the cultural models allow the group to adapt to its environment so as to increase the chances of group survival. See Laughlin and Brady 1978 *Extinction and Survival in Human Populations*. Of course, some models are more open to modification than others. On the modification of underlying models based on empirical modification, see especially Laughlin, McManus, and d'Aquili 1990.

13. See also Maturana and Varela 1988 *The Tree of Knowledge: The Biological Roots of Human Understanding*; and, Shore 1996, 47.

14. Foley 1997 *Anthropological Linguistics: An Introduction*.

15. Jok 2004 *Sudan at the Crossroads: Promoting Physical and Human Security*, 3–4.

16. See the very useful studies collected in Aoi, de Coning, and Thakur 2007 *Unintended Consequences of Peacekeeping Operations*; and Malone 2004 *The UN Security Council: From the Cold War to the 21st Century*.

17. Reisman 1993 "The constitutional crisis in the United Nations," 85–86.

18. See, for example, Murphy 1990 "Creating the appearance of consensus in Mende political discourse"; Smith 1985 "Commonwealth cross sections: prenegotiation to minimize conflict and develop cooperation"; Gulliver 1979 *Disputes and Negotiations: A Cross-Cultural Perspective*; Caplan 1995 *Understanding Disputes: The Politics of Argument.*

19. Personal communication, Brian Urquhart, 15 November 2003.

20. Like many root metaphors, which have fuzzy boundaries, there is no single accepted definition of "humanitarian space." Rather there is a variety of overlapping conceptualizations. This approach leaves the scope and nature of legitimate action open ended and ill defined. The United Nations Office for the Coordination of Humanitarian Affairs defines "humanitarian space" only by implication. See Bowden and Ironside 2003 *OCHA Glossary of Humanitarian Terms in Relation to the Protection of Civilians in Armed Conflict*, 14. Lewis Sida gives several overlapping definitions (2005 "Challenges to humanitarian space: a review of humanitarian issues related to the UN integrated mission in Liberia and to the relationship between humanitarian and military actors in Liberia," Annex I, 24).

21. Pouligny 2006 *Peace Operations Seen from Below: UN Missions and Local People*, 184–88.

22. See, for example, Gluck 2004 *Coalition Forces Endanger Humanitarian Action in Afghanistan*; Kelly and Rostrup 2002 "Identify yourselves: coalition soldiers in Afghanistan are endangering aid workers."

23. For example, Barry and Jefferys 2002 *A Bridge too Far: Aid Agencies and the Military in Humanitarian Response*, 15:

> Questions need to be faced concerning the proper roles of military forces and humanitarian actors in conflict situations, and the relationship between them. The issues confronting both sides encompass fundamental principles, as well as concerns around the cost effectiveness and appropriateness of the military delivery of aid, and the security and access implications that cooperation with the military raises. Yet despite these problems, the nature of modern conflict and the evolving political and strategic agendas of the major intervening powers mean that "cooperation" in one form or another is likely to remain a feature of the aid response, at least in key politically strategic areas such as the Balkans or Afghanistan.

24. See, for example, Barry and Jefferys 2002, 15–20; UNHCR 1995 *UNHCR Handbook for the Military on Humanitarian Operations*, chapter 4.

25. Rubinstein, Keller, and Scherger, nd. "Culture and interoperability in integrated missions."

26. One of the contributing factors to this pattern is the frequent changes in personnel on both sides of the conversation, especially among military participants whose tours are relatively brief and whose interest in working through the difficulties is based on the obligations of the role that they fill by direction rather than by choice.

27. African Civil Military Coordination Programme 2006 *CIMIC in UN and African Peace Operations: Resources*.

28. This is true of nearly all of this literature and also in the conversations of military officers who have worked with NGOs in the field. Based on his experiences as the administrator in Mitrovica, Kosovo, General William L. Nash described the differences this way: Militaries are quick, cohesive, well organized, well resourced and pursue clear missions. But NGOs are slow, underresourced, and have confused lines of responsibility, accountability, and authority (personal communication, 23 April 2001). See also UNHCR 1995.

29. Stuart Gordon notes, in addition, that the doctrines of the United States and French militaries follow this pattern of privileging strategic over humanitarian imperatives (2007 "Unintended consequences of civil-military cooperation in peace operations," especially, 112–13).

30. Sandra Whitworth, Charlene Cook, and Donna Winslow have suggested that a gender-based analysis helps illuminate this move as well. See Whitworth 2004 *Men, Militarism and UN Peacekeeping: A Gendered Analysis*; and Cook and Winslow 2007 "The role of gender in civil-military cooperation: a unique opportunity for change."

31. On southern Lebanon, see Heiberg 1990 "Peacekeepers and local populations: some comments on UNIFIL." On Nicaragua, James Quesada, (personal communication, 17 February 1990), On Kosovo, Elizabeth Callendar (personal communication, 1 June 2002). For Cairo, my own field research. And see Ammitzboell 2007 "Unintended consequences of peace operations on the host economy from a people's perspective."

32. For a guide to these activities, see Aoi, de Coning, and Thakur 2007.

33. Chopra and Hohe 2004 "Participatory intervention."

34. The success of the United Nations in leading efforts for decolonization and self-determination is held out as a signal achievement for the organization during the second half of the twentieth century. See, for example, Urquhart 1989 *Decolonization and World Peace*.

35. In the case of Kosovo and East Timor, this trajectory was intensified because the missions were deeply involved with the administration of society and employed models that contradicted local structures, perhaps more than earlier missions. Tanja Hohe Chopra, personal communication, 2 September 2007.

36. Ammitzboell 2007; Chopra 2000 "The UN's kingdom of East Timor."

37. Michael Bhatia gives a similar account in relation to international groups working in Afghanistan. He observes, "In addition to the over 30,000 soldiers deployed to Afghanistan as part of ISAF, NATO and the United States, there are thousands of expatriates in Afghanistan, predominantly concentrated in Kabul. Yet many foreign 'helpers' live sheltered from daily life in Afghanistan—rarely traveling outside of Kabul and only interacting with Afghans as colleagues, servants or beneficiaries. Closeness is prevented by guardposts, compound walls, restaurants and the closed doors of white landcruisers." See Bhatia 2007 "Shooting Afghanistan: beyond the conflict (II)," *The Globalist*, 28 August 2007, http://www.theglobalist.com/StoryId.aspx?StoryId=6417.

38. Clearly there are those in a society who benefit from the extra income that the inflated rents and salary might bring. Indeed, as Tanja Hohe Chopra (personal communication, 2 September 2007) notes, in her experience in East Timor, some families found this income to be critical to their survival and reestablishment of normal life.

39. See, for examples, Findlay 2002 *The Use of Force in UN Peace Operations*; Heiberg 1990; Urquhart 1993 *Ralph Bunche: An American Odyssey*; and discussions earlier in this book.

40. At times, this lack of attention to local level concerns was not a mere by-product of preoccupation with other factors—attention to such factors was actively discouraged. For contemporaneous critique of this tendency in international affairs in the 1980s and 1990s, see Foster and Rubinstein 1986 *Peace and War: Cross-Cultural Perspectives*; and Rubinstein and Foster 1997 *The Social Dynamics of Peace and Conflict: Culture in International Security*.

41. See, for instance, Chopra 1999 *The Politics of Peace-Maintenance*.

42. That there are only imprecise understandings about what constitutes peacekeeping and other operations other than war contributes to this confusion. It is still the case that "a definitional haze surrounds the varieties of peace operations, with a flurry of descriptions, terms and operational evolutions resulting in general confusion of peacekeeping, with peace enforcement, and UN sanctioned unilateral interventions." Bhatia 2003 *War and Intervention: Issues for Contemporary Peace Operations*, 11.

43. Aoi, de Coning, and Thakur 2007; Chopra 2002; Ghosh 1994 "The global reservation: notes toward an ethnography of international peacekeeping"; Rehn and Sirleaf 2002.

44. Sida 2005, 16.

45. Mersiades 2005 "Peacekeeping and legitimacy: lessons from Cambodia and Somalia." Mersiades' analysis of legitimacy is based on political theory, especially focusing on social contract theory, and thus differs in derivation from the cultural analysis presented here.

46. Hohe 2003 "Justice without judiciary in East Timor," 346.

47. Especially insightful work on the issues of engaging local political understandings and governance structures can be found in Hohe 2002a "Clash of paradigms: international administration and local political legitimacy in East Timor"; Hohe 2002b "Totem polls: indigenous concepts of 'free and fair' elections in East Timor"; and Hohe 2003.

48. Chopra 2002; Ghosh 1994; Nordstrom and Fetherston 1995 "Overcoming *habitus* in conflict management: UN peacekeeping and war zone ethnography."

Chapter 9

1. This is a widely repeated aphorism (see International Commission on Intervention and State Sovereignty 2001 *The Responsibility to Protect: Report of the International Commission on Intervention and State Sovereignty*, 181). It has been repeated so often that it is sometimes mistakenly credited to others (e.g., Anderson 2000 "The savage war of peace—an uncertain future we can't ignore").

2. Auden 1966 foreword. See also Stolpe 1966 *Dag Hammarskjöld: A Spiritual Portrait*.

3. Sahlins 1999 "Two or three things that I know about culture," 400.

4. International Commission on Intervention and State Sovereignty 2001.

5. O'Brien and Topolski 1968 *The United Nations: Sacred Drama*.

6. For this reason, the drive to streamline the United Nations and to make it conform to one particular vision of administrative efficiency is extremely dangerous. While administrative reform is clearly needed in an organization that has become bloated by redundancy and postings that are rightfully seen as sinecures, it is also important that the diversity that leads to the creative and moral tensions in the institution not be squelched.

7. Brahimi 2000 *Report of the Panel on United Nations Peace Operations*.

8. See, for example, Chopra 1999 *The Politics of Peace-Maintenance*.

9. Last says, "Peacekeeping and imperial policing are not the same. Peacekeeping . . . respects the control of the community over the instruments of coercion. Imperial policing is more coercive and imposes structures that serve external interests, usually for economic gain" (translation by David Last; 2006 "Marcher sur la corde raide: le maintien de la paix et le maintiende l'ordre impérial" 63–88).

10. Ralph Bunche 1950 "Nobel lecture: some reflections on peace in our time." Similar observations have been made about the role of peacekeeping in Grist 2001 "More than eunuchs at the orgy: observation and monitoring reconsidered," and by those who note that contemporary efforts to spread democracy through expeditionary force contain the seeds of their own failure.

References

All URLs in the references and notes are current as of February 2008.

Aall, P., D. Miltenberger, and T. G. Weiss. 2000. *Guide to IGOs, NGOs, and the Military in Peace and Relief Operations*. Washington, DC: United States Institute of Peace Press.

Aarvik, E. 1997. The Nobel Peace Prize 1988, presentation speech by Egil Aarvik. In *Nobel Lectures in Peace 1981–1990*. Edited by I. Abrams, 207–32. Singapore: World Scientific Publishing.

Abiew, F. K., and T. Keating. 1999. NGOs and UN peacekeeping operations: strange bedfellows. *International Peacekeeping* 6:89–111.

Ablon, J. 1977. Field methods in working with middle-class Americans: new issues of values, personality, and reciprocity. *Human Organization* 36:69–72.

Abu-Lughod, L. 1986. *Veiled Sentiments: Honor and Poetry in a Bedouin Society*. Berkeley, CA: University of California Press.

African Civil-Military Coordination Programme. 2006. *CIMIC in UN and African Peace Operations: Resources. Fifth Draft*. KwaZulu-Natal, South Africa: African Centre for the Constructive Resolution of Disputes.

Ammitzboell, K. 2007. Unintended consequences of peace operations on the host economy from a people's perspective. In *Unintended Consequences of Peacekeeping Operations*. Edited by C. Aoi, C. de Coning, and R. Thakur, 69–89. Tokyo: United Nations University Press.

Anderson, D. E. 2000. The savage war of peace—an uncertain future we can't ignore. *Air Force Journal of Logistics* 29:28.

Aning, K. 2007. Unintended consequences of peace operations for troop-contributing countries for West Africa: the case of Ghana. In *Unintended Consequences of Peacekeeping Operations*. Edited by C. Aoi, C. de Coning, and R. Thakur, 133–55. Tokyo: United Nations University Press.

Aoi, C., C. de Coning, and R. Thakur, eds. 2007. *Unintended Consequences of Peacekeeping Operations*. Tokyo: United Nations University Press.

Apter, M. J. 2001. An introduction to Reversal Theory. In *Motivational Styles in Everyday Life: A Guide to Reversal Theory*. Edited by M. J. Apter, 3–35. Washington, DC: American Psychological Association.

———. 2005. *Personality Dynamics: Key Concepts in Reversal Theory*. Loughborough, United Kingdom: Apter International, Ltd.

174

———. 2007. *Reversal Theory: The Dynamics of Motivation, Emotion and Personality.* Second edition. Oxford: Oneworld Publications.

Apter, M. J., D. Fontana, and S. Murgatroyd. eds. 1985. *Reversal Theory: Applications and Developments.* Cardiff, United Kingdom: University College Cardiff Press.

Auden, W. H. 1966. Foreword to *Markings,* by D. Hammarskjöld. Translated by L. Sjöberg and W. H. Auden. New York: Alfred A. Knopf.

Austin, J. H. 2001. *Zen and the Brain: Toward an Understanding of Meditation and Consciousness.* Cambridge, MA: MIT Press.

Avruch, K. 1998. *Culture and Conflict Resolution.* Washington, DC: United States Institute of Peace.

———. 1999. Civilian perspectives on the analysis of civil military interactions: introductory remarks. In *Analysis of Civil-Military Interactions.* Edited by A. Woodcock and D. Davis, 87–91. Clementsport, NS: Canadian Peacekeeping Press.

Avruch, K., J. Narel, and P. C. Siegel. 1999. *Information Campaigns for Peace Operations.* Washington, DC: Department of Defense C41 SR Cooperative Research Program.

Babcock, B. 1978a. Introduction to *The Reversible World: Symbolic Inversion in Art and Society.* Ithaca, NY: Cornell University Press.

———, ed. 1978b. *The Reversible World: Symbolic Inversion in Art and Society.* Ithaca, NY: Cornell University Press.

Barry, J., and A. Jefferys. 2002. *A Bridge too Far: Aid Agencies and the Military in Humanitarian Response.* London: Humanitarian Practice Network, Overseas Development Institute.

Barth, F. 1969. Introduction to *Ethnic Groups and Boundaries: The Social Organization of Culture Difference.* Edited by F. Barth, 9–38. London: Allen and Unwin.

Bartlett, T. 2000. UN medal parade, http://www.diggerz.org/~adaa/unm.htm.

Bateson, M. C. 1988. Compromise and the rhetoric of good and evil. In *The Social Dynamics of Peace and Conflict: Culture in International Security.* Edited by R. A. Rubinstein and M. L. Foster, 35–46. Boulder, CO: Westview Press.

Beeman, W. O. 1986. "Conflict and belief in American foreign policy. In *Peace and War: Cross-Cultural Perspectives.* Edited by M. L. Foster and R. A. Rubinstein, 333–42. New Brunswick, NJ: Transaction Books.

Bell, C. 1997. *Ritual: Perspectives and Dimensions.* Oxford: Oxford University Press.

Ben-Ari, E. 1998. *Mastering Soldiers: Conflict, Emotions and the Enemy in an Israeli Military Unit.* Oxford: Berghahn Books.

———. 2001. Blue helmets and white armor: multi-nationalism and multi-culturalism among UN peacekeeping forces. *City and Society* 13:271–302.

Benedict, R. 1934. *Patterns of Culture.* New York: Houghton Mifflin.

———. 1946. *The Chrysanthemum and the Sword.* Boston: Houghton Mifflin.

Bercuson, D. 1996. *Significant Incident: Canada's Army, the Airborne, and the Murder in Somalia.* Toronto: McClelland and Stewart.

Bhatia, Michael V. 2003. *War and Intervention: Issues for Contemporary Peace Operations.* Bloomfield, CT: Kumarian Press.

———. 2007. Shooting Afghanistan—beyond the conflict. *The Globalist* http://www.theglobalist.com/StoryId.aspx?StoryId=6417.

Bidney, D. 1967. *Theoretical Anthropology*. New York: Schocken Books.

Blum, H. 2003. *The Eve of Destruction: The Untold Story of the Yom Kippur War*. New York: HarperCollins.

Boas, Franz. 1919. Scientists as spies. *The Nation* 109:797.

Boatner, M. M. 1956. *Military Customs and Traditions*. Westport, CT: Greenwood Press.

Bond, M. H. 2002. Reclaiming the individual from Hofstede's ecological analysis— a 20-year odyssey: comment on Oyserman et al. (2002). *Psychological Bulletin* 128:73–77.

Bourdieu, P. 1990. *The Logic of Practice*. Stanford, CA: Stanford University Press.

Bourdieu, P., and L. J. D. Wacquant. 1992. *An Invitation to Reflexive Sociology*. Chicago: University of Chicago Press.

Boutros-Ghali, B. 1992. *An Agenda for Peace: Preventive Diplomacy, Peacemaking and Peace-keeping*. New York: United Nations.

Bowden, M. 1999. *Black Hawk Down: A Story of Modern War*. New York: Penguin Books.

Bowden, M., and P. Ironside. 2003. *OCHA Glossary of Humanitarian Terms in Relation to the Protection of Civilians in Armed Conflict*. New York: United Nations Office for the Coordination of Humanitarian Affairs.

Brahimi, L. 2000. *Report of the Panel on United Nations Peace Operations*. New York: United Nations.

Brasset, D. 1997. Values and the exercise of power: military elites. In *The Social Dynamics of Peace and Conflict: Culture in International Security*. Edited by R. A. Rubinstein and M. L. Foster, 81–90. Dubuque, IA: Kendall/Hunt Publishing.

Brett, J. M. 2001. *Negotiating Globally: How to Negotiate Deals, Resolve Disputes, and Make Decisions Across Cultures*. San Francisco: Jossey-Bass.

Briggs, C. 1986. *Learning How to Ask: A Sociolinguistic Appraisal of the Role of the Interview in Social Science Research*. Cambridge: Cambridge University Press.

Britt, T. W., and A. B. Adler, eds. 2003. *The Psychology of the Peacekeeper*. Westport, CT: Praeger.

Bunche, Ralph. 1950. "Nobel lecture: some reflections on peace in our time," December 11, http://nobelprize.org/nobel_prizes/peace/laureates/1950/bunche-lecture.html.

Caesaris, C. I. 1881. *Commentarii de bello civili*. Erklärt von Friedrich Kranner. Achte Auflage von Dr. Friedrich Hofmann. Berlin: Weidmannsche Buchhandlung.

Caplan, P., ed. 1995. *Understanding Disputes: The Politics of Argument*. Oxford: Berg Publishers.

Chagnon, N. 1968. *Yanomamo: The Fierce People*. New York: Holt, Rinehart, and Winston.

Chandler, D. 2004. Imposing the "rule of law": the lessons of BiH for peacebuilding in Iraq. *International Peacekeeping* 11:312–33.

Chayes, A., A. Chayes, and G. Raach. 1997. Beyond reform: restructuring for more effective conflict intervention. *Global Governance* 3:117–45.

Chomsky, Noam. 2006. *Failed States: The Abuse of Power and the Assault on Democracy*. New York: Metropolitan Books.

Chopra, J. 1999. *Peace-Maintenance: The Evolution of International Political Authority*. London: Routledge.

———. 2000. The UN's kingdom of East Timor. *Survival* 42:27–40.

Chopra, J, ed. 1999. *The Politics of Peace-Maintenance*. London: Routledge.

Chopra, J., and T. Hohe. 2004. Participatory intervention. *Global Governance* 10:289–305.

Ciechanski, J. 1994. Restructuring the UN Security Council. *International Peacekeeping* 1:413–39.

Cohen, A. 1974. *Two-Dimensional Man: An Essay on the Anthropology of Power and Symbolism in Complex Society*. Berkeley, CA: University of California Press.

Cohen, R. 1990. *Culture and Conflict in Egyptian-Israeli Affairs: A Dialogue of the Deaf*. Bloomington, IN: Indiana University Press.

———. 1997. *Negotiating Across Cultures*. Revised edition. Washington, DC: United States Institute of Peace.

Cook, C., and D. Winslow. 2007. The role of gender in civil-military cooperation: a unique opportunity for change. *Peace and Conflict Studies* 14:58–72.

Costa, G. 1995. The United Nations and reform of the police in El Salvador. *International Peacekeeping* 2:365–90.

Cunningham, R. B., and Y. K. Sarayrah. 1993. *Wasta: The Hidden Force in Middle Eastern Society*. Westport, CT: Praeger.

d'Andrade, R. G. 1984. Cultural meaning systems. In *Culture Theory: Essays on Mind, Self, and Emotion*. Edited by R. A. Shweder and R. A. LeVine, 88–119. Cambridge: Cambridge University Press.

———. 1990. Cultural cognition. In *Foundations of Cognitive Science*. Edited by M. I. Posner, 795–830. Cambridge, MA: MIT Press.

d'Aquili, E. G., and C. D. Laughlin. 1979. The neurobiology of myth and ritual. In *The Spectrum of Ritual: A Biogenetic Structural Analysis*. Edited by E. G. d'Aquili, C. D. Laughlin, and J. McManus. New York: Columbia University Press.

d'Aquili, E., C. D. Laughlin, and J. McManus, eds. 1979. *The Spectrum of Ritual: A Biogenetic Structural Analysis*. New York: Columbia University Press.

Dallaire, R. 2004. *Shake Hands with the Devil: The Failure of Humanity in Rwanda*. New York: Carroll and Graf Publishers.

Dayal, R. 1976. *Mission for Hammarskjöld: The Congo Crisis*. Princeton, NJ: Princeton University Press.

Debrix, F. 1999. *Re-Envisioning Peacekeeping. The United Nations and the Mobilization of Ideology*. Minneapolis: University of Minnesota Press.

DeWitte, L. 2001. *The Assassination of Lumumba*. London: Verso.

Dobbins, J., S. G. Jones, K. Crane, A. Rathmell, B. Steele, R. Teltschik, and A. Timilsina. 2004. *The UN's Role in Nation-Building: From the Congo to Iraq*. Santa Monica, CA: RAND Corporation.

Dolgin, J. L., D. S. Kemnitzer, and D. M. Schneider, eds. 1977. *Symbolic Anthropology: A Reader in the Study of Symbols and Meanings*. New York: Columbia University Press.

Donald, D. 2002. Neutrality, impartiality and UN peacekeeping at the beginning of the 21st century. *International Peacekeeping* 9:21–38.

Donini, A. 1996. Asserting humanitarianism in peace-maintenance. *Global Governance* 4:81–96.

Druckman, D., J. A. Wall, and P. F. Diehl. 1999. Conflict resolution roles in international peacekeeping missions. In *The New Agenda for Peace Research*. Edited by H. W. Jeong, 105–34. Aldershot, United Kingdom: Ashgate.

Duffey, T. 2000. Cultural issues in contemporary peacekeeping. *International Peace-keeping* 7:142–68.

Durch, William J. 1996. Introduction to anarchy: humanitarian intervention and "state-building" in Somalia. In *UN Peacekeeping, US Policy and the Uncivil Wars of the 1990s*. Edited by W. J. Durch, 311–66. New York: St. Martin's Press.

———. 2007. *Twenty-first-Century Peace Operations*. Washington, DC: United States Institute of Peace Press.

Earley, P. C. 2006. Leading cultural research in the future: a matter of paradigms and taste. *Journal of International Business Studies* 36:922–32.

Eide, E. B., A. T. Kaspersen, R. Kent, and K. von Hipple. 2005. *Report on Integrated Missions: Practical Perspectives and Recommendations. Independent Study of the Expanded UN ECHA Core Group*. Oslo: Norway Ministry of Foreign Affairs and Norwegian Institute of International Affairs.

Eidelson, R. J. 2003. *Modeling Crowd Behavior: The Core Beliefs of Crowd Members and Control Force Agents*. Working paper. Philadelphia: Solomon Asch Center for the Study of Ethnopolitical Conflict, University of Pennsylvania.

Elron, E., N. Halevy, E. Ben-Ari, and B. Shamir. 2003. Cooperation and coordination across cultures in the peacekeeping forces: individual and organizational integrating mechanisms. In *The Psychology of the Peacekeeper: Lessons from the Field*. Edited by T. W. Britt and A. B. Adler, 262–82. Westport, CT: Praeger.

Erickson, P. A., and L. Murphy. 2003. *A History of Anthropological Theory*. Second edition. Orchard Park, NY: Broadview Press.

Erskine, E. A. 1989. *Mission with UNIFIL: An African Soldier's Reflections*. New York: St. Martin's Press.

Fábos, A. 2008. *"Brothers" or Others: Muslim Arab Sudanese in Egypt*. Oxford: Berghahn Books.

Fauconnier, G., and M. Turner. 2002. *The Way We Think: Conceptual Blending and the Mind's Hidden Complexities*. New York: Basic Books.

Fenner, F., ed. 1989. *Smallpox and Its Eradication*. Geneva: World Health Organization.

Fetherston, A. B. 1994. *Towards a Theory of United Nations Peacekeeping*. New York: St. Martin's Press.

Findlay, T. 2002. *The Use of Force in UN Peace Operations*. Oxford: Oxford University Press.

Fisher, G. 1988. *Mindsets: The Role of Culture and Perception in International Relations*. Yarmouth, ME: Intercultural Press.

Fiske, A. P. 2002. Using individualism and collectivism to compare cultures—a critique of the validity of measurement of the constructs: comment on Oyserman et al. (2002). *Psychological Bulletin* 128:78–88.

Foley, W. A. 1997. *Anthropological Linguistics: An Introduction*. Malden, MA: Blackwell.

Foster, M. L. 1988. Cultural triggering of psychological reversals. In *Progress in Reversal Theory*. Edited by M. J. Apter, J. H. Kerr, and M. Cowles, 63–75. Amsterdam: Elsevier.

———. 1993. Reversal theory and the institutionalization of war. In *Advances in Reversal Theory*. Edited by J. Kerr, S. Murgatroyd, and M. Apter, 67–74. Amsterdam: Swets and Zeitlinger.

———. 1994. Symbolism: the foundation of culture. In *Companion Encyclopedia of Anthropology: Humanity, Culture and Social Life*. Edited by T. Ingold, 366–95. London: Routledge.

Foster, M. L., and S. Brandes, eds. 1980. *Symbol as Sense: New Approaches to the Analysis of Meaning*. New York: Academic Press.

Foster, M. L., and R. A. Rubinstein, eds. 1986. *Peace and War: Cross-Cultural Perspectives*. New Brunswick, NJ: Transaction Books.

Ghosh, A. 1994. The global reservation: notes toward an ethnography of international peacekeeping. *Cultural Anthropology* 9:412–22.

Glasser, B. G., and A. L. Strauss. 1967. *The Discovery of Grounded Theory: Strategies for Qualitative Research*. Chicago: Aldine.

Gluck, K. 2004. *Coalition Forces Endanger Humanitarian Action in Afghanistan*. Médecins Sans Frontières, http://www.msf.org/countries/page.cfm?articleid=409F102D-A77A-4C94-89E0A47D7213B4D5.

Goffman, E. 1959. *The Presentation of Self in Everyday Life*. New York: Doubleday.

Goldschmidt, W. 1990. *The Human Career: The Self in the Symbolic World*. Oxford: Blackwell.

Gonzalez, N. 1986. Ethnic targeting as a defense strategy. In *Peace and War: Cross-Cultural Perspectives*. Edited by M. L. Foster and R. A. Rubinstein, 119–32. New Brunswick, NJ: Transaction Books.

Goodwin, Deborah. 2005. *The Military and Negotiation: The Role of the Soldier-Diplomat*. London: Frank Cass.

Gordon, S. 2007. Unintended consequences of civil-military cooperation in peace operations. In *Unintended Consequences of Peacekeeping Operations*. Edited by C. Aoi, C. de Coning, and R. Thakur, 109–29. Tokyo: United Nations University Press.

Goulding, M. 1993. The evolution of United Nations peacekeeping. *International Affairs* 69:451–64.

———. 1996. The use of force by the United Nations. *International Peacekeeping* 3:1–18.

Graves, K. 2006. Who can keep the peace? In http://news.sky.com/skynews/article/0,,30000-1228278,00.html.

Greig, J. M. 2001. Recognizing conditions of ripeness for international mediation between enduring rivals. *Journal of Conflict Resolution* 45:691–718.

Grist, R. 2001. More than eunuchs at the orgy: observation and monitoring reconsidered. *International Peacekeeping* 8:59–78.

Gulliver, P. H. 1979. *Disputes and Negotiations: A Cross-Cultural Perspective*. New York: Academic Press.

Gusterson, H. 1993. Exploding anthropology's canon in the world of the bomb: ethnographic writing on militarism. *Journal of Contemporary Ethnography* 22:59–79.

———. 1997. Studying up revisited. *Political and Legal Anthropology Review* 20:114–19.

Hajjar, R. 2006. The Army's new TRADOC Culture Center. *Military Review* (November–December): 89–92.

Hall, E. 1967. *Beyond Culture*. New York: Anchor Books.

Hannerz, U. 1996. *Transnational Connections: Culture, People, Places*. London: Routledge.

Harbottle, M. 1970. *The Impartial Soldier*. London: Oxford University Press.

Harris, M. 2001. *The Rise of Anthropological Theory: A History of Theories of Culture*. Updated edition. Walnut Creek, CA: AltaMira Press.

Hatch, E. 1973. *Theories of Man and Culture*. New York: Columbia University Press.

Hawkins, J. P. 2001. *Army of Hope, Army of Alienation: Culture and Contradiction in the American Army Communities of Cold War Germany*. Westport, CT: Praeger.

Heiberg, M. 1990. Peacekeepers and local populations: some comments on UNIFIL. In *The United Nations and Peacekeeping. Results, Limitations and Prospects: The Lessons of 40 Years of Experience*. Edited by I. J. Rikhye and K. Skjelsbaek, 147–69. London: Macmillan.

———, ed. 1994. *Subduing Sovereignty: Sovereignty and the Right to Intervene*. London: Pinter Publishers.

Heiberg, M., and J. Holst. 1986. Peacekeeping in Lebanon: comparing UNIFIL and the MNF. *Survival* 28:410–11.

Heikal, M. 1976. *The Road to Ramadan*. New York: Ballantine Books.

Herman, A. P. 1937. An answer to criticisms of the lag concept. *The American Journal of Sociology* 43:440–51.

Hillen, J. 1998. *Blue Helmets: The Strategy of UN Military Operations*. Washington, DC: Brassey's.

Hirsch, J. L., and R. B. Oakley. 1995. *Somalia and Operation Restore Hope: Reflections on Peacemaking and Peacekeeping*. Washington, DC: United States Institute of Peace Press.

Hochschild, A. 1998. *King Leopold's Ghost: A Story of Greed, Terror, and Heroism in Colonial Africa*. New York: Houghton Mifflin.

Hofstede, G. 1991. *Culture and Organizations, Software of the Mind: Intercultural Cooperation and Its Importance for Survival*. London: McGraw-Hill.

———. 2006. What did GLOBE really measure? Researchers' minds versus respondents' minds. *Journal of International Business Studies* 36:882–96.

Hohe, T. 2002a. Clash of paradigms: international administration and local political legitimacy in East Timor. *Contemporary Southeast Asia* 24:569–89.

———. 2002b. Totem polls: indigenous concepts of "free and fair" elections in East Timor. *International Peacekeeping* 9:69–88.

———. 2003. Justice without judiciary in East Timor. *Conflict, Security and Development* 3:335–57.

Holland, D., and N. Quinn, eds. 1987. *Cultural Models in Language and Thought*. Cambridge: Cambridge University Press.

Holm, T. T., and E. B. Eide, eds. 2000. *Peacebuilding and Police Reform*. London: Frank Cass.

Hopkins, J. 1989. *The Eradication of Smallpox: Organizational Learning and Innovation in International Health*. Boulder, CO: Westview Press.

Houghton, R. B., and F. G. Trinka. 1984. *Multinational Peacekeeping in the Middle East*. Washington, DC: Foreign Service Institute, US Department of State.

House, R. J., P. J. Hanges, M. Javidan, P. W. Dorfman, and V. Gupta, eds. 2004. *Culture, Leadership, and Organizations: The GLOBE Study of 62 Societies*. Thousand Oaks, CA: Sage Publishers.

Humphrey, N. 1984. *Consciousness Regained: Chapters in the Development of Mind.* Oxford: Oxford University Press.

International Commission on Intervention and State Sovereignty. 2001. *The Responsibility to Protect: Report of the International Commission on Intervention and State Sovereignty.* Ottawa: International Development Research Centre.

International Peace Academy. 1984. *Peacekeeper's Handbook.* Third edition. New York: Pergamon Press.

Javidan, M., R. J. House, P. W. Dorfman, P. J. Hanges, and M. S. de Luque. 2006. Conceptualizing and measuring cultures and their consequences: a comparative review of GLOBE's and Hofstede's approaches. *Journal of International Business Studies* 36:897–914.

Joint Nordic Committee for Military UN Matters. 1986. *Nordic UN Stand-by Forces.* Third edition. Stockholm: Norstedts Tryckeri.

Joint Warfighting Center. 1997. *Joint Task Force Commander's Handbook for Peace Operations.* Fort Monroe, VA: Joint Warfighting Center.

Jok, J. M. 1998. *Militarization, Gender and Reproductive Health in South Sudan.* Lewiston, ME: Edwin Mellen Press.

———. 2004. *Sudan at the Crossroads: Promoting Physical and Human Security.* Medford, MA: The Fletcher School, Tufts University.

Kalb, M. G. 1982. The U.N.'s embattled peacekeeper. *New York Times Magazine*, 19 December, 45–48, 52–53, 59–60.

Kashima, Y. 1997. Culture, narrative, and human motivation. In *Motivation and Culture.* Edited by D. Munro, J. F. Schumaker, and C. C. Stuart, 16–30. London: Routledge.

Katz, P. 1990. Emotional metaphors, socialization, and roles of drill sergeants. *Ethos* 18:457–80.

Kelly, M., and M. Rostrup. 2002. Identify yourselves: coalition soldiers in Afghanistan are endangering aid workers. *The Guardian*, 1 February, 19, http://www.guardian.co.uk/society/2002/feb/01/comment.

Kent, V. 2007. Protecting civilians from UN peacekeepers and humanitarian workers: sexual exploitation and abuse. In *Unintended Consequences of Peacekeeping Operations.* Edited by C. Aoi, C. de Coning, and R. Thakur, 44–66. Tokyo: United Nations University Press.

Kertzer, D. I. 1988. *Ritual, Politics, and Power.* New Haven, CT: Yale University Press.

Kim, H. S., and D. K. Sherman. 2007. Express your self: culture and the effect of self-expression choice. *Journal of Personality and Social Psychology* 92:1–11.

Kinzer, S. 2006. *Overthrow: America's Century of Regime Change from Hawaii to Iraq.* New York: Times Books, Henry Holt and Company.

Kirsch, I. 1999. Response expectancy: an introduction. In *How Expectancies Shape Experience.* Edited by I. Kirsch, 3–13. Washington, DC: American Psychological Association.

Kleiboer, M. 1994. Ripeness of conflict: a fruitful notion? *Journal of Peace Research* 31:109–16.

———. 1998. *The Multiple Realities of International Mediation.* Boulder, CO: Lynne Rienner Publishers.

Koch, B. J. 1983. Presentation as proof: the language of Arabic rhetoric. *Anthropological Linguistics* 25:47–60.

Kochman, T. 1981. *Black and White Styles in Conflict*. Chicago: University of Chicago Press.

Kroeber, A. L., and C. Kluckhohn. 1952. *Culture: A Critical Review of Concepts and Definitions*. Cambridge, MA: Peabody Museum Papers.

Krulak, C. C. 1999. The strategic corporal: leadership in the three block war. *Marines Magazine*. (January): http://www.maxwell.af.mil/au/awc/awcgate/usmc/strategic_corporal.htm.

Kuper, A. 1999. *Culture: The Anthropologists' Account*. Cambridge, MA: Harvard University Press.

Lakoff, G., and M. Johnson. 1980. *Metaphors We Live By*. Chicago: University of Chicago Press.

Langholtz, H. J, ed. 1998. *The Psychology of Peacekeeping*. Westport, CT: Praeger.

Last, D. 2006. "Marcher sur la corde raide: le maintien de la paix et le maintiende l'ordre impérial," in *Guide du maintien de la paix 2007*. Edited by J. Coulon, 63–88. Outremont, QC: Athéna Editions.

Laughlin, C. D., and I. Brady, eds. 1978. *Extinction and Survival in Human Populations*. New York: Columbia University Press.

Laughlin, C. D., and E. d'Aquili. 1974. *Biogenetic Structuralism*. New York: Columbia University Press.

Laughlin, C. D., J. McManus, and E. d'Aquili. 1990. *Brain, Symbol and Experience: Toward a Neurophenomenology of Human Consciousness*. Boston: Shambala Publications.

Laughlin, C. D., J. McManus, R. A. Rubinstein, and J. Shearer. 1986. The ritual transformation of experience. *Studies in Symbolic Interaction* 7:107–36.

Leeds, C. A. 2001. Culture, conflict resolution, peacekeeper training and the D mediator. *International Peacekeeping* 8:92–110.

Lehmann, I. 1999. *Peacekeeping and Public Information: Caught in the Crossfire*. London: Frank Cass Publishers.

LeVine, R. A. 1984. Properties of culture. In *Culture Theory: Essays on Mind, Self, and Emotion*. Edited by R. A. Schweder and R. A. LeVine. Cambridge: Cambridge University Press.

Lex, B. 1979. Neurobiology of ritual trance. In *The Spectrum of Ritual: A Biogenetic Structural Analysis*. Edited by E. d'Aquili, C. D. Laughlin, and J. McManus, 117–51. New York: Columbia University Press.

Liddy, L. 2005. The strategic corporal: some requirements in training and education. *Australian Army Journal* 11:139–48.

Lindley, D. 2004. Untapped power? the status of UN information operations. *International Peacekeeping* 11:608–24.

Lovell, J. P. 1990. The United States as ally and adversary in East Asia: reflections on culture and foreign policy. In *Culture and International Relations*. Edited by J. Chay, 89–102. Westport, CT: Praeger.

Lutz, C. 2001. *Homefront: A Military City and the American Twentieth Century*. Boston: Beacon Press.

Mackinlay, J., and J. Chopra. 1993. *A Draft Concept of Second Generation Multinational Operations*. Providence, RI: Thomas J. Watson Institute for International Studies, Brown University.

Makinda, S. 1993. *Seeking Peace from Chaos: Humanitarian Intervention in Somalia*. Boulder, CO: Lynne Rienner Publishers.

Malinowski, B. 1941. An anthropological analysis of war. *American Journal of Sociology* 46:521–50.

———. 1961 [1922]. *Argonauts of the Western Pacific: An Account of Native Enterprise and Adventure in the Archipelagoes of Melanesian New Guinea*. New York: Dutton.

Malone, D., ed. 2004. *The UN Security Council: From the Cold War to the 21st Century* Boulder, CO: Lynne Rienner Publishers.

Maloney, Sean M. 2002. *Canada and UN Peacekeeping: Cold War by Other Means 1945–1970*. St. Catherines, Ont.: Vanwell Publishing.

Maturana, H. R., and F. J. Varela. 1988. *The Tree of Knowledge: The Biological Roots of Human Understanding*. Boston: New Science Library.

McClelland, C. A., ed. 1960. *The United Nations: The Continuing Debate*. San Francisco: H. Chandler.

McDermott, A. 1999. Japan's financial contribution to the UN system: in pursuit of acceptance and standing. *International Peacekeeping* 6:64–88.

McFarland, M. 2005. Military cultural education. *Military Review* 85 (March–April): 62–69.

McFate, Montgomery. 2005. Anthropology and counterinsurgency: the strange story of their curious relationship. *Military Review* 85 (March–April): 24–38.

McLeod, J. 1987. *Ain't No Makin' It: Leveled Aspirations in a Low-Income Neighborhood*. Boulder, CO: Westview Press.

Mead, M. 1942. *And Keep Your Powder Dry: An Anthropologist Looks at America*. New York: W. Morrow and Company.

Mersiades, Michael. 2005. Peacekeeping and legitimacy: lessons from Cambodia and Somalia. *International Peacekeeping* 12:205–11.

Munro, D. 1997. Levels and processes in motivation and culture. In *Motivation and Culture*. Edited by D. Munro, J. F. Schumaker, and C. C. Stuart, 3–15. London: Routledge.

Murphy, G. R., S.J. 1979. A ceremonial ritual: the Mass. In *The Spectrum of Ritual: A Biogenetic Structural Analysis*. Edited by E. d'Aquili, C. D. Laughlin, and J. McManus, 318–41. New York: Columbia University Press.

Murphy, W. P. 1990. Creating the appearance of consensus in Mende political discourse. *American Anthropologist* 92:24–41.

Murthy, C. S. R. 2007. Unintended consequences of peace operations for troop-contributing countries from South Asia. In *Unintended Consequences of Peacekeeping Operations*. Edited by C. Aoi, C. de Coning, and R. Thakur, 156–70. Tokyo: United Nations University Press.

Myint-U, Thant, and Elizabeth Sellwood. 2000. *Knowledge and Multilateral Interventions: The UN's Experience in Cambodia and Bosnia-Herzegovina*. London: The Royal Institute of International Affairs.

Nachmani, Amikam. 1990. *International Intervention in the Greek Civil War: The United Nations Special Committee on the Balkans, 1947–1953*. New York: Praeger.

Nader, L. 1969. Up the anthropologist—perspectives gained from studying up. In *Reinventing Anthropology*. Edited by D. Hymes, 284–311. New York: Pantheon.

Nordquist, J. 1997. *Pierre Bourdieu: A Bibliography*. Santa Cruz, CA: Reference and Research Services.

Nordstrom, C., and A. B. Fetherston. 1995. Overcoming *habitus* in conflict management: UN peacekeeping and war zone ethnography. *Peace and Change* 20:94–119.

Nordstrom, C., and A. C. G. M. Robben, eds. 1996. *Fieldwork Under Fire: Contemporary Studies of Violence and Survival*. Berkeley, CA: University of California Press.

Nzongola-Ntalaja, G. 2002. *The Congo from Leopold to Kabila: A People's History*. London: Zed Books.

O'Brien, C. C. 1962. *To Katanga and Back: A UN Case History*. New York: Simon and Schuster.

O'Brien, C. C., and F. Topolski. 1968. *The United Nations: Sacred Drama*. New York: Simon and Schuster.

Oakley, R. B., M. J. Dziedzic, and E. M. Goldberg, eds. 1998. *Policing the New World Disorder: Peace Operations and Public Security*. Washington, DC: National Defense University Press.

Ogburn, W. F. 1922. *Social Change*. New York: Viking Press.

Ortner, S. 1973. On key symbols. *American Anthropologist* 75:1,338–46.

Otterbein, K. 1970. *The Evolution of War: A Cross-Cultural Study*. New Haven, CT: HRAF Press.

Oyserman, D., H. M. Coon, and M. Kemmelmeir. 2002. Rethinking individualism and collectivism: evaluation of theoretical assumptions and meta-analyses. *Psychological Bulletin* 128:3–72.

Palmer, M., A. Leila, and E. S. Yassin. 1988. *The Egyptian Bureaucracy*. Syracuse, NY: Syracuse University Press.

Paris, Roland. 1997. Peacebuilding and the limits of liberal internationalism. *International Security* 22:54–89.

———. 2000. Broadening the study of peace operations. *International Studies Review* 2:27–44.

———. 2002. International peacebuilding and the "mission civilisatrice." *Review of International Studies* 38:637–56.

———. 2003. Peacekeeping and the constraints of global culture. *European Journal of International Relations* 9:441–73.

Pelcovits, N. 1984. *Peacekeeping on the Arab-Israeli Fronts: Lessons from Sinai and Lebanon*. Boulder, CO: Westview Press.

Pepper, S. C. 1942. *World Hypotheses: A Study in Evidence*. Berkeley, CA: University of California Press.

Perito, R. M. 2004. *Where Is the Lone Ranger When We Need Him? America's Search for a Postconflict Stability Force*. Washington, DC: United States Institute of Peace Press.

———. 2007. *Guide to Participants in Peace, Stability, and Relief Operations*. Washington, DC: United States Institute of Peace Press.

Peterson, B. 2004. *Cultural Intelligence: A Guide to Working with People from Other Cultures.* Yarmouth, ME: Intercultural Press.

Picco, G. 1994. The U.N. and the use of force: leave the secretary general out of it. *Foreign Affairs* 73:14–18.

Plunkett, M. 1998. Reestablishing law and order in peace-maintenance. *Global Governance* 4:61–79.

Pouligny, B. 2006. *Peace Operations Seen from Below: UN Missions and Local People.* Bloomfield, CT: Kumarian Press.

Pritchard, G. 1995. Caught in the crossfire. In *Protection Force.* Ottawa: National Film Board of Canada.

Pruitt, D. G. 1997. Ripeness theory and the Oslo talks. *International Negotiation* 2:237–50.

Pugh, M., ed. 1996. *The UN, Peace and Force.* Reprint of a special issue of *International Peacekeeping* 3, no. 4. London: Frank Cass.

Pulliam, L. 1997. Achieving social competence in the navy community. In *The Social Dynamics of Peace and Conflict: Culture in International Security.* Edited by R. A. Rubinstein and M. L. Foster, 91–106. Dubuque, IA: Kendall/Hunt Publishing.

Randall, A. 1986. The culture of United States military enclaves. In *Peace and War: Cross-Cultural Perspectives.* Edited by M. L. Foster and R. A. Rubinstein, 61–69. New Brunswick, NJ: Transaction Books.

Razack, S. 2004. *Dark Threats and White Knights: The Somalia Affair, Peacekeeping and the New Imperialism.* Toronto: University of Toronto Press.

Rehn, E., and E. J. Sirleaf. 2002. *Women, War, and Peace.* New York: United Nations Development Fund for Women.

Reisman, W. M. 1993. The constitutional crisis in the United Nations. *American Journal of International Law* 87:80–90.

———. 1999. Sovereignty and human rights in contemporary international law. In *Democratic Governance and International Law.* Edited by G. H. Fox and B. R. Roth, 239–58. Cambridge: Cambridge University Press.

Richburg, K. B. 1993. Somalia battle killed 12 Americans, wounded 78. *Washington Post*, 5 October, A1.

Rikhye, I. J. 1978. *The Sinai Blunder: Withdrawal of the United Nations Emergency Force Leading to the Six Day War, June 1967.* New Delhi: Oxford and IBH Publishing.

———. 1984. *The Theory and Practice of Peacekeeping.* London: C. Hunt and Company.

Rikhye, I. J., M. Harbottle, and E. Bjorn. 1974. *The Thin Blue Line: International Peacekeeping and Its Future.* New Haven, CT: Yale University Press.

Rothschild, M. 2003. Bush trashes the United Nations. *The Progressive* 67:19–22.

Rubin, J. Z. 1991. The timing of ripeness and the ripeness of timing. In *Timing the Deescalation of International Conflicts.* Edited by L. Kriesberg and S. J. Thorson. Syracuse, NY: Syracuse University Press.

Rubinstein, R. A. 1986. The collapse of strategy: understanding ideological bias in policy decisions. In *Peace and War: Cross-Cultural Perspectives.* Edited by M. L. Foster and R. A. Rubinstein, 343–51. New Brunswick, NJ: Transaction Books.

———. 1988. Cultural analysis and international security. *Alternatives* 13:529–42.

———. 1989. Culture, international affairs and peacekeeping: confusing process and pattern. *Cultural Dynamics* 2:41–61.

———. 1992. Culture and negotiation. In *The Struggle for Peace: Israelis and Palestinians*. Edited by E. W. Fernea and M. E. Hocking, 116–29. Austin: University of Texas Press.

———. 1993. Cultural aspects of peacekeeping: notes on the substance of symbols. *Millennium: Journal of International Studies* 22:547–62.

———. 1998. Methodological challenges in the ethnographic study of multilateral peacekeeping. *Political and Legal Anthropology Review* 21:138–49.

———, ed. 2001a. *Doing Fieldwork: The Correspondence of Robert Redfield and Sol Tax*. New Brunswick, NJ: Transaction Books.

———. 2001b. Reflection and reflexivity in anthropology. In *Doing Fieldwork: The Correspondence of Robert Redfield and Sol Tax*. Edited by R. A. Rubinstein, 1–35. New Brunswick, NJ: Transaction Books.

———. 2003a. Cross-cultural considerations in complex peace operations. *Negotiation Journal* 19:29–49.

———. 2003b. Politics and peacekeepers: experience and political representation among United States military officers. In *Anthropology and the United States Military: Coming of Age in the Twenty-First Century*. Edited by P. R. Frese and M. C. Harrell, 15–27. New York: Palgrave Macmillan.

Rubinstein, R. A., and M. L. Foster, eds. 1997. *The Social Dynamics of Peace and Conflict: Culture in International Security*. Dubuque, IA: Kendall/Hunt Publishing.

Rubinstein, R. A., D. M. Keller, and M. E. Scherger. nd. Culture and interoperability in integrated missions *International Peacekeeping*. Forthcoming.

Rubinstein, R. A., and S. D. Lane. 2000. Population, identity and political violence. *Social Justice: Anthropology, Peace and Human Rights* 3:130–52.

Rubinstein, R. A., and C. D. Laughlin. 1977. Bridging levels of systemic organization. *Current Anthropology* 18:459–63.

Rubinstein, R. A., C. D. Laughlin, and J. McManus. 1984. *Science as Cognitive Process: Toward an Empirical Philosophy of Science*. Philadelphia, PA: University of Pennsylvania Press.

Rubinstein, R. A., and S. Tax. 1985. Power, powerlessness, and the failure of "political realism." In *Native Power: The Quest for Autonomy and Nationhood of Indigenous People*. Edited by J. Brosted, J. Dahl, A. Gray, H. C. Gullov, G. Henriksen, J. B. Jorgensen, and I. Kleivan, 301–8. Bergen: Universitetsforlaget AS.

Rumelhart, D. 1980. Schemata: the building blocks of cognition. In *Theoretical Issues in Reading Comprehension: Perspectives from Cognitive Psychology, Linguistics, Artificial Intelligence, and Education*. Edited by R. J. Spiro, B. C. Bruce, and W. F. Brewer. Hillsdale, NJ: Lawrence Earlbaum.

Sahlins, M. 1999. Two or three things that I know about culture. *Journal of the Royal Anthropological Institute* 5:399–421.

Sahnoun, M. 1994. *Somalia: The Missed Opportunities*. Washington, DC: United States Institute of Peace Press.

Sanderson, J. M. 1998. The incalculable dynamic of using force. In *UN Peacekeeping in Trouble: Lessons Learned from the Former Yugoslavia*. Edited by W. Biermann and M. Vadset, 203–17. Aldershot, United Kingdom: Ashgate.

Saner, R., and L. Yiu. 2002. Porous boundary and power politics: contextual constraints on organisation development change projects in United Nations organisations. *Gestalt Review* 6:84–94.

Saxe, J. G. 1878. The blind men and the elephant. In *Poetry of America: Selections from One Hundred American Poets from 1776 to 1876*. Edited by W. J. Linton, 150–52. London: George Bell and Sons.

Saxena, S. 1978. *Namibia: Challenge to the United Nations*. Berkeley, CA: University of California Press.

Schauber, A. C. 2002. *Working with Differences in Communities: A Handbook for Those Who Care about Creating Inclusive Communities*. Corvallis, OR: Oregon State University Extension Service.

Schechner, R. 1994. Ritual and performance. In *Companion Encyclopedia of Anthropology: Humanity, Culture and Social Life*. Edited by T. Ingold, 613–47. London: Routledge.

Schlesinger, S. 2003. *Act of Creation: The Founding of the United Nations: A Story of Superpowers, Secret Agents, Wartime Allies and Enemies, and their Quest for a Peaceful World*. Boulder, CO: Westview Press.

Schoettle, E. C. B. 1993. Financing UN peacekeeping. In *Keeping the Peace in the Post–Cold War Era: Strengthening Multilateral Peacekeeping*. Edited by J. Roper, M. Nishihara, O. A. Otunnu, and E. C. B. Schoettle, 17–48. New York: Trilateral Commission.

Schön, D. 1983. *The Reflective Practitioner: How Professionals Think in Action*. New York: Basic Books.

Segal, D. R. 2001. Is a peacekeeping culture emerging among American infantry in the Sinai MFO? *Journal of Contemporary Ethnography* 30:607–36.

Segal, D. R., and M. W. Segal. 1993. *Peacekeepers and Their Wives: American Participation in the Multinational Force and Observers*. Westport, CT: Greenwood Press.

Seiple, C. 1996. *The U.S. Military/NGO Relationship in Humanitarian Interventions*. Carlisle, PA: US Army Peacekeeping Institute.

Selmeski, B. R. 1997. *Military Cross-Cultural Competence: Core Concepts and Individual Development*. Centre for Security, Armed Forces and Society, Occasional Paper Series No. 1. Kingston, ON: Royal Military College of Canada.

Sengupta, K. 2003. The Iraq conflict: US says flag incident was a "coincidence." *The Independent*, 11 April, 5.

Shore, B. 1996. *Culture in Mind: Cognition, Culture and the Problem of Meaning*. Oxford: Oxford University Press.

Sida, L. 2005. Challenges to humanitarian space: a review of humanitarian issues related to the UN integrated mission in Liberia and to the relationship between humanitarian and military actors in Liberia. Unpublished manuscript.

Simons, A. 1995. *Networks of Dissolution: Somalia Undone*. Boulder, CO: Westview Press.

———. 1997. *The Company They Keep: Life Inside the U.S. Army Special Forces*. New York: The Free Press.

Sion, L. 2006. Too sweet and innocent for war?: Dutch peacekeepers and the use of violence. *Armed Forces and Society* 32:148–71.

Skjelsbaek, K. 1990. UN Peacekeeping: expectations, limitations and results: forty years of mixed experiences. In *The United Nations and Peacekeeping: Results, Limitations and Prospects*. Edited by I. J. Rikhye and K. Skjelsbaek, 52–67. London: Macmillan.

Skogmo, B. 1989. *UNIFIL: International Peacekeeping in Lebanon, 1978–1988*. Boulder, CO: Lynne Rienner Publishers.

Slim, H. 1996. The stretcher and the drum: civil-military relations in peace support operations. *International Peacekeeping* 3:123–40.

Sluka, J. 1997. Loyal citizens of the republic: morality, violence, and popular support for the IRA and INLA in a Northern Irish ghetto. In *The Social Dynamics of Peace and Conflict: Culture in International Security*. Edited by R. A. Rubinstein and M. L. Foster, 107–25. Dubuque, IA: Kendall/Hunt Publishing.

Smith, A. 1985. Commonwealth cross-sections: prenegotiation to minimize conflict and develop cooperation. In *Multilateral Negotiation and Mediation: Instruments and Methods*. Edited by A. S. Lall, 53–73. New York: Pergamon Press.

Smith, P. B. 2006. When elephants fight, the grass gets trampled: the GLOBE and Hofstede Projects. *Journal of International Business Studies* 36:915–21.

Sobel, L. A, ed. 1974. *Israel and the Arabs: The October 1973 War*. New York: Facts on File.

Somalia Commission of Inquiry. 1997. *Dishonoured Legacy: The Lessons of the Somalia Affair. Final Report of the Commission of Inquiry into the Deployment of Canadian Forces to Somalia*. Ottawa: Canadian Government Publishing.

Spicer, E. H, ed. 1967. *Human Problems in Technological Change*. New York: John Wiley.

Stanton, M. 1994. A riot in Wanwaylen: lessons learned. *Army* 44:24–30.

———. 2001. *Somalia on $5.00 a Day: A Soldier's Story*. Novato, CA: Presidio Press.

Stolpe, S. 1966. *Dag Hammarskjöld: A Spiritual Portrait*. New York: Charles Scribner's Sons.

Tabory, M. 1986. *The Multinational Force and Observers in the Sinai: Organization, Structure, and Function*. Boulder, CO: Westview Press.

Tax, S, ed. 1967. *The Draft: A Handbook of Facts and Alternatives*. Chicago: University of Chicago Press.

Thakur, R. 2003. Reforming the United Nations. *International Peacekeeping* 10:40–61.

Tomforde, M. 2005. Motivation and self-image among German peacekeepers. *International Peacekeeping* 12:576–85.

Trainor, B. 1996. Suicide over a medal? an ex-general's view. *New York Times*, 20 May, 6.

Trostle, J. A. 2005. *Epidemiology and Culture*. Cambridge: Cambridge University Press.

Turner, M. 2001. *Cognitive Dimensions of Social Science*. Oxford: Oxford University Press.

Turner, V. 1967. *The Forest of Symbols*. Ithaca, NY: Cornell University Press.

———. 1969. *The Ritual Process: Structure and Anti-Structure*. Ithaca, NY: Cornell University Press.

Tversky, A., and D. Kahneman. 1982. Judgment under uncertainty: heuristics and biases. In *Judgment Under Uncertainty: Heuristics and Biases*. Edited by D. Kahneman, P. Slovic, and A. Tversky, 3–20. Cambridge: Cambridge University Press.

Ungerer, F., and H.-J. Schmid. 1997. *An Introduction to Cognitive Linguistics*. London: Longman.

UNHCR. 1995. *UNHCR Handbook for the Military on Humanitarian Operations*. Geneva: United Nations High Commissioner for Refugees.

United Nations Department of Public Information. 1996a. *The Blue Helmets. A Review of United Nations Peace-Keeping*. Third edition. New York: United Nations Department of Public Information.

———. 1996b. *United Nations and Somalia, 1992–1996*. New York: United Nations Department of Public Information.

United States Office of the Assistant Secretary of Defense. 1996. *Manual of Military Decorations and Awards*. Department of Defense 1348.33–M. Washington, DC: Office of the Assistant Secretary of Defense (Force Management Policy).

Urquhart, B. 1987. *A Life in Peace and War*. New York: Harper & Row.

———. 1989. *Decolonization and World Peace*. Austin: University of Texas Press.

———. 1990. Reflections by the chairman. In *The United Nations and Peacekeeping: Results, Limitations and Prospects*. Edited by I. J. Rikhye and K. Skjelsbaek, 17–21. London: Macmillan.

———. 1993. *Ralph Bunche: An American Odyssey*. New York: W. W. Norton.

Vadset, M. 1988. UNTSO and the future: reflections by the COS. *UNTSO News* 9:5.

van Gennep, A. 1960 [1909]. *The Rites of Passage*. Translated by M. Vizedom and G. Caffee. Chicago: University of Chicago Press.

Varhola, C. H. 2004. The US military in Iraq: are we our own worst enemy? *Practicing Anthropology* 24:39–42.

Varhola, C. H., and L. R. Varhola. 2006. Avoiding the cookie-cutter approach to culture: lessons learned from operations in East Africa. *Military Review* (November–December): 73–78.

Verrier, A. 1981. *International Peacekeeping. United Nations Forces in a Troubled World*. New York: Penguin.

Wallace, A. F. C. 1970. *Culture and Personality*. Second edition. New York: Random House.

Wallenius, C., C. Johansson, and G. Larsson. 2002. Reactions and performance of Swedish peacekeepers in life-threatening situations. *International Peacekeeping* 9:133–52.

Wallis, R. 1985. Institutions. In *The Social Science Encyclopedia*. Edited by A. Kuper and J. Kuper, 399–401. London: Routledge and Kegan Paul.

Washington Post. 1983. The Sharon-Weinberger factor. *Washington Post*, 5 February, A14.

Weiner, J. F. 1994. Myth and metaphor. In *Companion Encyclopedia of Anthropology: Humanity, Culture and Social Life*. Edited by T. Ingold, 591–612. London: Routledge.

Weiss, T. G. 1995. Military-civilian humanitarianism: the "age of innocence" is over. *International Peacekeeping* 2:157–74.

———. 1999. *Military-Civilian Interactions: Intervening in Humanitarian Crises*. Lanham, MD: Rowman & Littlefield.

White, L. A. 1949. *The Science of Culture*. New York: Farrar, Straus and Cudahy.

Whitehead, A. N. 1927. *Symbolism: Its Meaning and Effect*. New York: Fordham University Press.

Whitman, J. 1998. The UN specialized agencies, peacekeeping and the enactment of values. *International Peacekeeping* 5:120–37.

Whitworth, S. 2004. *Men, Militarism and UN Peacekeeping: A Gendered Analysis*. Boulder, CO: Lynne Rienner Publishers.

Wilcox, C. 2004. *Robert Redfield and the Development of American Anthropology*. Lanham, MD: Lexington Books.

Winslow, D. 1997. *The Canadian Airborne Regiment in Somalia: A Socio-Cultural Inquiry*. Ottawa: Canada Communications Group-Publishing.

———. 1999. Rites of passage and group bonding in the Canadian Airborne. *Armed Forces and Society* 25:429–57.

Wolf, E. R., and J. G. Jorgensen. 1970. Anthropology on the warpath in Thailand. *New York Review of Books* 15:26–35.

Woodhouse, T., and O. Ramsbotham. 2000. *Peacekeeping and Conflict Resolution*. London: Frank Cass.

Worsley, P. 1997. Images of the other. In *The Social Dynamics of Peace and Conflict: Culture in International Security*. Edited by R. A. Rubinstein and M. L. Foster, 69–80. Dubuque, IA: Kendall/Hunt Publishing.

Yamaguchi, M. 2004. Japan urges soldiers in Iraq to grow mustaches, bans pork and alcohol. *Associated Press Worldstream*, 5 February.

Zartman, W. I. 1985. *Ripe for Resolution: Conflict and Intervention in Africa*. Oxford: Oxford University Press.

Zerubavel, E. 1991. *The Fine Line: Making Distinctions in Everyday Life*. Chicago: University of Chicago Press.

Zucchino, D. 2004. Army stage-managed fall of Hussein statue. *Los Angeles Times*, 3 July, A28.

Index

Note: Page numbers in italics refer to figures and tables in the text.